# NATHAN BEDFORD
# FORREST'S
## ESCORT AND STAFF

# NATHAN BEDFORD
# FORREST'S
# ESCORT AND STAFF

## MICHAEL R. BRADLEY

PELICAN PUBLISHING COMPANY

GRETNA 2009

First printing, November 2006
Second printing, December 2009

**Library of Congress Cataloging-in-Publication Data**

Bradley, Michael R. (Michael Raymond), 1940-
  Nathan Bedford Forrest's escort and staff / Michael R. Bradley.
    p. cm.
  Includes bibliographical references and index.
  ISBN-13: 978-1-58980-363-3 (hardcover : alk. paper)
  1. Forrest, Nathan Bedford, 1821-1877—Friends and associates.
2. Generals—Confederate States of America—Staffs. 3.
Confederate States of America. Army. Cavalry—Biography. 4.
United States—History—Civil War, 1861-1865—Cavalry opera-
tions. 5. United States—History—Civil War, 1861-1865—Veterans.
I. Title.
  E467.1.F72B73 2006
  973.7'3092—dc22

                                                2006009802

Printed in the United States of America
Published by Pelican Publishing Company, Inc.
1000 Burmaster Street, Gretna, Louisiana 70053

*To William Andrew Warren, that my grandson may
not be ignorant of those from whom he is sprung*

# Contents

|  |  |  |
|---|---|---|
|  | Preface | 9 |
|  | Acknowledgments | 15 |
| Chapter 1 | Legendary Deeds Produce a Legend | 21 |
| Chapter 2 | Birth and Baptism of the Escort and Staff: 1862 | 33 |
| Chapter 3 | Recognition, Revolt, Renaissance: 1863 | 63 |
| Chapter 4 | Trial by Fire: 1864-65 | 91 |
| Chapter 5 | Years of Turmoil, Days of Peace: 1877-1909 | 137 |
| Appendix A | Roster of Escort at Organization | 195 |
| Appendix B | Members of the Escort Present at the Surrender | 197 |
| Appendix C | Complete Roster of Forrest's Escort and Staff | 199 |
| Appendix D | Forrest in Literature | 209 |
| Appendix E | Forrest and Race | 215 |
| Appendix F | George L. Cowan's History of the Escort | 221 |
| Appendix G | Abbreviations Used in Citations | 225 |
|  | Bibliography | 227 |
|  | Index | 231 |

# Preface

During the War Between the States, all general officers at or above the rank of major general were allowed to have an escort, or bodyguard, unit. For the most part, these units were simply detached from existing cavalry regiments and were used to provide camp security and to supplement the number of couriers who could be dispatched to carry orders to various subordinate officers. Likewise, general officers were allowed a staff of administrative officers to carry out the various specialized functions demanded by a military organization. In addition to managing an administrative unit, such as ammunition or food supply, these staff officers were representatives of the general they served and were authorized to oversee the execution of his orders in the area under his command.

Most of the staff officers and escort members have faded into obscurity unless they wrote memoirs, such as Kyd Douglas's *I Rode with Stonewall* or W. W. Blackford's *War Years with Jeb Stuart*. Robert E. L. Krick has authored an annotated listing of the staff officers of the Army of Northern Virginia, but most staff officers remain in the shadows of history. There is no history of an escort unit.

One group stands as an exception to these general observations. Even during the war, the Escort Company and Staff Officers of Nathan Bedford Forrest were held in awe by men on both sides of the conflict. These men were not merely headquarters guards, couriers, or administrative officers; they were an elite strike force, the closest thing the Western Confederacy had to a Delta Force. In a cavalry corps known for hard riding and fierce fighting, the Escort and Staff of Forrest rode harder and fought more fiercely than any others. In a situation where a regiment seemed called for, Forrest would send in his Escort Company and always achieved the desired results. These men became a legend among their contemporaries (I say "contemporaries" because they had no peers). Until now, the story of this legendary force had not been told.

Of those who rode with Forrest, Lord Garnet Joseph Wolseley,

Commander in Chief of Her Majesties' Army, later wrote:

> They were reckless men, who looked on him as their master, their leader, and over whom he had obtained the most complete control. He possessed that rare tact—unlearnable from books—which enabled him not only effectively to control those fiery, turbulent spirits, but to attach them to him personally "with hooks of steel." In him they recognized not only the daring, able, and successful leader, but also the commanding officer who would not hesitate to punish with severity when he deemed punishment necessary. . . . They possessed as an inheritance all the best and most valuable fighting qualities of the irregulars, accustomed as they were from boyhood to horses and the use of arms, and brought up with all the devil-may-care lawless notions of the frontiersman. But the most volcanic spirit among them felt he must bow before the superior iron will of the determined man who led them. There was something about the dark gray eye of Forrest which warned his subordinates he was not to be trifled with and would stand no nonsense from either friend or foe. He was essentially a man of action, with a dauntless, fiery soul, and a heart that knew no fear. (Wyeth, 174-75)

In part, this group became a legend because they served a legendary figure. There is no debate that Nathan Bedford Forrest is such a figure. There is, however, continuing debate over the nature and content of that legend.

Forrest was a legend from birth. He was of legendary size and strength, apparently from boyhood. It is documented that more than once during the war years Forrest scooped up from the ground unwilling, struggling enemies; slung them behind him on his horse, and used them as a shield as he broke out of a surrounding ring of steel. Forrest killed twenty-nine armed opponents in face-to-face combat, ending the war with his right arm in a sling from a wound inflicted by the last of these adversaries. During these encounters, thirty horses were killed under him.

Enlisting as a private at age forty, Forrest rose to the rank of lieutenant general in less than four years. He organized a regiment of cavalry in the early days of the war, broke out of the perimeter at Fort Donelson before it surrendered, and increased his command to the size of a brigade. Stripped of his men in September 1862, he raised another brigade and, when stripped of that in October 1863, raised another, which he increased to the size of a division. By the end of the war, he commanded a corps of cavalry. His victories in north Mississippi and west Tennessee in 1864 are even today considered gems of strategy and tactics. His skilled and determined guarding of the rear of the shattered Army of Tennessee on its retreat from Nashville in December 1864 is still studied as an example of the proper conduct of a rear-guard action.

This legendary figure has been an inspiration for writers of both biography and fiction for over a century and a quarter. During that time, the nature of the books about Forrest has evolved from dealing with wartime controversies and personalities, to romantic views of a picturesque, and picaresque, hero, to an analysis of his social and military significance. Despite this historical maturation process, legends, half-truths, and whole lies still cluster around Forrest, while some authors are so overcome by their passions against him as to depart from the standards of the historian to become mere propagandists.

As one example of the legend of Forrest, the motto so often attributed to him, "Git thar fustest with the mostest," is sheer gibberish. No Southerner ever spoke in such a ridiculous fashion. The persistent connection of these words with Forrest shows a stubborn desire not to understand the man, his times, or his home country but to create a legend of fantastic proportions.

Equally unbelievable is the positive assertion that Forrest ordered a massacre of black troops at Fort Pillow, Tennessee, in April 1864. Obviously something bad happened at Fort Pillow, but the reasons why it happened were not uncovered by a wartime investigation by the United States Congress, and they are beyond recovery today. What is clear is that human life had become a cheap commodity in the South by the spring of 1864. The provost marshal records of the United States Army show large-scale deportation of civilians from strategic zones around railroads, the establishment of "free fire" areas, executions of hundreds of civilians without trials, local genocides, and even the use of torture against Confederate citizens by Union officials. Rape committed by Northern troops was a common occurrence. These acts make it difficult to accept at face value Lincoln's words at his second inauguration, "with malice toward none." There was a great deal of malice toward the South during the war, and after; and such malevolence can even be seen today. It is instructive to note that Fort Pillow is widely cited as evidence of Southern racism, but most Civil War historians have ignored the provost marshal records, with their accounts of war crimes perpetrated against Southern civilians by the United States armed forces. (Before any of my Rebel brothers objects to my use of the term *Civil War,* let me point out that this is the name "Ole Bedford" applied to the conflict in his famous farewell address to his men at Gainesville, Alabama, in May 1865.) These historical records make it clear that many people joined Mr. Lincoln's armies because their malice caused them to desire to wreak havoc on Dixie. They make it clear that Northern hands are far from clean of innocent blood. An honest, impartial reading of the records places Fort Pillow in a clearer historical context.

The often-repeated statement that Forrest founded the Ku Klux Klan flies in the face of solid historical evidence. John Morton in *The Artillery of Nathan Bedford Forrest's Cavalry* states that Morton inducted Forrest into the Klan some eighteen months after the organization's founding. Forrest did become the Grand Dragon of the Klan and, using the authority of that position, ordered the Klan to disband in 1870.

The complexities of nineteenth-century attitudes toward race relations are illustrated by a contrasting pair of quotes. The first quote says, "I will say, then, that I am not, nor ever have been, in favor of bringing about in any way the social and political equality of the white and black races—that I am not, nor ever have been, in favor of making voters or jurors of Negroes, nor of qualifying them to hold office, nor to intermarry with white people; and I will say in addition to this that there is a physical difference between the white and black races which prevents them from living together on terms of social and political equality. And inasmuch as they cannot so live, while they do remain together there must be the position of superior and inferior, and I as much as any other man, am in favor of having the superior position assigned to the white race."

The second quote says:

I came here with the jeers of some white people, who think that I am doing wrong. I believe I can exert some influence, and do much to assist the people in strengthening fraternal relations and shall do all in my power to elevate every man—and to depress none. I want to elevate the colored people to take positions in law offices, in stores, on farms, and wherever you are capable of going. I have not said anything about politics today. I don't propose to say anything about politics. You have a right to elect whom you please; vote for the man you think best, and I think, when that is done, you and I are freemen. Do as you consider right and honest in electing men for office. I came to meet you as friends. When I can serve you I will do so. We have but one flag, one country; let us stand together. We may differ in color, but not in sentiment. Go to work, be industrious, live honestly and act truly, and when you are oppressed I'll come to your relief.

The first quote is from Abraham Lincoln, the second from Forrest. Minds can, and do, change over time.

If many false ideas about Nathan Bedford Forrest persist, then the state of knowledge about those who "rode with Forrest" is even more abysmal. The officers and men who followed "the wizard of the saddle" are usually painted with the same brush as Forrest, for good or ill. For, if Forrest has become a legend, so have those who fought under him. Well into the twentieth century, men considered it a badge of honor to say, "I rode with Forrest," and many today are proud to say that of their forbears. Forrest was a leader who was feared but was fearless, vicious in battle but usually victorious, charismatic in personality but careful with the lives of his soldiers. Such a one attracts daring followers.

So there rises the eternal, cyclical question: did Forrest create a legendary fighting force, or did a legendary fighting force create Forrest? I propose that each created the other. There existed a symbiotic relationship between Forrest and his men; each fed off the other. Forrest attracted men ready to fight; fighting men needed a general like Forrest.

Though raised an untutored child in a frontier society, Forrest rose to a level of wealth and authority that brought an appreciation of education, if not of culture. He made friends among the wealthy, educated people of his time and place and, when war came, called on these same people to use their talents as members of his Staff.

Innocent of military training, Forrest still valued discipline and instilled it into the character of his soldiers. His command was not a band of lawless, untrained guerrillas fighting "bushwhacker" style but a highly mobile strike force comprised of units trained to operate together or independently of one another. Such forces require the highest level of discipline to function effectively, and Forrest's command was spectacularly successful. The Escort accepted and practiced the necessary discipline more thoroughly than any other of "Ole Bedford's" units.

This book is intended to give a clear picture of the members of the Escort and Staff, so far as the available historical records permit. In this book, these men are allowed to speak for themselves, to "tell their side of the story." Contemporary historians will note that not all sides of controversies are presented. The members of the Escort and Staff saw one side, their side.

These men, many of them really only boys, had the closest possible association with Forrest during the war. The Escort and Staff were picked men, chosen for their ability to perform under combat conditions and to make a military unit function smoothly. This body would be a military extension of Forrest himself. This book deals with these men and their exploits. They would indeed become "a band of brothers, native to the soil." The bonds of brotherhood would survive the war.

Soon after the end of the conflict, veterans on both sides began to form associations, formal and informal, to perpetuate the bonds forged during the war. In time, an organization for all Confederate veterans, the United Confederate Veterans (UCV), would be formed. The local groups of the UCV were called "bivouacs." Wives and daughters of veterans formed the United Daughters of the Confederacy (UDC) in 1890. The sons and descendants of veterans would form the Sons of Confederate Veterans (SCV) in 1896. In addition to these large, formal organizations, the old soldiers held reunions of their regiments, brigades, divisions, and army corps. Surgeons and chaplains met to share their common experiences of the war. In 1877, the surviving members of the Escort and Staff formed a veterans association to keep alive their memories of the valiant days of their youth. The history of this association is also a part of this book. The men who belonged to the Escort and Staff Veterans Association were involved in numerous other veterans groups and attended many reunions, but they valued most highly of all their right to say, "I rode with Forrest."

# Acknowledgments

Many people contributed to the making of this book. They did their best to help me, and if I have made mistakes, such are my responsibility alone.

Heath Mathews of Franklin, Tennessee, should be thanked above all others for making this book possible. Heath helped me acquire a copy of the unpublished minutes of the association formed by the Escort and Staff in 1877.

Brian Allison is the current staff historian at Carnton Plantation in Franklin and he made available to me a most exciting find. In February 2005 the staff found and opened a safety deposit box, which contained papers of George Limerick Cowan, the secretary of the Veterans Association for many years. Among those papers were two roll books, which date from after the war but in which are many notes about the fate of various members of the group, and a short history of the Escort written in a small notebook in Cowan's hand. This history covers only the first few weeks of the Escort's formation.

Dr. James Jones, Tennessee Historical Commission, helped find many obscure facts and was always courteous and enthusiastic. Dr. Lonnie Maness, professor emeritus at the University of Tennessee—Martin, offered encouragement and suggestions. Professor Maness knows more about Forrest than any other person now alive.

I have had a delightful relationship with Dr. Bruce Bickley at Florida State University in which we have discussed Southern postbellum writers and the role of Forrest in various pieces of fiction. Lee Millar of Memphis, Tennessee, has collected material about the Escort Company for several years. When he learned of my project, he immediately and generously offered to share his information.

Ronnie Mangrum of Franklin, Tennessee, provided an invaluable service when he shared with me letters written by an enlisted man in the Escort, Johnston C. Ryall of Bedford County. These letters added a spark of life to the history of the Escort. Bill Harris of Lewisburg helped me identify veterans of the Escort who applied for pensions after the war.

David Fraley and Thomas Cartwright of the Carter House in Franklin, Tennessee, made me welcome and shared resources with me. George Stone shared with me his vast knowledge of the families of Moore and Bedford counties. Dr. Randall Black used his skills in Internet research to my great advantage.

My friend and neighbor, O. B. Wilkinson, not only ran down numerous loose ends but over the years frequently gave me a kick in the pants by asking, "Are you working on the Forrest Escort book yet?" Jason Morgan and Russell Sells of my SCV camp, Dr. J. B. Cowan Camp #155, tramped through area cemeteries looking for the final resting place of "Ole Bedford's Boys." Joyce Bateman of the Crouch Library at Motlow College was always cheerful, efficient, and willing to help with the numerous arcane requests I made of her for interlibrary loans.

Skip Erle, past commander, Tennessee Division, SCV, offered encouragement and support. The staffs at Belle Meade Plantation and Travellers Rest, both in Nashville, shared their knowledge of events that occurred on those historic properties. Many members of the SCV and UDC contributed information about their families. I have also found a warm welcome in the Tennessee State Library and Archives and, most especially appreciated, in the libraries of small towns where I went searching for newspaper accounts of meetings of the association and for obituaries of members of the Escort and Staff. Lasting gratitude is due Kay Muse, who prepared the index for this book.

And, most of all, there has been "The Carolina Belle," my consort since 1963, who is eternally patient with my Confederate enthusiasms. She is a true daughter of her ancestors, Sgt. John Newton Todd of Orr's South Carolina Rifles and Pvt. Elias Alexander of the First South Carolina Cavalry. I hope Pvt. Andrew Jackson Bradley of Turney's First Tennessee Infantry is proud of his offspring, too. We have no need to be ashamed of our Confederate ancestors. I am conscious of the need to be sure they have no cause to be ashamed of us.

Through the help of all these people, the Escort and Staff ride once again with Forrest, in war and in peace.

"Keep the skeer on 'em."

# NATHAN BEDFORD
# FORREST'S
## ESCORT AND STAFF

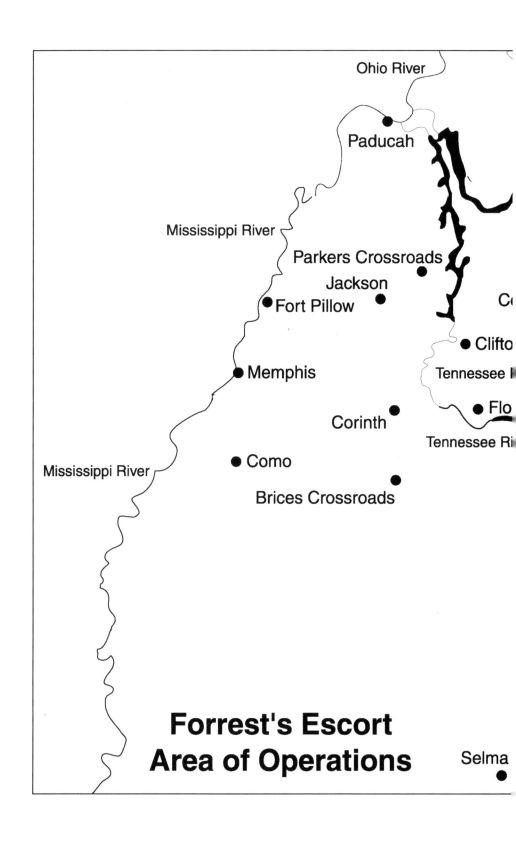

Ohio River

Paducah

Mississippi River

Parkers Crossroads

Jackson

Fort Pillow

Clifto

Tennessee I

Memphis

Corinth

Flo

Tennessee Ri

Mississippi River

Como

Brices Crossroads

**Forrest's Escort
Area of Operations**

Selma

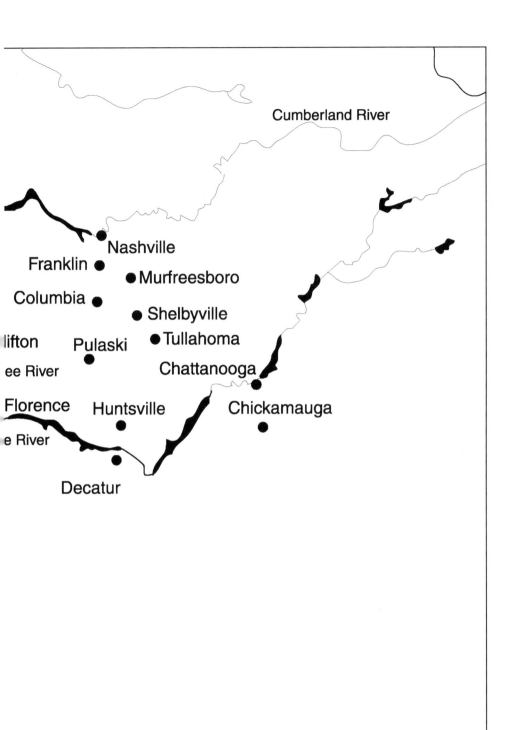

Cumberland River

Nashville

Franklin

Columbia

Murfreesboro

Shelbyville

lifton

Pulaski

Tullahoma

ee River

Chattanooga

Florence

Huntsville

Chickamauga

e River

Decatur

na

# CHAPTER 1

# Legendary Deeds Produce a Legend

Legends are born in the most unlikely places. The dusty village of Chapel Hill, Tennessee, was one such place, for there, on July 13, 1821, Nathan Bedford Forrest was born. This infant was destined to become a legend in his own lifetime and remains one today.

Forrest is remembered today as a fierce fighter, an implacable foe, even a "butcher." Forrest was a product of his time and place, sharing the virtues and vices of both. He was also one of the greatest fighting men ever produced by an American army.

In times of danger such men are seen as valuable assets; but in times of peace they are viewed in a different light, especially by people of a different time and place. During the War Between the States, his enemies called him "that devil, Forrest," while his friends dubbed him "the wizard of the saddle." Many years later, when Forrest's portrait was hung in the state capitol in Nashville, one of his officers, John Morton, would say:

> Forrest, like a ruthless besom of destruction, made the air livid with his maledictions as he hurled himself upon the foe. He was indeed "the Wizard of the Saddle," self-reliant and aggressive with the conscious power of one who always knew when, how, and where to strike. . . . His fame, deeds, and genius . . . ever will be the theme of eager discussion in every camp and school where military skill and science enlist a thought. (CV 11: 398-99)

For so long as that conflict raged, Forrest blazed his way across the landscape of Tennessee, Mississippi, Alabama, and Kentucky, destroying Union supplies, disrupting rail travel, capturing hundreds of Union soldiers, and spreading chaos in the ranks of Union strategists. On these campaigns and raids, after September 1862, Forrest would be accompanied by a devoted band of followers, his Escort and his Staff. This "official family" would become as legendary as their leader. "The Forty Thieves," the Escort was sometimes called; "they were as adept at foraging as they were at fighting and at fighting they had no equals," one contemporary commented.

Also accompanying Forrest on these forays was a group of Confederates whose existence many would like to deny or, at least, forget. These were black men, men who drove wagons loaded with food, ammunition, and equipment, men who sometimes took a weapon in hand and went in harm's way. These were men whose labor allowed white men to fight.

Indeed, riding with Forrest as combat soldiers were a handful of African-Americans, some of whom were members of the general's personal bodyguard. Of the black men who served under him, Forrest would later say, "There were no better Confederates." Though many of this group are now lost to history, some are to be found in the available records (see Appendix E). The bonds these black men forged on the anvil of war with the white members of the Escort endured into the times of peace, for some of the black Confederates joined the Veterans Association established by the Escort and Staff. At least one of them became an officer of that body. Astonishing as it may seem today, white and black Confederate veterans met in integrated assemblies in the postwar years, while to the North, the reunions of veterans were segregated by race. Of course, the Confederates had fought side by side, while the Union soldiers served in units that represented only one race. Obviously, there was a side of the personality and character of Forrest that appealed to the black cavalrymen who "rode with Forrest." Equally obvious, the matter of race in the Old South was not as simple as some would like to think.

## Military Career

The speed at which Forrest rose through the ranks was also legendary. He joined the army as a private in 1861, became a colonel by 1862, was a brigadier before that year was out, and was a lieutenant general when the war ended in 1865. He did not lead from the rear; that was part of his legend. At least two dozen Yankees fell to his hand in personal combat, he was wounded four times, and thirty horses were shot from under him in battle. This legendary combat record attracted fighters who would themselves become legends.

Forrest's financial rise and fall were also the stuff of legends. Born in poverty in an area still a raw frontier, and left without a

father at an early age, Forrest became a millionaire through plant-
ing, real-estate sales, and slave trading. At the end of the war he
had lost all his worldly goods and lived out his last years in a modest log house on land he rented, though he constantly planned
and worked to recoup his finances through railroad construction
and land development.

Before the war, Forrest had only a small circle of family and
friends in northern Mississippi, and though these family roots had
ties back to his birthplace in middle Tennessee, he was not a
famous man. He also had made friends in commercial circles in
Memphis, but he was not considered to be a "civic leader" in that
town, nor did Forrest show any ambition to enter politics. As a
man of wealth and personal accomplishment he was known to
political leaders, but they did not seek his advice. Relatively few
people knew Forrest when the war began.

Modesty and patriotism led Forrest to enlist as a private in
Confederate service in June 1861, but his ability and reputation
among those who did know him soon made him an officer
assigned the task of raising a cavalry regiment, a task for which he
was well suited. The unit Forrest raised was officially designated
the Third Tennessee Cavalry, but its members would always refer
with pride to having been a part of "Forrest's Old Regiment."

In organizing this force in the summer and fall of 1861, Forrest
put into practice several tactics he would use throughout the war.
First, he sent agents widely into the surrounding country to gather news and bring in recruits; then, in search of supplies, he went
behind enemy lines. The weapons and equipment Forrest wanted
were in short supply in Memphis, where numerous cavalry units
were forming. Withdrawing a large sum in cash from his personal
bank account, Forrest rode alone to Kentucky, shopping for pistols and saddles in several towns, including Louisville. In the
Bluegrass State, Forrest met with groups of Southern sympathizers, whom he recruited into his nascent command and whom he
utilized as couriers to carry his supplies back to Tennessee.

By the end of October 1861, Forrest and his regiment were on
duty along the outpost line of the Confederate forces. In what
would become another staple of Forrest's tactics, his men
ambushed a steamboat on the Ohio River and seized supplies for
themselves. On another occasion they challenged the gunboat
*Conestoga* and sent so much small shot through its gunports that
the commander of the vessel decided to retire. On December 26

Forrest fought a sizable skirmish near the village of Sacramento, Kentucky. Here another staple on his strategic menu was developed.

Hearing from civilians, including a young woman, that a Union force was in Sacramento, Forrest advanced boldly until confronted by a line of defenders under the cover of heavy woods. Forrest dismounted part of his men to engage the center of this line and, from a location unobservable by the Yankees, sent a detachment around each of their flanks. When these detachments attacked from the rear of the Union line, Forrest charged from the front. A stampede resulted, but a temporary stand by the bluecoats produced another scenario that would become standard Forrest fare: Forrest had outrun the rest of his men, found himself surrounded, and engaged several enemies in hand-to-hand combat. At the end of this encounter, Forrest had killed three men. Maj. D. C. Kelley described this scene, and the basic elements of his word picture would be repeated many times by other observers throughout the war.

> Forrest seemed in desperate mood and very much excited. His face was flushed till it looked like a painted warrior, and his eyes, usually mild in expression, glared like those of a panther about to spring upon its prey. He looked as little like the Forrest of the mess-table as the storm of December resembles the quiet of June. (Wyeth, 44)

## Early 1862

At Fort Donelson, Forrest showed he was capable of performing the duties of a cavalryman as defined by the regular army. On February 12, 1862, Forrest was placed in temporary command of a force of about 1,300 cavalrymen, who fought a series of skillful delaying actions against the advance guard of Grant's force moving from Fort Henry toward Fort Donelson. Using most of his men to fight dismounted, Forrest repeatedly identified, occupied, and defended tactical positions while retaining a portion of his men on horseback to protect his flanks.

Again, on the thirteenth, Forrest was constantly on reconnaissance, although the Confederate forces had withdrawn within the entrenched perimeter of Fort Donelson. On February 15 Forrest commanded the cavalry shield of the Confederate assault column, which drove back Grant's right flank and opened an escape route for the besieged Rebs, if only they had chosen to use it. During the attack, which lasted several hours, Forrest's men captured two batteries of artillery and Forrest had his horse killed under him, the first of thirty such animals to meet that fate. That night, informed of the infantry commanders' plan to surrender, Forrest made the decision that would launch his widespread fame. "To hell with that," he snorted. "I did not come here to surrender." Nor did he. During the darkness of February 15-16, Forrest led his command, and as many others who cared to join him, out of the besieged fort, escaping to Nashville. This became the one bright ray to shine from that gloomy event for the South, and the Forrest legend began to grow.

Placed in command of the city of Nashville by General Floyd, Forrest showed his skill as an organizer and administrator. Forrest stationed guards at all depots of government property, who once used a fire engine to hose down a mob and extinguish their desire for loot. Food and ammunition were sent south to Franklin on the Tennessee & Alabama Railroad, while other trains were directed down the Nashville & Chattanooga Railroad to Murfreesboro. Wagons poured out of the town along every pike leading south and east. Even after Union infantry arrived on the opposite bank of the Cumberland River, Forrest remained in Nashville an additional twenty-four hours, until Yankee gunboats arrived to protect the troop crossing and he was forced to act.

Falling back to Huntsville, Alabama, Forrest allowed his command to disperse so the men could spend two weeks at their homes in middle Tennessee and north Alabama. At a time when Southern fortunes were declining, allowing men to go home would seem to be an invitation to mass desertion, but on the day set for the rendezvous, the furloughed men came back, bringing new recruits with them. Something about Forrest aroused fierce loyalty among his command.

After occupying Nashville, the Union commander committed a classic blunder, dividing his troops and separating his command. Don Carlos Buell left Nashville for a push toward Chattanooga, while Grant moved up the Tennessee River (south) toward a vital railroad junction at Corinth, Mississippi. Confederates under Albert Sidney Johnston used the network of rail lines to concentrate forces from all over the Deep South at Corinth. The Battle of Shiloh was a counterattack designed to destroy one part of the Union army before it could be supported by the other. The plan almost worked.

Forrest did not play an important role in the advance from Corinth to Shiloh, but on April 6, the first day of battle, he supported the Confederate right flank and once joined in an infantry attack on a Union battery. Later in his military career Forrest was asked what was the best way to attack a battery of artillery. He replied, "Since Shiloh I've knowd they ain't no best way. Hell, they ain't even no good way." The heavily wooded nature of the battlefield did not provide much scope for cavalry, but a reconnaissance on the night of the sixth allowed Forrest to report the arrival of Union reinforcements. The Union army had reunited just in time to avoid disaster.

April 7, the second day of the battle, was a repeat of the previous day for Forrest. On the eighth, however, he came into his glory leading the Confederate rear guard. His tactics of ambush and sudden assault checked the Union pursuit only a couple of miles from the battlefield. This engagement at a creek crossing called Fallen Timbers brought Forrest his first serious wound—a rifle shot that entered his right side above the point of his hip joint and lodged on the left side of his spine—and led to the death of his second horse. Forrest recuperated in Memphis until April 29, returned to his command, had the ball removed, and then spent two weeks recovering from the operation.

Forrest returned from his medical leave the first week of June. On the eleventh he was ordered to report to Chattanooga to organize a cavalry brigade to operate against the Union advance on that key city. After slowly advancing against and capturing Corinth, the Union forces had concentrated at Nashville and advanced nearly to the Tennessee River, while repairing the Nashville & Chattanooga Railroad to serve as their supply line for an advance to Chattanooga. Gen. Braxton Bragg was preparing to move the Confederate army to Chattanooga, but something had to slow the Yankee juggernaut first. That something was Forrest.

## Rise to Fame

Forrest was delighted to return to his roots in middle Tennessee, but he was sorry to have to leave behind his "Old Regiment." Arriving in Chattanooga on June 19 Forrest found he had a core cadre of veterans on which to build. His new command would include the Eighth Texas or Terry's Texas Rangers, the

Second Georgia Cavalry, the Second Georgia Battalion, and 100 Kentuckians under the command of Lieutenant Colonel Woodward. To this core would be added new recruits and some units of less-experienced men.

Using the organizational and administrative skills that he possessed in abundance (though historians have not commented on them before), Forrest had his new command organized in only two weeks. On July 6 he moved toward middle Tennessee. As Forrest crossed the Tennessee River and moved into the Cumberland Mountains, which form the eastern plateau of the central part of the state, he followed an established pattern that the coming years would only strengthen. He sent ahead of his force a number of scouts, who would contact sympathetic civilian residents and bring back accurate information about road conditions; the placement of Yankee pickets, patrols, and troop encampments; and the location of forage and fodder for Forrest's men and animals. These scouts brought interesting news about the Union garrison at Murfreesboro.

There were two Union infantry regiments at Murfreesboro, the Ninth Michigan and the Third Minnesota. They were supported by four guns of a Kentucky battery, while the task of patrolling was done by the Seventh Pennsylvania Cavalry. Because of friction among the commands, the Minnesota infantry and Kentucky battery were camped on the banks of Stones River north of town while the Michigan infantry and Pennsylvania cavalry were ensconced on the Maney family farm, "Oaklands," some two miles away on the east side of town. A third detachment of Yankees occupied the town square, where the courthouse provided administrative office space for Gen. Thomas T. Crittenden and where a number of military and political prisoners were held in the town jail. Forrest decided to exploit the error the Union forces had made in dispersing their men.

Careful intelligence gathering, strategic maneuvering, and tactical finesse were already evident as basic elements of Forrest's military operations and show him to be a much more sophisticated soldier than the "first with the most" folktales indicate.

On the evening of July 12 Union soldiers relaxed in their Murfreesboro camps, assured that no Confederates were within striking distance. That would be the last sound sleep for any Yankee in Tennessee for many months. The events of the next twenty-four hours showed Forrest might be lurking anywhere, ready to pounce on the unsuspecting and the unprepared.

Forrest had left McMinnville about noon on July 12. About midnight his command entered the village of Woodbury, where they were fed—and enraged. Along with good food the cavalry-men received the news that the Union provost, Capt. Oliver Cromwell Rounds, had arrested all the men and boys in the village and imprisoned them in the Murfreesboro jail. Some of these civilians were sentenced to hang on the next morning. Forrest promised he would celebrate his birthday, July 13, by freeing these innocent Confederates.

Pushing on the remaining nineteen miles to Murfreesboro, Forrest silently captured the Yankee pickets and assigned his command their tasks. The Texans were to take on the Michigan infantry and Pennsylvania cavalry at the Maney farm. The Georgia troops would charge the town square, freeing the civilians from the jail and capturing the Yankee command structure. The rest of the command was to attack the Minnesota and Kentucky encampment.

The fight at the Maney farm became a stalemate. The infantry camp was overrun and the Pennsylvania cavalry captured, but most of the infantry force barricaded itself behind a stout fence and the Texans had no artillery to open the way for them.

On the square the jail was taken, but not before the soldier in charge had set it on fire and run off with the keys to the cells. Apparently, burning to death Southern civilians was an acceptable act in some Yankee minds. The courthouse, which is still in use today, was captured by a storming party who battered down the door with axes, occupied the ground floor, and then lit a fire to smoke out the Yankees on the upper floors. Unlike the Confederate prisoners in the jail, there was no chance of the Yankees burning to death; the brick building was fireproof. Hay was piled in the stairwell to produce a smoky fire.

The Minnesota and Kentucky troops fought stubbornly, even after Forrest led an attack from the rear that captured their camp and set it on fire. It took Forrest three charges to capture this camp, and in the process, he killed another man in personal combat. Even with their camp in flames behind them, the Northern troops held firm on a ridge. Forrest left only enough men to pin them in place and concentrated the rest of his men against the Yankees on the Maney farm.

After making all apparent preparations for an assault, Forrest sent in a note that contained wording soon to be familiar from repetition on dozens of fields. The Union troops were told they must surrender immediately or face the consequences. The "consequences" were that the assault force would accept no surrender once the attack began. This demand was fully in keeping with the established rules of war of the day, which stated that if a position refused a demand to surrender and was carried by assault, the attacking troops were under no obligation to accept as prisoners those who, by their continued resistance, had forced the assault to be made. The Union commander knew that since he harbored a man who had attempted to burn to death civilians in violation of the rules of war, Forrest had every reason to be serious about his intention to kill those who resisted a successful attack. The same knowledge of Union atrocities would weigh on the mind of many officers called on to surrender to Forrest.

The demand for surrender was successful and the news of the capitulation of the Michigan troops was carried to the still-resisting men of Minnesota and Kentucky. After a brief conference, they joined their comrades as prisoners of war.

Before leaving Murfreesboro, Forrest and his Staff met with the Union officers in the Maney house, Oaklands, for a meal of sweet potatoes and black-eyed peas, all the food Yankee foragers had left on the place. This meal is still served at Oaklands each July 13 in celebration of Forrest's birthday, the anniversary of his victory at Murfreesboro. Also, Forrest made a roll of the names of the prisoners captured. As this roll was called, the name of the soldier who had set fire to the jail was announced. "That's all right," said Forrest. "Pass on" (Lytle, 95-96). The summary justice of a drumhead court-martial was already a part of the conflict.

What the escape from Fort Donelson had begun, the capture of Murfreesboro completed. The Forrest legend was made.

In the late summer of 1862, Braxton Bragg conceived and executed one of his best strategic plans. Using the rail net to transport his troops to the area of Chattanooga, he concentrated a force that he then led across the Cumberland Mountains and Cumberland River into Kentucky. This obliged many of the Union troops in Tennessee to fall back toward the Ohio River to meet the Confederate move. Forrest, still growing into the skills and responsibilities of command, played a role in screening the army on its northern move. However, in doing this, he made a tactical error.

At Guest Hollow, near Morrison, Tennessee, a Union stockade guarded a bridge on an important branch of the Nashville and Chattanooga line. Railroad fortifications were something new for Forrest. Because the Union forces depended so heavily on the rails for logistical support, every culvert, every bridge, was coming to be protected by blockhouses or stockades. These fortifications would provide effective protection against raiders or guerrillas but would be vulnerable to a force supplied with artillery. At this point Forrest had no artillery but he saw that most of the Yankee garrison was outside the stockade, lolling on the grass and eating. Forrest assumed a sudden attack would stampede the Yanks and they could be overrun before they got under cover. He was wrong, and thirteen of his men paid the price for his false assumption. Forrest was not infallible—he did make mistakes—but he learned from them. Never again would he order such an attack. When such a role was forced on him in December 1862 by Gen. Joseph Wheeler at Dover, Tennessee, Forrest rebelled and refused ever to serve under Wheeler again.

Though Forrest was an effective and growing officer, the commander of the army was not happy with him and decided to place all the cavalry under the command of Joseph Wheeler. The younger Wheeler did not have Forrest's record of combat success, but he had the educational credentials from West Point, which Bragg trusted. As a result, Forrest was removed from his command and assigned to return to the area of middle Tennessee to raise more men. For the second time in four months, Forrest became an officer without a command.

## Maturing Ability as a Commander

By this point, Forrest had become one of the first officers to recognize the realities of modern war. Forrest abandoned the use of the traditional cavalry weapons, sabers and carbines, in favor of pistols and rifles. When his men needed to attack on horseback, pistols were more effective than edged weapons; when they needed to fight on foot, rifles gave them more firepower than did carbines.

The day of the cavalryman taking on artillery and jumping over breastworks was over. Forrest developed the use of artillery as an effective offensive weapon by attaching cannon to his command

and by using them at ranges as short as sixty yards to blast a hole in enemy lines or fortifications. He knew that if the line of supply was destroyed, even the largest enemy force would have to retreat, so he became a master of disrupting Yankee logistics systems. Psychology was also an important tool, even if the word itself was not in Forrest's vocabulary. He would soon adopt as his battle cry, "Keep the skeer on!" Forrest knew too that the civilian population had become a military target. He despised the suffering inflicted on those he considered "innocent victims" of war and used his full fury to suppress those who committed atrocities against civilians. This practice made him a hero in the South, even as it made him a villain in the North.

Recognition of the realities of modern war did not mean a hesitancy to fight when fighting could be done to an advantage. In 1862 Forrest selected an officer's sword from among captured booty. In disgust he found the weapon to be sharp for only a few inches from the point. Forrest called for a grindstone and, with an aide, proceeded to put a razor edge on the blade. One of Forrest's more formally educated officers intervened, telling him swords were more for show than for fighting. Forrest replied with a comment that still exemplifies the essence of war:

> Damn such nonsense. War means fightin' and fightin' means killin'. Turn the grindstone.

The national motto of Scotland is: "No one insults me with impunity." Forrest agreed with that attitude, even if he never heard the words spoken. He demonstrated the same spirit when, in the spring of 1863, one of his own officers shot Forrest in a fit of anger during an argument. Forrest went after his assailant with a pocket knife, roaring, "No damn man kills me and lives!" That attitude would attract as recruits men who were hardy, inventive, dedicated, and dangerous—men who understood the realities of war and laughed at those same realities. Forrest would spread men imbued with this spirit across the entire cavalry force of the Army of Tennessee, as he frequently was forced to turn over his command to another and begin again to raise, equip, and arm a new force.

By the autumn of 1862, Forrest's deeds had created a legend. Personal leadership, exercised from the front; a fit application of analysis leading to the formulation of effective plans; skillful maneuvering followed by fierce attacks and implacable pursuit of a retreating foe; an uncanny ability to discern the position and intentions of the enemy; a shrewd use of psychology—Forrest had put all on display North and South. These traits had begun to attract men whose spirits admired and emulated that of Forrest. Their presence in the ranks of his command would create a symbiotic relationship in which commander and commanded fed off the other. No single unit would have a greater share of that spirit than the Escort.

As Forrest made his way back to middle Tennessee, he sent a relative of his wife to the county in which he had been born. There the call went out for adventurous, active men who wanted to follow a fighter. Despite the presence of numerous Northern sympathizers and a Union garrison still occupying Nashville, the men Forrest wanted began to rally. Shelbyville, Tennessee, would be their first camp. There a new part of the Forrest legend would be born.

## CHAPTER 2

# Birth and Baptism of the Escort and Staff: 1862

As Forrest began yet another mustering of men to raise a command he was also gathering about him some close associates who would form the heart of his "military family." Some of the officers who would make up his Staff had been with him in his earlier commands, some as early as his original regiment; others would be joining Forrest as part of his new organization.

The social background of the members of the Staff and Escort is informative about them as a group and about the South in general. While the economy of the South was dominated by agriculture, this was by no means the only facet of the economy. Neither did slave owners dominate the ranks of farmers. According to the 1860 census, South-wide, about 10 percent of white citizens owned slaves. Of course, in some areas the incidence of slave owning was much higher, but there were many areas where the number of slave owners was lower. If all members of a slave owner's family, including children, are included in the figure, about one in four white Southerners had direct involvement with slave owning.

Of the slaveholding minority, three-quarters held between 1 and 9 slaves, with 4 being the most common number. A person who held 20 to 30 slaves was part of a small economic elite, while only one-tenth of 1 percent of slave owners held as many as 100 slaves. The picture of a "plantation aristocracy" living in the lap of luxury, supported by the labor of numerous slaves, is largely the stuff of fiction. The typical slave owner did not sit in a rocking chair on the front porch of a white-columned mansion listening to the sweet spirituals sung by the field hands. He picked cotton, pulled corn, and cut tobacco alongside his slaves.

The size of farms reflected the incidence of slaveholding. In the 1860 census, 75 percent of all farms were 160 acres or less, the amount of land one would expect to be owned and worked by a non-slaveholding family.

A great many trades were practiced in the South because these skills were essential in any developed society, even a predominantly agricultural one. Smiths and millers were rather common, as were carpenters, cabinetmakers, printers, wholesale factors, and store clerks. The men of the Escort and Staff had among them representatives of all these backgrounds.

When Forrest chose those who would serve on his Staff, he turned to men he knew whose prewar experience prepared them for their military duties. Except for aides, he did not draw on planters for staff members. Of course, many businessmen engaged in farming as well as commerce. For example, Charles W. Anderson was a railroad executive but he owned several hundred acres and held twenty slaves.

Staff members and Escort officers tended to come from backgrounds of greater wealth and to have more education than did the enlisted men. However, John Eaton, a popular officer, owned no slaves, and Nath Boone is also not listed as a slaveholder in the 1860 census. Many of the enlisted men were not of legal age and it is no surprise that they owned no property, including slaves. However, over 85 percent of the enlisted men of the Escort came from families that owned no slaves.

The Escort, like the rest of the Confederate forces, was made up mostly of yeomen, led by better-educated and wealthier men. This characteristic is not unique to Confederates; it was common in the Union army and is a profile of the U.S. armed forces of today.

Charles W. Anderson was born in Kentucky in 1825 and moved with his family to Nashville when he was about ten years old. He had at one time been the captain of a riverboat but then had gone to work as an officer with the Nashville & Chattanooga Railroad. Because of this experience, Anderson first served in the transportation department of the Confederate government. His skill as an organizer was demonstrated in carrying out the assignment he received shortly after the surrender of Fort Donelson. Stationed in Chattanooga at the time, Anderson received a telegram from Gen. Albert Sidney Johnston telling him to prepare for about 1,200 sick and convalescent soldiers being evacuated from Nashville. At that time there was not a single army hospital in Chattanooga. Yet, with the help of citizens, three large buildings were taken over, cleaned, and supplied. Although there were no beds available when the first soldiers arrived, Mrs. Ben Hardin Helm took charge of getting women to sew sacks to be stuffed for mattresses while Anderson oversaw the building of bed frames. Within a week each evacuee had been housed, was being fed, and had his own bed (CV 4: 289-90).

Soon Anderson found it necessary to return to his home to attend to his wife, who was seriously ill. This placed him within Union lines, and he was soon discovered and made a prisoner. Because of a prewar friendship with Andrew Johnson, who was just being named Union governor of occupied Tennessee, Anderson was placed on parole so he could stay with his wife.

When the Union forces retreated from middle Tennessee in response to Bragg's move into Kentucky, Anderson again found himself in the path of the war.

> Forrest was following close on the heels of Buell's army; and after the Federals had all gone by, my first meeting with General Forrest took place on the pike near my home. Introducing myself, I rode with him a mile or more toward LaVergne and expressed a desire to join his command. The day Buell passed my home myself and family were on a visit to a neighbor some four miles away. McCook's cavalry formed in front of my house, and soon every building as well as my residence was in flames. They took my portraits out, of which I had two, smashed the frames, tacked the canvas to trees, and jabbed their sabers through the eyes. They drove my negroes out of their houses and fired the buildings. (CV 18: 84)

Anderson was chosen for the Staff when Forrest found he could write orders in a clear and precise fashion. As assistant adjutant and inspector general, Anderson would spend more time in Forrest's company than any other member of the Staff and would also take on the duty of being the general's personal secretary (CV 16: 26).

As inspector general, Anderson would visit every unit in Forrest's command. His duties as assistant adjutant often took him into positions of great danger, for example, carrying a flag of truce into an enemy position to demand an unconditional surrender, or leading a small body of troops, such as the Escort Company, to block the escape route of an enemy force. Anderson was once assigned the distasteful duty of protecting the home of Col. Fielding Hurst of Purdy, Tennessee, after the Union colonel had used his Sixth U.S. Tennessee Cavalry to burn the homes of many Confederates in the area (CV 23: 451). Anderson was very influential in persuading Forrest to stay in the South when the war came to an end instead of going to Mexico with the governor of Tennessee, Isham Harris. At the time of the surrender, Anderson took Forrest's roughly developed ideas and put them into the polished farewell address that was issued to the command.

After the war, Anderson remained a close friend of Forrest and was very active in various veterans organizations until his death in 1908 (CV 9: 494). He worked for the Nashville & Chattanooga Railroad until 1879, when poor health limited his activity. He managed his farm for the remainder of his life (*Memphis Commercial Appeal,* May 16, 1905).

John P. Strange of Memphis had served in Forrest's first regiment, the "Old Regiment," as sergeant major, but after the reorganization following Fort Donelson he became adjutant for the brigade with the rank of major. He would serve in this capacity for the duration of the war (Lindsley 2: 761). Major Strange was wounded and captured at Parkers Crossroads and saw a good deal of hard service but was still with the Staff at the surrender in 1865. He was active in the Veterans Association for many years, while also serving as a judge in Memphis. Major Strange may have had tuberculosis, since he was excused from duty in the spring of 1864 because of a "hemorrhage of the lungs." He died before 1900 (CV 8: 237).

Maj. C. S. Severson served as brigade quartermaster. He proved quite adept at his job, especially in procuring horses for the artillery. At Chickamauga, the battery once commanded by Captain Freeman went into combat with all guns drawn by matched teams. Because of poor health, Major Severson resigned his commission in 1864 (CV 8: 14).

Capt. George V. Rambaut, born in Petersburg, Virginia, in 1837, had been manager of a Memphis hotel before the war. When the war began he joined Forrest's "Old Regiment" as a private. Captain Rambaut recalled later that on the night before Shiloh, when he was a young and inexperienced soldier, his command turned out of their blankets and fell into line to receive an attack by the Yankees. The attack had been announced by the steady sound of tramping feet approaching the camp. When the "attackers" came close enough to be seen, they proved to be a single artillery horse that had slipped its tether. When Forrest was promoted to brigadier in 1862, Rambaut was asked to become chief commissary officer, utilizing his prewar hotel experience in Memphis. Combat soon seasoned the captain. Rambaut was captured near Columbia, Tennessee, in February 1863, when he took a wrong turn while leading an advance party and blundered into a Yankee detachment. Soon exchanged, he was promoted to major and served the rest of the war. Rambaut was in the process of writing a biography of Forrest when he died shortly after the close of the war (CV 3: 187, 5: 277).

Maj. J. B. Cowan, a cousin of Forrest's wife, was practicing medicine at Meridianville, Alabama, near Huntsville, when the war began. He was a native of Fayetteville, Tennessee, and the son of a prominent Cumberland Presbyterian minister. He had graduated from the New York Medical College in 1855.

Cowan's first assignment in the Confederate army was to the Ninth Mississippi Infantry, but he joined Forrest in December 1861. He would eventually become chief surgeon on Forrest's Corps, but before that he would remove from Forrest's back the rifle bullet that hit him near the spine at Fallen Timbers on the retreat from Shiloh. Cowan would also be present when Forrest had his furious and profane interview with Bragg following the Battle of Chickamauga. Cowan liked to be where the action was and, while the fighting was in progress, was frequently found in the front lines instead of at the hospital. Despite being older than many of the Staff, Cowan was a jokester and often the liveliest man around the headquarters campfire. Following the war Cowan moved to Tullahoma, Tennessee, where he was active in several veterans organizations and was a founding member of the Escort and Staff Veterans Association. When Cowan died on July 24, 1909, he was survived by only one member of the Staff. Cowan had been feeling unwell for several days but on that day felt better and walked down the street to a drugstore. He presented the pharmacist with a prescription he had written for himself, and while waiting for it to be filled, he fell dead (CV 17: 424).

George Dashiel of Memphis became paymaster under Forrest. In his official capacity he was not often called on for battlefield duty, but the "boys" were always glad to see Captain Dashiel coming when the government in Richmond decided to issue their pay. Dashiel was born in Maryland on January 10, 1828, and his family moved to Bedford County, Tennessee, in 1838. When Fort Sumter was fired on, Dashiel was living in Memphis and was sent by Gov. Isham Harris as a special agent to New York City to purchase blankets and other military supplies for the state forces of Tennessee. In this task he was successful (*Memphis Commercial Appeal*, May 16, 1905). When Tennessee left the Union, he enlisted as a private in Company B, 154th Tennessee Infantry, one of the militia units that received permission to keep its prewar numerical designation. Soon the War Department transferred Dashiel to the cavalry and ordered him to report to Gen. Leonidas Polk. The "Fighting Bishop" made the cavalryman paymaster for Cheatham's Division, a post he occupied until the spring of 1863, when his services were requested by Forrest. Captain Dashiel served with Forrest for the remainder of the war (CV 9: 99).

Sixteen-year-old William M. Forrest served his father as aide-de-camp. Since this was his only son and Forrest was concerned for his moral development, the general "borrowed" the sons of Bishop James Otey of the Episcopal Church and Brig. Daniel Donelson, adding them to his command so "Willie" could have appropriate companions. Willie was only nineteen when the war was over. The presence of both her husband and only son in combat must have given Mrs. Forrest many sleepless nights. Following the war, Forrest sent his son to study law at the University of Mississippi, where he became one of the first students to graduate under the tutelage of L. Q. C. Lamar. The war made Willie restless and he did not do well in the practice of law. He went west to drive a stagecoach and run a ranch. He later returned to Memphis, where he owned a company that built railroads and levees (*Memphis Commercial Appeal*, May 16, 1905).

On the night of the day on which Fort Sumter was fired on, Samuel Donelson left the University of North Carolina at Chapel Hill to return to Tennessee and offer his services to the state forces. He served on the staff of his father, Daniel Donelson, until the general was killed in April 1863. Samuel joined the Staff in January 1864 and held the rank of first lieutenant. His "mess" included Willie Forrest and Mercer Otey and was called by the rest of the Staff the "Infants Mess." Before the end of the war, Donelson would be assistant inspector general and Otey would assist in the adjutant's work (CV 9: 107).

Capt. Sam Freeman commanded Forrest's artillery, guns Forrest had captured at Murfreesboro on his raid of July 13, 1862. In many cases, the commander of a battery would not be considered to have any connection with the staff, but Forrest maintained strategic, and sometimes tactical, control over his artillery, so that

Freeman acted as if he were in a staff position. The survivors of the Staff certainly thought the artillery was a part of them because John W. Morton, Freeman's successor, was invited to join the Veterans Association. An attorney, Freeman was born near Nashville, attended Franklin College, and read law in Nashville. Before he became an attorney, Freeman had taught school at Mill Creek Academy near Franklin and at Mount Juliet Academy near Lebanon.

On April 10, 1863, a force under Forrest and Van Dorn attacked Franklin. While marching down the Lewisburg Pike near Douglas Church, the Confederate column was surprised by a sudden attack by the Fourth U.S. Regular Cavalry. Freeman was among those captured. The prisoners were forced to run back toward the Union lines, and when Freeman could not keep up with the mounted Union soldiers, one of them shot him in the face, killing him instantly (CV 19: 308, 21: 407, 25: 358). W. H. Whitsett was a soldier in Company F, Starnes Fourth Tennessee. He conducted Freeman's funeral the next day and said that Forrest cried "like a woman" during the service (CV 25: 359). Freeman was a very popular member of the Staff, and the Escort would not forget the manner of his death.

Replacing Freeman as artillery commander was John W. Morton. Under his command the "Bull Pups" of Forrest's artillery become famous across the western theater of the war. Morton was a student at Western Military Institute in Nashville when the war began. He enlisted in Maney's First Tennessee Infantry but was sent home when that unit went to western Virginia, because the regiment's colonel did not think Morton could handle campaigning in such rugged terrain. Before reaching home Morton joined Porter's Battery, the unit with which he fought at Fort Donelson. Captured there, he spent several months in Federal prisons before being exchanged and joining Forrest in the autumn of 1862.

When Morton first reported to Forrest, the general was very suspicious of him on two accounts. Since Morton was attempting to transfer to Forrest from Wheeler's command, Forrest thought Bragg might be trying to interfere in his command, perhaps even to plant a spy. Second, Morton was not an imposing physical specimen. Forrest described him as "a whey-faced boy," and it was only when the "boy" rode over a hundred miles in under twenty-four hours to get a formal discharge from Wheeler's command that Forrest began to feel there might be some potential in him. Allowing Morton to accompany his command on the first west Tennessee raid, Forrest promised to "capture some guns for him." Two guns captured during the December 1862 raid became the nucleus of "Morton's Bull Pups."

Having joined while still eighteen years of age, Morton did not celebrate his twenty-first birthday until September 19, 1863, right in the middle of the Battle of Chickamauga. On that birthday, a hungry mule chewed up a new uniform he had stored in a wagon, all three of his personal mounts were taken out of action through being hit by gunfire, and his personal servant got scared and ran away with all his rations. Morton was with the command from 1862 until the surrender. After the war, he was active in the Klan and is the person who initiated Forrest into that organization. He was also active in the veterans groups formed by the Escort Company and Staff (Morton, *Artillery,* passim; CV 7: 44) and served for many years as the secretary of state of Tennessee.

Capt. Charles S. Hill served as chief of ordnance on the Staff. Since Forrest frequently rearmed his men with superior captured weapons, such a post must have been a challenging one. On most occasions, both the cavalrymen and the artillery were supplied with a wide variety of weapons (CV 26: 103).

Capt. John G. Mann was the chief engineer. No one seems to think of engineers in connection with Forrest, yet the general is widely known for the rapid construction of bridges over bodies of water both broad and swift, using locally available materials. Clearly, a good engineer officer was an asset in such enterprises. Mann had originally enlisted in Company G, "The Jackson Greys," of the Sixth Tennessee Infantry. Following Shiloh, he was assigned to the staff of Gen. Benjamin Franklin Cheatham as captain of engineers. Forrest found him here and had him assigned to his own staff (CV 12: 426; Lindsley, 216).

There was no official chaplain on Forrest's staff. Many people continue to assume that the rough, profane Forrest had no use for religion, but this supposition is false. Maj. (later Col.) David C. Kelley served with Forrest from the beginning of the war and filled the role of chaplain, although in an unofficial capacity. Born in 1833 in Leeville, Wilson County, Tennessee, Kelley early decided to enter the ministry of the Methodist Episcopal Church, South. In the pursuit of that profession, he came to possess a talent unique in Forrest's cavalry, if not the entire Confederate army. Kelley spoke Chinese. He was sent to China by his church and served there for several years before returning to the South. When the war began, Kelley was pastor of a Methodist church in New Market, Alabama, not far from Huntsville. In that village, he raised a company of cavalry known as "Kelley's Troopers" and led them to Memphis, where they became part of Forrest's original regiment (CV 20: 36, 19: 291, 7: 421).

Although a minister, Kelley had no desire to be a chaplain. He had observed chaplains at work in China and felt that these men did not receive treatment that was dignified or that recognized their value to the units they served. So Kelley became known as "Forrest's fighting preacher." He often shared a tent with Forrest and always held morning and evening prayers, with Forrest usually in attendance. During the war, Kelley was often called on to conduct funerals for the men of his regiment or for others who fell in battle. Writing in *The Methodist Review* in April 1900, Kelley recalled of Forrest:

> He was an impressive speaker, and on several occasions I have heard him deliver an address in most effective manner. I was a messmate with Forrest for more than a year in the early part of the war. During this time a blessing was always asked at the table and a prayer offered before retiring, while on more than one occasion Forrest declared that his hope of safety and success rested more on the prayers of his mother and wife than in any skill of his own. He never failed during his whole military service to encourage preaching to his troops. Whenever requested a general order was issued from headquarters announcing special services and urgently inviting the attendance of his command. When possible, he was always himself present, a reverent listener.

Kelley was noted for his ability to conduct small unit operations and frequently won engagements against heavy odds. His motto was: "In the path of duty there is no danger." This attitude made him ready to follow all orders—the ideal soldier, in the opinion of Forrest. His bravery won the loyalty of the men in the regiment he came to command. Years after the war, one of them said, "Kelley would fight when there was fighting to do and would preach to us when there was leisure" (CV 3: 41, 102, 278, 479, 6: 24). Kelley's coolness under fire was first noted at Fort Donelson. One of his comrades recalled:

> I was there when the enemy tried to pass the Fort with his fleet. Our regiment being cavalry could not be used in defense of the fort. So we were placed back to await orders. During this bombardment and when it looked like the furies of hell were turned loose on us, I looked down the line, and saw Kelley sitting on a camp stool leaning against a tent pole reading his Bible. My curiosity was at once excited, and wondering if it were possible for a man to be interested even in reading God's word under such circumstances, I walked to where he was, stood close to him until I was satisfied that he was deeply interested in the Book. I went back and called some comrades' attention to it, and after going close to him they returned in perfect amazement, that any man could be so composed amid such roaring of cannon shots, and screaming shells. (CV 3: 41)

From Columbia, Frank C. Dunnington decided to volunteer as an aide-de-camp on Forrest's staff. He had already begun a career as a journalist and would later become the brother-in-law of the famous journalist and orator Edward W. Carmack (CV 4: 84).

During the spring of 1864, W. H. Brand joined the Staff to assist Major Strange as acting adjutant general. Strange was in poor health during some of this time, and Brand signed most of the orders and reports coming from Forrest's command. Brand had been in the Trans-Mississippi and had served with Sterling Price, coming east with that general at the time of the Corinth Campaign. When Strange was able to resume his duties for Forrest, Brand would become adjutant of one of the brigades in the cavalry command (CV 5: 278; OR 39: 279).

The Staff was about to get some new comrades-in-arms with whom they would become close associates: the Escort Company. Both groups would live at headquarters, and members of the Escort Company would accompany Staff officers on special assignments. Even before the Kentucky Campaign had cleared middle Tennessee of Yankees, Montgomery Little had been given the responsibility of going to Bedford County, Tennessee, and raising a body of young men to serve as a bodyguard, or escort, for Forrest. Little was born in Rowan County, North Carolina, on July 18, 1825, and his family moved to Smith County, Tennessee, in 1829. Left an orphan at an early age, Little received assistance from an elder brother to attend St. Mary's College in Kentucky. For a time he was a planter in Mississippi, but Little was in business in Memphis when the war began. He was a Union man until Lincoln called for troops to invade the South; then he became a supporter of Southern independence and joined Forrest. Like Forrest, Little had relatives in Bedford County and, using their plantation as a base of operations, he began recruiting men for the Escort under the very nose of the Federal garrison in Shelbyville. When Union troops withdrew from Shelbyville in September 1862, Little called his recruits together (Henry, 130).

One of the young men Little recruited was Johnston S. Ryall. He had not joined the Confederate forces in the first wave of enlistments following secession but had stayed at home on the family farm, Woodlawn, in Bedford County, Tennessee. However, he had ties of friendship with many who had enlisted, and he heard the call to enlist before he took his oath to the Confederacy as part of the Escort. As early as January 1862, Ryall had written the following to Nathan Boone:

> Long has it been my desire to be with you, and share the burden borne by you since your company first left Shelbyville. I have been arranging my affairs so that I might join and suffer in or rejoice with you in accord with fates decree. I have been behind longer than I expected when you left, yet, busy all the time, and now I am about ready to come to you, feeling that I shall soon learn the soldiers duty and be prepared for assisting actively if soon called upon. So far perhaps I have done better for myself and country by being at home but I cannot stay here in comparative safety, while my friends and companions are exposed to danger. What ever is to be borne by those I love, my shoulders are ready and willing to bear their part. If success crown their efforts, let my voice mingle in the joyful sound, if not, let us all rest in one grave together. . . . I met Montgomery Little and Bill at a dancing party at Joe Thompsons last evening. (Ryall, January 24, 1862)

It seems Little was active in going to the places where young men were to be found and working on their consciences to encourage enlistment.

As soon as the band had gathered and a company was organized, elections were held for officers. Little became the captain of the Escort Company, with Nathan Boone, Matthew Cortner,

Daniel Dunaway, George L. Cowan, and John Eaton as lieutenants.

Nathan Boone, usually called "Nath," was from Booneville in Lincoln County. He was a descendant of Daniel Boone and showed much of the resourcefulness of that old pioneer. He had joined the Tennessee volunteers to fight in Mexico when he was only sixteen years old and served for three years in that war. He was described as "fat, fair, forty, and fearless . . . his courage knew no bounds, his heart no fear." When the Union army under Gen. Don Carlos Buell occupied Shelbyville in early 1862, Boone was living on his farm at Boons Hill south of Shelbyville. That town became one of the distribution points for Federal garrisons scattered across middle Tennessee. Boone gathered five young men and made a raid on the small Union force that was guarding the supplies. Pinning the garrison inside the depot, Boone and his little band loaded two wagons with tents and camp equipment, set fire to the rest of the accumulated stores, and escaped into the hills. These were just the sorts of men Little was anxious to recruit (Cowan).

Although a good soldier, Boone was not ambitious for rank. He began and ended the war as a lieutenant, although he was in command of the Escort on numerous occasions when other officers were disabled by wounds or illness. When Captain Little was killed, Boone was next in line for the command, but he suggested the post go to J. C. Jackson. Boone was wounded more than once during the war, his last injury being received in the fighting around Selma in 1865. Attacked by several Union cavalrymen wielding sabers, Boone received a severe blow to the head, which left a scar the size and shape of a horseshoe. His horse carried him out of the fight as he lay fainting on the saddle horn. He later said the horse had "exercised uncommon good judgment in taking me away from such a mix-up when all the Yankees had said was 'Go to the rear, damn you!'" (CV 25: 6). Following the war, Boone served as sheriff of Lincoln County, Tennessee, and was appointed warden of the State Prison in Nashville by Governor Marks. He was also active in the movement to prohibit the manufacture, sale, and consumption of liquor. Boone died at his home in Booneville on November 21, 1898 (CV 7: 175, 2: 308).

Matthew Cortner came from a prominent family in Bedford County, Tennessee, and originally had joined the Seventeenth Tennessee Infantry, where he became captain of Company B. On May 8, 1862, that regiment reenlisted for the duration of the war, and Cortner was not reelected captain. He returned home for a short time but soon became part of the nucleus of the Escort Company (CV 31: 47; Lindsley, 351).

George L. Cowan was born in County Derry, Ireland, in 1842 and came with his family to America in 1850. His parents,

Lt. George L. Cowan

Robert and Hannah Cowan, had four sons and six daughters and became respected citizens of Bedford County, Tennessee, although they were not wealthy. The Cowans do not appear in the 1860 list of slaveholders in that county. The 1860 census lists George as "about age 15" and living in Nashville, where he was assisting one of his older brothers in running a dry-goods company. At about age nineteen, he enlisted in the company formed by Nathan Boone and served with the Escort Company from start to finish. After the war he became a wholesale merchant in Nashville and married, in 1884, Hattie McGavock, the daughter of John McGavock of Carnton Plantation in Franklin. Cowan was active in various veterans associations following the war, serving as recording secretary of the Escort and Staff Veterans Association for many years. He died in Franklin on September 1, 1919 (CV 20: 79).

Attaching himself to the Escort as Cowan's body servant was Jones Greer, born in Lincoln County, Tennessee, in 1844. Greer was awarded a pension for his Confederate service by the state of Tennessee. At that time, he was living in Marshall County in the village of Belfast and was farming ten acres of land (*Confederate Pension Records*).

John Eaton, of Tullahoma, rose to the rank of second lieutenant in the Escort (CV 5: 183), as did J. H. Crenshaw, J. O. Crump, and Daniel P. Dunaway (CV 12: 426). Thomas Jackson Eaton, called Jack, joined the Escort with John Eaton. During Forrest's 1864 foray into middle Tennessee, Jack paid an exciting visit home.

> Jack Eaton, Henry Lipscomb, and Robert Terry went to the home of Eaton's father for their dinner. While there twenty-five or thirty Yankees run upon them. While crossing a field Henry Lipscomb got off his horse and laid down the fence, while Jack and Bob turned on their horses and held the enemy at bay until Henry "opened the gap" and mounted his horse. They rode away, leaving three or four of the enemy wounded, while the others were awestruck at their failure to capture or injure any of the three. (CV 9: 260)

The character of the enlisted men may be further assessed by the record of T. R. Priest, of Maury County, Tennessee. Priest joined the Maury Artillery at Columbia in the spring of 1861. He was captured with his unit at Fort Donelson and sent to prison. Exchanged in 1863, he was assigned to Port Hudson, where he was captured a second time. Rapidly exchanged, the Maury Artillery was disbanded, but Priest, tired of surrendering with the artillery, joined the Escort Company. He was wounded in the fighting around Selma, Alabama, in April 1865 and was not paroled from the hospital until June of that year. He died at his home in Franklin, Tennessee, on June 22, 1920 (CV 29: 188).

Martin Livingston Parks had joined Peter Turney's First Tennessee on April 29, 1861, at age thirty-two. When his one-year enlistment was up, he elected to return to Tennessee, where he had left his wife and children. On October 27, 1862, he joined the Escort and became first sergeant of the unit (Watt).

W. W. Strickland was serving in the Twenty-seventh Tennessee Infantry but was very much attracted to the life of a cavalryman, especially one in the Escort. While home on furlough, he joined the Escort, only to be tracked down by the provost marshal and arrested to be returned to his regiment. Forrest had become attached to Strickland, so he sent seven conscripts to take his place in the infantry, enabling Strickland to stay with the Escort. Strickland would die in combat at Anthonys Hill near Pulaski on Christmas Day 1864, during Hood's retreat from Tennessee (Jordan and Pryor, 460).

Robert Cannon Garrett hailed from the community of Rover in Bedford County, the home of the future commander of the Escort, John Jackson. Garrett enlisted in the Confederate forces in 1862 at age eighteen. He fought with the Escort until the end of the war, being twice wounded. His pension application to the state of Tennessee notes that the injury received at Chickamauga was to the right arm and caused a partial disability, which had grown worse with the passage of time. At the time of the application, Garrett was a member of the Tennessee General Assembly (McCullough).

M. A. Enochs joined Peter Turney's First Tennessee Confederate infantry at the age of seventeen. At the Battle of Seven Pines, outside Richmond, he was wounded in the right leg but was taken to Richmond, where he began his recovery at the home of citizens who took him in until he could come back to Bedford County, Tennessee. Since the Union army under Gen. Don Carlos Buell was occupying the area, he was hidden by his mother until fully recovered, by which time the Kentucky Campaign of 1862 had cleared the area of Yankees. Returning to

Virginia, Enochs rejoined his regiment and took part in Pickett's Charge on the third day at Gettysburg. He was wounded twice in the charge and captured when Lee fell back to Virginia. Like many of the Gettysburg prisoners, he was exchanged in the early fall, returned to middle Tennessee (now occupied by Union forces), and recuperated at home. Once his health permitted, he made his way through the lines to north Mississippi, where he joined the Escort and served with them until the end of the war. Enochs became a medical doctor following the war and died at his home in Bedford County in 1918 (CV 26: 216).

J. B. Erwin was also a teenaged boy in Bedford County who was attracted to the Escort. Following the war he became a Methodist minister and served the congregation in Shelbyville for many years (CV 9: 297).

Polk Arnold of Shelbyville joined the Escort in 1863 at the age of nineteen. He served as a private until his death at Harrisburg, Mississippi, on July 17, 1864. His widow, CaldoniaArnold, received a pension years later (*Confederate Pension Records*). The pension application states that Arnold was a Negro.

Another testimony of the spirit of the Escort Company would be the service record of Thomas C. Little, the nephew of Montgomery Little. Thomas came from a wealthy family in Bedford County, Tennessee, whose home was some two miles from Shelbyville on the Lewisburg Turnpike. Thomas had been too young to take part in the early days of the war, but when Forrest came into the area in September 1864 on his raid against the Nashville & Chattanooga Railroad, the youth ran away from home to join. Assigned to the Escort Company, he fought with them for a time before being sent to Saltville, Virginia, with the Fourth Tennessee. From Saltville he opposed Sherman's march for a time and was then sent back west. There the Escort met the Army of Tennessee at the Tennessee River, as the battered remnants of that once-proud force fell back from Nashville. Thomas served with the Escort until the surrender. He was sixteen when he first joined (Dyer and Moore, 3: 1369-71) and lived until 1933. During most of his postwar life, Little was the minister of the Church of Christ in Lincoln County, Tennessee.

Marcus Black served during the first part of the war as an infantryman in the Eighth Tennessee but came back to his home after Perryville and joined the Escort (CV 11: 447). D. R. Bedford of Lincoln County followed the same path. After the war he and his wife moved to Texas, where they lived for many years. Mrs. Bedford wrote to *The Confederate Veteran* in 1918 to say they enjoyed reading about the other old soldiers and to recall how she had spent the war knitting gloves and socks for "the boys in gray" (CV 26: 44).

Hugh L. W. Boone also fought in the Eighth Tennessee before joining the Escort. His obituary says:

> Entering the Confederate service as a private in the Eighth Tennessee Regiment at its organization, he served with that regiment until Forrest's escort was raised. He was transferred to this company, and served with it until the surrender at Gainesville, Ala., May 12, 1865. Hugh was one of the bravest of Forrest's Cavalry, discharging every duty with a cheerfulness that showed his heart was in his work. He was known in the company as "Uncle John" and was a favorite with his comrades. (CV 7: 175)

Luke E. Wright joined the Escort as a heavy artilleryman. After Wright served at New Madrid in 1862, his command was transferred to Vicksburg and he was captured there. Sent to the exchange camp at Demopolis, Alabama, many members of the heavy artillery were given furloughs before being ordered to reassemble. Wright, like many others, refused to return to the artillery service and joined Forrest. He served with the Escort until the end of the war. In later years, Wright would become secretary of war under Pres. Theodore Roosevelt (CV 30: 470; Horn, 1: 121).

W. F. Buchanan joined the Escort in Shelbyville, survived the war, and returned to Shelbyville, where he became active in the local bivouac of the United Confederate Veterans. In 1909, he served as president of the Escort and Staff Veterans Association (CV 8: 34; 17: 359).

W. T. Green and Thomas J. Brown joined from the area around Lynchburg, Tennessee. These men came home in 1864 in a very tragic fashion. They were scouting for Forrest during his raid against the Nashville & Chattanooga Railroad when they were captured by Union forces, who accused them of being "bushwhackers." They were captured about four miles from Lynchburg. Green had been mounted on the same horse as Bill Davis, a civilian who was guiding them, when they were captured.

After the men surrendered, the Union commander rushed up to the soldiers, demanding that the men be shot immediately. Green tackled the officer, took away his pistol, and killed him. The rest of the Union force riddled Green with bullets. Davis and Brown were then given a "drum-head" court martial and were also shot on the spot (CV 4: 330).

Crockett Hudson was living near Eagleville when he joined the Escort. His spirit was not broken by combat nor by his experience in prison after his capture. Incarcerated at Camp Morton, Indiana, Hudson was forced to participate in a "dress parade" put on for the benefit of visiting civilian dignitaries, both male and female. One of the women visitors stopped her carriage near where Hudson stood in the ranks of the "parade" and loudly inquired why the "Rebels wore such ragged clothes." Hudson replied, "Gentlemen of the South have two suits, one they wear among nice people and one we wear when killing hogs. It is the latter we are wearing today" (CV 21: 58). The carriage drove on in silence.

From Rippa Villa plantation in Spring Hill, Thomas Gorum Cheairs joined the Escort. His father would also be associated with the Staff at intervals during the war. Of Thomas Cheairs, it was said:

> He enlisted in Forrest's Escort in February, 1863, and served until he was paroled May 18, 1865. He was General Forrest's ideal of a good soldier. Ever near his chief, he was ready to go and do whatever ordered, however dangerous it might be. (CV 17: 609)

Lee H. Russ was known as "the baby of the Escort" (CV 14: 253), being just sixteen when he joined it. His brother, William, was a sergeant in Company C, Fifth U.S. Tennessee Cavalry. This group of "galvanized Yankees" was recruited in Bedford County and was something of a terror to its Confederate neighbors. While William was visiting the family home, Lee got up in the middle of the night, stole his brother's pistols, boots, horse, and saddle, and, so equipped, rode to Dalton, Georgia, where he joined the Escort shortly after the Battle of Chickamauga (*Nashville Banner*, September 6, 1894). After the war, Lee moved to Birmingham, Alabama, and became a journalist with the *Age-Herald* newspaper. In 1906, he delivered one of the welcoming speeches when the surviving veterans of Forrest's Corps met in Memphis (CV 14: 253).

## The Escort Goes to War

On October 5, 1862, 105 enlisted men and twenty-one officers left Shelbyville to join Forrest at Murfreesboro (see Appendix A). On the first day of this journey, the unit marched about twelve miles toward Murfreesboro and camped at Ransom's Spring. Early the next day, the bivouac was roused by the sound of gunfire coming from the north and soon learned that a fight was going on at LaVergne. Arriving at Murfreesboro, Captain Little formed the men for an inspection by Forrest.

> What a fine body of men, Captain[, Forrest said]. Have you any more where these came from? Captain Little, proud of his men, said, No, General, they can't be found that will equal my boys. (Cowan)

Events were to prove the truth of this boast. Although these "boys" were not veterans and were mostly armed with shotguns, their determination, bravery, and ingenuity would soon make the Escort Company a legend.

Born at Shelbyville, the Escort Company would be baptized in west Tennessee, at Lexington, Trenton, Union City, and Parkers Crossroads. The occasion would be Forrest's first raid into the western part of the state. The main body of Forrest's command as it stood in the closing weeks of 1862 was the Fourth Tennessee Cavalry led by Col. James W. Starnes, a physician in civilian life; the Eighth Tennessee under George G. Dibrell; the Ninth Tennessee under Col. J. B. Biffle; the Fourth Alabama under Col. A. A. Russell; Freeman's Battery; and the Escort Company (Wyeth, 90). Soon the Escort would have a reputation to equal that of the brigade of which it was a part.

The raid into west Tennessee would begin with Forrest crossing the Tennessee River at Clifton between December 13 and 15. Col. Nicholas Nichols Cox had been leading a battalion of cavalry in that area for some time, operating between the mouth of the Duck River and the town of Savannah. Cox was born in Bedford County, like so many of Forrest's associates, was left fatherless at the age of only a few months, and was raised by his mother, who brought up thirteen children without ever remarrying. Cox graduated from Cumberland College in Lebanon, Tennessee, in 1858 and was practicing law in Perry County, just across the river from Clifton, when the war began (BCHQ 2: 49-50). He was called on to find the best spot to cross the river and to prepare the means for doing so. Cox chose Clifton, which had a steamboat landing and a ferry. Carpenters collected materials and built two small flat-boats, each capable of carrying about twenty-five men. These were hidden in a slough until the command arrived on December 13 (Lindsley, 883-85).

In a rain that had fallen steadily for several days, Forrest's command, led by the general and his Escort, rode into Clifton on that afternoon. The soldiers occupied all the public buildings in the village in an attempt to stay dry while the entire brigade came up. On the morning of the fourteenth, part of Forrest's brigade crossed at the steamboat landing and the rest just below the town at a place called Double Islands (the islands have long since been washed away by the river). While the crossing was in progress, John Morton approached Forrest and asked if he and the few men he had recruited for his promised artillery battery could be issued weapons so they could fight as cavalry until some cannon were captured. Forrest looked long and hard at the officer he had just called "a whey-faced boy" a few days earlier and then sent an order to Captain Freeman to "loan" Morton two guns (Morton, *Artillery,* 47-48). The river crossing was completed on December 15, and the command moved north.

On December 17, near Livingston, Forrest overtook the command of Union colonel Robert Ingersol. The Yankees were still forming in a defensive position when Forrest charged with Dibrell's and Biffle's regiments, four companies of the Fourth Alabama under Capt. Frank Gurley, and the Escort Company. Breaking the left of the Union line, Forrest and the Escort swung around to attack the other flank, which was made up of Tennessee Unionists. The field suddenly cleared of blue soldiers.

This engagement was described by V. Y. Cook.

> I was a boy at the time, just past my fourteenth birthday, and had not then joined the army; but was on a runaway from home, with a few choice associates for that purpose, trying to get South through the Federal lines, being closely followed by my father, who, while in perfect accord with the Southern cause, objected to my entering its army on account of youth.
>
> Thus on the 17th of December, 1862, we were caught almost in the very jaws of the two hostile forces. Having quit the main road for a few miles to avoid a collision with a Federal cavalry column

moving southward, upon coming into the road again we gladly, though unexpectedly, met General Forrest's advance, composed of four companies of Russell's 4th Alabama Cavalry, commanded by Capt. Frank B. Gurley, then near Lexington, in West Tennessee, and which in a very few minutes thereafter encountered the 3d Battalion of the 5th Ohio Cavalry, some three hundred strong, commanded by Capt. James C. Harrison, which command Captain Gurley charged and drove rearward at a furious gait until the eastern limits of Lexington were reached, making many captures. There strong epaulments had been hastily erected for the Federal artillery, with dismounted cavalry on each flank and in support.

Here Captain Gurley formed for battle and paused for alignment, at which juncture General Forrest arrived with the main body of his command, and, with an eye and judgment equal to any emergency, ordered the position on the Federal left carried, which order was promptly and gallantly executed by his ever-willing and resolute Tennesseans and with their characteristic impetuosity and dash, which nothing in blue withstood that day.

I sat upon my horse and stared with boyish wonderment at what appeared an apparition, the most inspiring personage my eyes had ever beheld. It was General Forrest superbly mounted upon a spirited animal, which seemed to catch the inspiration of its master as he led his battalions by our position rightward toward the Federal left; and soon we heard heavy firing in that direction, accompanied by the Rebel yell, which transmitted the result to those sturdy soldiers where we were, and they in turn announced its significance to us. At that moment Captain Gurley ordered our line forward, which, coming within the zone of the Federal artillery fire, was quickly dismounted and advanced in splendid style.

The 7th Tennessee Federal Cavalry, commanded by Lieut. Col. Isaac R. Hawkins, occupied the Federal left, in what was considered a strong position; but when the Tennessee Confederates advanced toward them, their line vanished like vapor, and thus the position occupied by Colonel Ingersol with the 11th Illinois Cavalry, dismounted, was flanked and enfiladed, and he and most of his officers and men captured, together with all his artillery, small arms, and ammunition. . . .

General Forrest might have been defeated, for his armament was very ineffective, being a mixture of flintlock muskets, double-barrel shotguns, and Derringer pistols, and supplied with only a few rounds of ammunition. He was therefore in poor condition to encounter such formidable equipment as Ingersol's men possessed. . . . My father now put in his appearance, which had a decided tendency to calm my military aspirations, . . . and I started back to "My Old Kentucky Home" somewhat crestfallen. (CV 15: 54-55)

Among the spoils of war Forrest gathered from this field were two three-inch Rodman rifles, which became the nucleus of Morton's Battery (Jordan and Pryor, 195). The 300 cavalrymen eagerly exchanged shotguns and antiquated pistols for modern arms.

On his own, deep in enemy-held territory, Forrest did not hesitate to trust his tactical judgment and so utilized the combination of a frontal feint and rear assault that he had developed as early as Sacramento.

Robert Ingersol, commander of the Eleventh Illinois, was a well-known agnostic who had gained a national reputation through his writings and lectures challenging orthodox Christianity. He was a "guest" of Forrest's cavalry for three days and, as an officer, messed with the Staff. In the evenings, a game of four-card-draw poker was a regular feature of the Staff mess. By the end of the second evening, Ingersol was broke and Dr. J. B. Cowan loaned him $100 in Confederate notes so he could keep playing. Several years after the war, Ingersol was delivering a lecture in Nashville and met Dr. Cowan. Ingersol remembered the incident and promptly handed

Standing, left to right: Lt. William Forrest, Capt. John Morton. Seated, left to right: Col. D. C. Kelley, Dr. J. B. Cowan, Capt. Charles W. Anderson

Cowan a check for $100. Loaning Confederate notes and collecting in U.S. currency was good business! (Morton, *Artillery,* 58; Henry, 508)

Trenton had the largest Union garrison between Corinth, Mississippi, and Columbus, Kentucky, commanded by Col. Jacob Fry, and Forrest determined to take that post next. Major Cox had been sent with his force of raw, poorly armed volunteers to burn the railroad trestle at Trenton. On his way there, Cox was warned by civilians that the town was heavily garrisoned and that the Union defenses centered around the railroad depot. This news was sent to Forrest, who brought up his Escort of about ninety men and two guns. At about 1:00 P.M. Forrest approached Trenton and sent a force under Major Cox to the east end of the town to attack the railroad depot. Since this was a focus of the Union defense, the building was barricaded with cotton bales and hogsheads of tobacco. With only the Escort following him, Forrest charged into Trenton itself, and with the women of the town showing the way by waving their handkerchiefs toward the depot, Forrest forced the defenders into their breastworks. A short match between sharpshooters cleared the way for Maj. John Strange to bring up Morton's artillery. Near the corner of Second and Brownsville streets in Trenton today stands Considine's Grocery. This was one of the buildings that had Union sharpshooters posted on its roof. About a hundred yards away once stood a tobacco stemmery. A sharpshooter from the Escort posted there exchanged ten rounds with a Union soldier, and at the eleventh round the Union man disappeared. When his body was recovered the next day, he was identified as Sam Piper, 122nd Illinois Infantry (Hill-Freeman). Three rounds fired from Morton's guns into the depot sent cotton bales and tobacco hogsheads flying, and soon several white flags were waving over the position.

The Escort had played the leading role in capturing 400 Union soldiers, 1,000 horses and mules, 20,000 rounds of artillery ammunition, 400,000 rounds of small-arms ammunition, 100,000 food rations, and other quartermaster stores. They also saw the first of their number fall, Felix Grundy Motlow (CV 3: 322; Wyeth, 100-101; Jordan and Pryor, 201). Motlow was born in what is now Moore County, Tennessee. In 1861 he, with two brothers, joined Peter Turney's First Tennessee Infantry and served in Virginia for his one-year term of enlistment. In 1862 he returned to Tennessee and joined the Escort. He was twenty-six at the time of his death.

The Staff, represented by Adjutant Strange, played a combat role at Trenton and had an even greater success the following day. Maj. G. V. Rambaut, chief commissary officer, was moving down a country road with his wagon train and a few men whose horses had gone lame when he came upon a Yankee stockade defending Kenton Station. Rambaut promptly used his men to surround the stockade and pin down the defenders until Forrest and his Escort could arrive with Freeman's Battery. One salvo from Freeman brought a surrender offer from the boys in blue. This must have been a proud day indeed for a commissary officer, and it was the second success in two days for the Escort (Wyeth, 102; Jordan and Pryor, 203).

The following day brought the Escort yet more glory. Accompanied by Major Cox's volunteers, soldiers who were rapidly becoming veterans after only two days' service, and an independent company commanded by Capt. Jeffrey Forrest, the Escort Company led the attack on Union City. An exchange of shots, followed by a demand to surrender unconditionally, transformed the Union garrison into Confederate prisoners (Wyeth, 105).

While the Escort and Staff had been busy with these duties, other elements of Forrest's force had demonstrated against Jackson to keep that large garrison occupied, and other units had wrecked miles of railroad, burning numerous trestles and bridges, and captured several additional Union garrisons.

By now, Yankees were swarming like hornets from a nest smacked with a stick, so Forrest decided to head back toward the Tennessee River. Recalling his men from the targets to which they had been assigned, and collecting his military booty, the general moved into the Obion River Bottoms, wrecking the numerous bridges behind him while making temporary repairs to causeways and bridges on the lesser roads he needed to follow. With most of the command engaged in road work, the Escort Company provided the advance guard.

## Parkers Crossroads

After a day of rest, on December 29 Forrest's command moved to a location about four miles from Parkers Crossroads. At the same time, two Union brigades, Fuller's and Dunham's, arrived in Huntington, twelve miles northeast. On December 30, Col. James

Starnes' regiment made a reconnaissance on the Huntington road but found no Union movement on that route. During this time, one of Forrest's regiments, Biffle's, was fighting near Trenton and William Forrest was leading a Confederate unit in an attack on Dunham's Union force near Clarksburg. These engagements gave the Union command a good idea of the location of Forrest's main body.

By December 31, Forrest was confronted by his pursuers at Parkers Crossroads. After sending out a small force to scout his rear for any approaching threat, Forrest attacked the Union force commanded by Col. C. T. Dunham, comprising about 1,800 men. When Dunham personally reached Parkers Crossroads he ordered the 122nd Illinois to take position at the crossroads and across the road leading west from there. The Thirty-ninth Iowa was posted across the Huntington road north of the crossroads. Dunham moved the Fiftieth Indiana and the Eighteenth Illinois Mounted Infantry northwest up the McLemoreville road and positioned them on a ridge overlooking a field belonging to the Hicks family. These Yankees were supported by the Seventh Wisconsin Battery.

Across the Hicks field were Dibrell's Eighth Tennessee Cavalry and Russell's Fourth Alabama, supported by one gun from Morton's Battery, commanded by Sgt. Nat Baxter, Jr. When Baxter opened fire, he dismounted one of the Union guns and engaged the Wisconsin battery for almost ninety minutes, before reinforcements arrived under Captain Freeman and Lieutenant Morton. Under the intense artillery fire, Dunham's Northern boys withdrew from their position northwest of Parkers Crossroads to a new spot 1,200 yards southwest of the crossroads.

In his new position, Dunham placed the Thirty-ninth Iowa on his left flank, facing the Lexington road. The 122nd Illinois was placed just north of the Iowa regiment, the Eighteenth Illinois to their right, and the Fiftieth Indiana north of these three regiments, extending across the road. The brigade wagons were in a hollow to the rear of the three regiments, guarded by two infantry companies.

Forrest moved along the Pleasant Exchange road to gain the rear of the Union position, and Dunham responded about 11:00 A.M. by ordering his brigade to move north about eigh hundred yards and to establish a new line running east and west on the north side of the road. Forrest had disposed of his artillery on his flanks and center, placing the guns in advance of his dismounted troopers. The fire from Freeman and Morton forced Dunham to abandon his artillery and make a charge on Forrest's batteries. The Fiftieth Indiana and 122nd Illinois charged the guns to the east and were raked by canister as well as by rifle fire. A general advance by Forrest drove these men back to a rail fence behind the ridge crest but still above the hollow where their wagons were parked. Twice more the Union force advanced up the ridge toward the Confederate artillery, and both times they were repulsed. The fire from the Confederate guns sent splinters flying from the rail fence, and these inflicted many wounds on the Union defenders.

Taking advantage of the confusion in the Yankee ranks, Forrest began to encircle their position, sending Russell's Fourth Alabama and Woodward's Kentucky Battalion to come up in the Union rear. Forrest then thinned his ranks facing south in order to send men to confront the Union left flank. An attempt by Dunham to break this thin line was repulsed by a crossfire of artillery and rifles. A general advance by Forrest then split the Union defenders into two groups. The Thirty-ninth Iowa broke and was ridden down by Starnes' regiment, which then broke into the wagon park, spreading confusion in all directions.

Dunham's force had been roughly handled and surrounded and terms for surrender were being discussed when Col. Charles Carroll, a member of the Staff, informed Forrest, "A heavy line of infantry is in our rear; we're between two lines of battle. What are we going to do?" Forrest is said to have replied, "Charge both ways."

The orders given the force guarding Forrest's rear had not been clearly worded, and while the force had obeyed their orders, they had not prevented the second Union force from reaching the field, nor did they give adequate warning of the approaching force. Recovering quickly from his surprise, Forrest took seventy-five men from his Escort and another fifty men from Dibrell's regiment, ordered those men who had not yet been issued arms to join to swell his numbers, and charged the approaching Union force. This bold move took the wind out of the Yankee sails and they went into a defensive position, allowing Forrest to escape the tight spot he found himself in, although with the loss of 250 prisoners (Jordan and Pryor, 209-11; MCHQ 30: 2).

Forrest had also taken a severe tongue lashing from an old lady living in the area. While forming his men for the attack, Forrest maneuvered a unit through this lady's backyard. The unit, while going into line, turned over the ash-hopper, in which wood ashes were collected to help in making lye for household uses. The old lady came out on her porch and loudly berated Forrest for "allowing his horse critters to ruin her ash-hopper while making a streak of fight" (CV 15: 55).

One of the prisoners Forrest left in Yankee hands was J. M. Metcalf of Lincoln County, Tennessee, who had joined Forrest's artillery just a short time before the west Tennessee expedition began. Although he was nineteen years old, Metcalf was of such slight build that he looked to be at least three years younger. As a young man with a desire to see something of the world, he found the early part of the raid exhilarating, with days filled with rapid movement, just enough fighting to be exciting, and constant victories that allowed him to equip himself in proper military fashion, even though when he got a pair of cavalry boots from the stores captured at Trenton he found one boot to be larger than the other. His luck changed at Parkers Crossroads. He has been assigned the duty of driver of the near swing horse on a gun team. The gun was being moved to a new position when the second Union force came up behind Forrest. The change of position suddenly became an effort to break out of the closing ring of Union steel. When Forrest and the Escort Company charged to cut their way out, the gun joined in the charge, only to have the lead and wheel drivers shot off their horses. Metcalf could not control the team from his position as swing driver and soon found himself hanging on while the team ran parallel to the Yankee line. His position was that of a duck in a shooting gallery, but that was preferable to what happened next. The gun hit a log and Metcalf was thrown off his mount, only to be run over by the wheel team, the limber chest, and the gun. Captured, he was taken to a hospital but received no care for several days. When the surgeons did get to him, they discovered he had several broken ribs and a broken collarbone. These wounds, plus internal injuries, got Metcalf a parole, and he made his way back to Lincoln County, unfit for any further service during the entire war (CV 16: 338).

Another casualty caused by an accident rather than enemy fire involved Johnston Ryall. Just a few days after the battle at Parkers Crossroads, Ryall wrote to his father:

> Lying on my back I will endeavor to let you know that I am in good spirits and health save a broken leg. I feel pretty low this morning since I have had my leg splinted. I spent rather a bad time from yesterday two o'clock in the morning, lying on the floor of a negro cabin with little cover on me, no fire scarcely, and helpless. I can't say the Yankees are kind to the helpless. I had dismounted with John Bryant, a messmate who was wounded in the shoulder, on the field and the captain commanding told me to get on my horse and leave him which I did, and on reaching the company (still under fire) Tom Story's mare kicking with great force, struck me on the left leg, four inches below the knee and shivered the shin bone. The doctor that dressed it this morning says he thinks it will get well before a great while. I was fearful from the pain that I would have to lose it, now with care I hope not. I tried to stay on my mare when kicked, but she was unmanageable and having no use of one leg I could not stick on so I tumbled off and scrambled in a fence corner (I was in a lane) and there had to lie till picked up. I shall try to be conveyed to a Mr. Fearson's house, some two miles from here towards Lexington, and remain there till I get able to travel, and then I will work my way home, be exchanged if able, if not, perhaps can assist on the farm. You need not be uneasy. I think I shall not want for anything to make me comfortable. I hope in some five or six weeks I may move about. I much regret that after the fight was so near over I should have been kicked by a horse. I wish the leaders in this war could feel the suffering around me. There are many much worse wounded than I. (Ryall, undated)

The Escort and Staff did themselves proud at Parkers Crossroads. Adjutant John Strange single-handedly captured eighteen wagons loaded with ammunition and received the surrender of the twenty-two men guarding the train. However, when he dismounted to take an inventory of the contents of his capture, the second Union force arrived on the field and took him prisoner. Strange found himself in company with Col. N. N. Cox and R. P. Newly, who were also taken prisoner. The three men were moved to several places until they finally reached the prison camp at Cairo, Illinois. A detachment of Federal soldiers came one afternoon and called out five of Forrest's men, including these three. Already Forrest was being charged with various violations of the rules of war, and the Yankees were talking of retaliation. Strange thought he had been chosen as one of the victims, an idea reinforced when he was placed in a foul cell no better than a dungeon. After staying there for only one afternoon, he was taken out, along with Cox and Newly, and placed on a boat bound for the prison camp at Alton, Illinois (CV 16: 73).

The Union force that had attacked Forrest from the rear almost captured the general too. Capt. J. C. Jackson told how he helped Forrest escape. Jackson had gone to look for two companies of men Forrest had sent toward his own rear but found a Yankee force advancing instead. Reporting this to the general, he then accompanied Forrest toward the threat. When they reached a road crossing where some ammunition wagons were parked, Jackson said, "I would not go any farther if I were you." Forrest replied, "Sir?" and rode on, leaving Jackson slightly behind. Almost immediately, Forrest was faced with a group of Yankees who came out from behind a barn and demanded his surrender. Forrest said, "All right, I'll go back and get what few men I have left." Riding away as slowly as an old farmer going to the mill, Forrest had not gotten to the wagons when Jackson charged up with some members of the Escort and pitched into the Union line. The Yanks soon broke and Forrest and the Escort rode out of the trap (CV 2: 308).

Jackson, from Rover, Tennessee, had been an infantry officer but was so badly wounded at Shiloh that he could no longer serve in that branch of the army. Unwilling to accept garrison duty, he resigned his commission and went to see Forrest. Saying that their fathers had been neighbors, Jackson asked for a place in the command. Forrest had no vacancies for officers, so Jackson stayed on as a private. He was actually still an enlisted man when he saved Forrest at Parkers Crossroads. Later, upon the death of Capt. Montgomery Little, he would be chosen to command the Escort Company (CV 2: 308, 6: 370).

After Parkers Crossroads, Forrest successfully fell back to the Tennessee at Clifton, brushing aside Union opposition. On New Year's Day, at noon, the raiders began crossing the river on their way back to middle Tennessee. The flatboats previously built had been sunk to hide them from Yankee gunboats or roving cavalry patrols. The boats were now raised, and the men began the slow trip back to the "safe" side of the river. John Allan Wyeth describes the crossing.

The men poled and rowed the boats upstream from Clifton toward the town, then out into the river so that the current swept them back downstream. It was the duty of the steersman to bring the boat to the Clifton side of the river. While the men were crossing two men in a canoe led a horse out into deep water where the animal had to swim, then the other horses were driven over the riverbank into the water. With the example of the swimming horse in front of them the rest followed. At one time over a thousand horses were swimming the 300 yard wide river. (Wyeth, 120)

Rev. J. N. Hunter would later comment, "The raid of two weeks may be summed up as follows: Three battles—Lexington, Trenton, and Parkers Crossroads—and innumerable skirmishes, many bridges destroyed, twenty stockades captured and burned, twenty-five hundred of the enemy killed and captured, ten pieces of artillery and fifty wagons and teams, ten thousand small arms, one million rounds of ammunition, and eighteen hundred blankets taken from the enemy, and then the Tennessee River recrossed" (CV 21: 315).

The command Forrest brought out of west Tennessee was far different from the one he took in. On December 15, Forrest commanded men who were raw soldiers, poorly armed, and unknown to each other as a brigade. On New Year's Day, he led a brigade of confident veterans armed and equipped with the best that the U.S. government could provide. Beyond that, his Staff had proved itself equal to emergencies and opportunities, and a legendary fighting force, the Escort Company, had been born and baptized.

# CHAPTER 3

# Recognition, Revolt, Renaissance: 1863

The Staff had shown itself capable of satisfying the demanding expectations of General Forrest, and he had shown he had equally high expectations of himself. It is notable that after the unclear orders that allowed a Union force to gain his rear at Parkers Crossroads, Forrest was very careful to issue orders that were sterling examples of clarity. The Escort had quickly become veterans, with the greatest confidence in their leader and in themselves. This confidence, coupled with almost constant success, bred morale of the highest order. The year following the first west Tennessee raid would boost that confidence, polish the abilities of the Staff and Escort, and lead to a confrontation at the highest levels of command, which would result in a rebirth of Forrest's command.

While the Staff and Escort had been following Forrest all over west Tennessee the main Confederate army, commanded by Braxton Bragg, had fought the Union Army of the Cumberland under William S. Rosecrans along the banks of Stones River just outside Murfreesboro. At the end of the first day's fighting, the Union army was doubled back on itself, with its battle line literally standing in the road that it would have to use to retreat to Nashville in the event of defeat. The next day, little happened to bring about that defeat. On the third day of battle, the Confederates made an unwise and unauthorized attack on their opponent's left flank, which added to the casualty list but produced nothing of value to their cause. Soon after that, Bragg received a report from his cavalry chief, Joseph Wheeler, that Union reinforcements were approaching the Confederate right flank. Although the report was false, Bragg accepted it as valid information and ordered a retreat to the line of the Duck River. There Bragg and his army would stay for the next six months.

The Duck River rises in an area of middle Tennessee known as the Highland Rim. To the west of the Highland Rim, the land falls away into the Cumberland Basin, a fertile agricultural area in which are located the towns of Nashville, Franklin, Columbia, and Murfreesboro. East of the Rim rise the peaks and ridges of the Cumberland Plateau. The Rim itself is flat and geographically featureless, although the break from the Rim into the Basin provides defensible terrain for an army. By positioning his army along the Duck River as it nears the break of the Rim, Bragg was occupying good military positions. The problem was that he did not have enough men to guard all the passes through which roads led from Murfreesboro, where Rosecrans positioned his army, up onto the Rim.

Behind Bragg, to the east, the Cumberland Plateau offered terrain that appeared eminently defensible at first glance, until the logistics of operating in such rugged country were considered. The absence of railroads and the scarcity of good wagon roads made it impossible to supply an army positioned on the mountains, and no force could live off the countryside in the Cumberlands.

The logistics were further complicated for Bragg by the fact that the Confederate commissary general, Lucius Northrupp, had ordered all supplies behind Bragg to be sent to the Carolinas and Virginia. Bragg was to draw his supplies from country in front of, and beyond, his left flank. This area stretched from Columbia, Tennessee, to the west and north into a "no-man's land" not controlled by Union or Confederate forces.

While Bragg and his infantry commanders sent the troops into winter quarters at Shelbyville and Tullahoma, and argued with each other over who was to blame for recent failures at Perryville and Stones River, the cavalry was sent out to guard the flanks and secure the area from which the supplies were drawn.

Although well known for his exploits at Murfreesboro and in west Tennessee, Forrest had not won the confidence of Braxton Bragg, who thought of Forrest as a raider or guerrilla leader instead of a competent cavalryman. To make sure outposting, patrolling, and other duties were performed in a manner consistent with the latest West Point doctrine, Bragg placed Joseph Wheeler in charge of the entire cavalry force. Indeed, this was a case of a son commanding a father, since Wheeler was young enough to have been an offspring of Forrest. From the first, this command arrangement did not work well.

After a few weeks of scouting and patrol work in the vicinity of Columbia, Tennessee, Forrest was ordered to take about one thousand of his men and set up ambushes on the Cumberland River. General Rosecrans was attempting to build up a depot of supplies for his Army of the Cumberland, and some of those supplies were arriving by water. This move by Forrest was designed to cut off the river route. Soon, however, Wheeler joined Forrest and decided that an attack on the town of Dover, location of Fort Donelson, would be of greater value to stopping the flow of supplies to Rosecrans. Although this event is usually described as an attack on Fort Donelson, it actually was mounted on the village of Dover. The Union forces had constructed two lines of breastworks and rifle pits in a loop around the village, with each end of the loop resting on the Cumberland River. In the town itself was a redoubt mounting several heavy cannon (Jordan and Pryor, 227).

Forrest thought from the first that the attack was pointless. The capture of the place would immediately halt all boat traffic, but the relatively small Confederate cavalry force would soon be driven out of the town. Taking and holding Dover for a couple of days would cost lives and accomplish nothing of value. Forrest made his feelings clear to Capt. Charles Anderson of his Staff.

> I have a special request to make of you in regard to the proposed attack. I have protested against the move, but my protest has been disregarded, and I intend to do my whole duty, and I want my men to do the same. I have spoken to none but you on this subject, and I do not wish that any should know of the objections I have made. I have this request to make. If I am killed in this fight, you will see that justice is done me by officially stating that I protested against the attack, and that I am not willing to be held responsible for any disaster that may result. (Wyeth, 127)

When the fight opened early on February 3, 1863, Forrest indeed did his whole duty as did the men of the Staff and Escort. Driving the Yanks out of one line of works, they pressed on over the second line and up to the parapet of the redoubt (Jordan and Pryor, 228). It was here that a volunteer serving on the Staff was killed. Col. Frank McNairy had commanded the First Tennessee Cavalry Battalion until that unit was consolidated with some others to form a regiment. At that time, McNairy became a supernumerary officer and volunteered to serve with Forrest. He was killed advancing on the redoubt (CV 25: 178).

Literally under the muzzles of the heavy guns, Forrest, Captain Anderson of the Staff, and a dozen of the Escort Company sat on their horses and fired into the gun crews from a range of some thirty yards (Jordan and Pryor, 228). This was not enough. Ammunition was low throughout the command and, as darkness fell, a retreat was ordered. Anderson described what happened that night.

It was late when I reached headquarters at Yellow Creek Furnace. Arriving there I asked for General Forrest. The general, recognizing my voice, came to the door, and as I was too near frozen to dismount, he came out and helped me down and into the house. Without any ceremony he went to the only bed in the room, jerked the covering from two officers who were occupying it, and brusquely ordered them to get out. My boots were pulled off, I was rolled up in blankets and put in the vacated bed. General Wharton was sitting on the side of the fireplace opposite General Wheeler, who was dictating his report to one of his staff. Forrest had resumed his place, lying down on his water-proof coat in front of the fire, his head on a turned-down chair and his feet well on the hearth.

Words were exchanged between Wheeler and Forrest about the content of the report which Forrest felt was critical of his men. Forrest then said, "General Wheeler, I advised against this attack, and said all a subordinate officer should have said against it, and nothing you can now say or do will bring back my brave men lying dead or wounded and freezing around that fort tonight. I mean no disrespect to you; you know my feelings of personal friendship for you; you can have my sword if you demand it; but there is one thing I do want you to put in that report to General Bragg—tell him I will be in my coffin before I will fight again under your command." (Wyeth, 132-33)

Forrest was as good as his word. The general, his Staff, and the Escort Company would never again serve under Wheeler.

## Thompsons Station and Brentwood

Braxton Bragg divided his cavalry to protect his two widely separated flanks. To the west, protecting the area from which his food was drawn, he assigned Earl Van Dorn, with Forrest as second in command. Wheeler was sent to the east, to the area around McMinnville, Tennessee, to guard the approaches to the right flank. Under Van Dorn, Forrest had more flexibility of operations than he had enjoyed under Wheeler. This became obvious on March 4, 1863, when Van Dorn received news that a strong

Federal force was moving south along the Columbia Turnpike in the direction of Thompsons Station. Early the next morning, the Confederate cavalry was in position to intercept this force, with Forrest on the right flank. The ensuing engagement was, said J. R. Harris of the Fourth Tennessee, "one of the hardest fought of all my many battles" (CV 23: 495).

The intent of the Union move was to send a strong force of two regiments of cavalry, a brigade of infantry, and some artillery south from Franklin along the Columbia Pike to join a second force moving west out of Murfreesboro. The overall intent was to disrupt Confederate foraging activities and to take food for the use of the Union troops. The force from Franklin was led by Col. John Coburn of the Thirty-third Indiana Infantry.

On the morning of March 5, Colonel Coburn advanced against the waiting Confederates of Whitfield's brigade, who were positioned behind a stone wall. The Union charge was repulsed, and Forrest seized the opportunity that the resulting confusion created to move against the Union left. This move put part of the Yankee line in a crossfire. Confederate artillery under Captains Freeman and Morton swept the field over which the Union infantry had to pass. Colonel Coburn said, "In a moment a battery of the enemy, of four guns, which had heretofore been masked, opened on our flank, completely covering the ground upon which our infantry and cavalry were placed, and also completely flanking our guns" (OR 23: 81). Forrest's move forced the enemy to double back on its right flank and make a stand on a steep hill. Morton describes what happened next.

> By a quick movement Captain Morton got his guns into a position which commanded the new position taken by the Federals and at the same time cut off their retreat toward Franklin. General Forrest, forming his Escort, made a bold dash up the hill, but in the face of a galling fire; advanced up the steep slope of the ridge until within thirty paces of the Federal commander, whose surrender he demanded at the point of a leveled revolver. Colonel Coburn, seeing Jordan's Cavalry pushed from the Union left and the Indiana troops fleeing from the field in great disorder, was forced to succumb. General Forrest was on foot, his horse having been shot under him as he dashed up the ridge. (Morton, *Artillery*, 83)

The horse Forrest lost that day was his favorite, Roderick. When the Escort made its charge up the hill against the final

Union position, Roderick was hit three times. Forrest dismounted, turned his horse over to his son, Lt. Willie Forrest of his Staff, and went on with the men. Willie took Roderick back to the line of horse holders, took the saddle and bridle off the steed, and saw him revive somewhat. Roderick caught the sound of the fight still going on and broke away from Willie. Jumping three stone walls in the process, the horse dashed back to where the general was fighting and took a fourth, and fatal, wound just as he reached Forrest (Henry, 130).

Among the prisoners taken that day was Col. William Utley, Twenty-second Wisconsin. He wrote his report from captivity and said:

> During the engagement my lieutenant colonel from a safe position annoyed me by sending word to me to retire. Casting my eye to the right wing, I saw several companies headed by the lieutenant colonel in full retreat. I immediately started to head them off, which for a time made things very much worse; for when the men saw me run they all broke from the hill and ran after me, thus leaving the position entirely defenseless. I finally got them all halted and stepped to the front to align the ranks, and while thus engaged I saw a portion of the regiment again in full retreat at the double-quick, headed by the lieutenant colonel, and I could not overtake him this time. (CV 26: 448)

The victory for which they had done so much was not without cost to the Escort. Capt. Montgomery Little, the organizer of the Escort, fell dead (Jordan and Pryor, 234-35). D. M. Stegall of Forrest's command recalled another incident from the battle.

> Our command was fighting on foot while some of our men went around the Yankees to take them in the rear. I, being orderly sergeant, was number one, placed in command of the horse holders. Those dismounted formed in line of battle about fifty steps in front of the horse holders. While waiting for orders to move forward our captain, A. A. Dysart, came back to me and said: "Dug, I'll be killed today and I want you to take my watch and pocketbook and give them to Uncle Jim Dysart." He was killed, the only one in our foot attack to die. (CV 21: 487)

The captain was buried in the yard of Dr. Hiram Laws' house on the battlefield, and a cedar tree was later planted to mark his grave.

One of the regiments in Forrest's command was the Third Arkansas, and it experienced such an unusual occurrence that it must be told here, though it did not concern the Escort or Staff. When the battle began, Alice Thompson, age sixteen, started from her home to another place where she thought she would be out of danger. The opening shots of the engagement convinced her to take refuge in the cellar of the Banks home. This house was soon surrounded by some of the heaviest of the fighting. The Third Arkansas charged the Yankees, who were in a field beyond the Banks house, and were repulsed with some confusion. As the retreating Rebs passed the house, their color bearer was shot. Alice ran out of the cellar, picked up the flag, and began waving it over her head. Col. S. G. Earle, commander of the Third, saw what was happening and called out, "Boys, a woman has our flag." The soldiers stopped, escorted Alice back to the cellar, and turned to take care of the Yanks (CV 8: 263).

The Escort Company had been with Forrest every step of the way in the engagement and when the Union force surrendered. The unit was rapidly gaining recognition as an elite force that could be depended on as the best shock troops in the entire brigade, a compliment indeed among such a hard-fighting collection of soldiers.

The loss of their commander, Capt. Montgomery Little, cast a shadow over the pride the Escort felt for its actions. For a time, Lt. Nath Boone took command, but he felt he was not the person to lead the Escort. He preferred a secondary role. Boone suggested to Forrest that John Jackson be given the command.

Jackson was a farmer from the Versailles community, near Rover, in Bedford County. He was farming a plot called the "coffee lot place," a name apparently derived from the custom of making an ersatz brew from the acorns of the numerous oaks on the farm. Jackson had raised a company for the Twenty-fourth Tennessee Infantry, was seriously wounded at Shiloh, and was discharged. On recovering from his wound, he joined the Escort as it was organized under Montgomery Little. Since all the positions for officers were filled, Jackson enlisted as a private. Boone knew Jackson's record of bravery and insisted he be brought up from the ranks to become the commander. Forrest agreed. Jackson would pay for his commission with his blood, being wounded three more times before the end of the war, the last time during the retreat from Tennessee in 1864. While Jackson passed through Shelbyville,

Tennessee, near his own home, a Unionist acquaintance shot him in the face with a pistol. Jackson recovered from this wound in time to rejoin the Escort for its last campaign.

Deciding to "keep the skeer on," Forrest determined to move against two Union stockades guarding railroad bridges at Brentwood, Tennessee. Many of the men in these garrisons were the survivors of the fight at Thompsons Station. Forrest had learned some of the art of war since 1862. Recalling the repulse of his men at the Guest Hollow stockade, he took two cannon with him on this foray. Remembering the lessons of Parkers Crossroads, he sent a strong force to guard his rear while deploying yet more troops to block any Union retreat. On March 24 Starnes was ordered to get in position by daylight on the twenty-fifth to attack the first Union stockade at Brentwood from one side while Forrest attacked it from the other. This move was easy for Starnes since his home was less than five miles from where he would cross the Harpeth River. Starnes got into position on time, but Forrest was late in arriving. Not wanting to be so deep in Union lines during full daylight, Starnes fell back only a short time before Forrest led his force onto the field. Deducing that Starnes had given him up, Forrest proceeded to attack on his own.

Forrest sent a detachment to watch the road to Franklin in case Union reinforcements came from that way and sent yet other troops to block any Union retreat toward Nashville. All things being ready, Capt. Charles Anderson of the Staff was ordered to take a flag of truce and ride into the Union position to demand an unconditional surrender with the added threat of "no quarter" if the position was defended. There was an embarrassed pause while the Staff searched for a white cloth. Finally a single white handkerchief was produced and Anderson rode forward with it on the point of his saber. Anderson carried out his duty in delivering the message, but the demand was refused.

While Forrest's artillery was going into battery, the Union commander, Col. E. Bloodgood, tried to send his wagon train out of the stockade, thinking it could escape before Forrest completed his cordon around the post. Forrest and the Escort met the head of the wagon train before the tail end cleared the gate. Racing down the line of wagons, the Escort charged the stockade, while the Tenth Tennessee attacked from the other side (Wyeth, 148-49). Colonel Bloodgood took the path of reason and surrendered.

Again the Escort had led the way to Confederate victory.

Sending the prisoners and captured goods back toward his escape route, Forrest took the Fourth Mississippi, the Tenth Tennessee, the Escort, and Freeman's two guns to complete the mission. With this small force he raced toward the railroad bridge over the Harpeth River to take the stockade there. Surrounding the place, he fired an artillery salvo, which sent splinters flying from the palisade. Captain Anderson was again drafted to carry in the surrender demand. Searching everywhere, Anderson could not find the handkerchief he had just used at the first stockade. Forrest, trying to hide a smile, told his major to take off his shirt and "hope the laundry work had been good enough the Yankees could see that it had once been white." Tying his shirt to his saber, Anderson galloped forward. He came back with the surrender of 230 officers and men of the Twenty-second Michigan (Wyeth, 150). Forrest led this new batch of prisoners and booty in pursuit of the rest of his men.

The withdrawal from Brentwood began successfully. The last pike leading from Nashville had been crossed and the men, hungry from a night of marching and a morning of fighting, stopped for a late dinner. Suddenly the rear guard came stampeding down the road, with the blue soldiers of Gen. Green Clay Smith in close pursuit. These Yankees were making quite a racket, being armed with Burnside breech-loading carbines (CV 23: 317, 25: 359). Forrest dropped his dinner and, followed by the Escort, charged down the road toward the Yanks. Seeing that the Federals were killing the animals pulling the wagons loaded with his captured supplies, Forrest ignored the Third Commandment and turned the air blue (Bradley, *Tullahoma*, 42).

J. G. Witherspoon, one of the participants in the attack, recalled his thoughts many years later.

> The prisoners we had taken at Brentwood early that morning had just passed us, and I noticed that they were being hurried along pretty fast, but there was no special excitement. I was Second Sergeant and was in command of the rear guard that day. We were halted about halfway down a lane, with fields on each side fenced with stone and with other stone fences running off at right angles from the lane about a quarter of a mile north of us. Company A of our regiment (Biffle's 9th Tennessee) was stationed at a branch that crossed the road three or four hundred yards in front of us, I

understood, for our support. The other part of our regiment had gone on, at least was not in sight. All at once firing commenced in our rear. Looking back, I saw about two regiments of infantry coming in double-quick from toward the railroad and forming on the stone fences north of us. We mounted our horses and fired a few shots at their skirmishers as they advanced down through the fields. We retreated to the branch, but when we got there Captain Hill and his company were gone. We dismounted, got behind trees, and commenced firing on the skirmishers as they advanced toward us. In a few minutes a member of General Forrest's Escort came dashing up and told us to hold our ground; that the wagon train which had been captured at Brentwood that morning had been attacked, that the guards had been stampeded, and that Biffle was off on the right, or somewhere, cut off but fighting like hell. This was the first we had heard of the fighting in front of us. The Escort member pleaded with us to hold our ground and, with his help, we did hold them back. In a very short time General Forrest came charging up the pike with the rest of his Escort, cursing a blue streak as he came. He had picked up a considerable force of men of different commands. He had a flag in his hand which he waved over his head. As he came up I heard him say, "Fall in, every damn one of you." We fell in, we couldn't have stayed out even if we had wanted to. I dropped in immediately to his rear and we charged up the pike like the Old Scratch was after us. When we got within good long range of their muskets which we could see glistening behind the stone fence, outnumbering us three to one, I began to think, "Old Man, I wonder if you are going to charge those fences in the shape we are in" for we were then in column by fours. Just then he reined up his horse and gave the command to "Halt." Turning his horse, he looked back down the line as if he wanted to see how many men he had with him, then said as coolly as if he were simply on his way to church: "Boys, I'll be damned if it will do to charge that position." Then I thought, "Old Man, you have certainly said something." In an instant he gave the command: "March to the left flank! Double-quick!" And when we had cleared their right he threw us into line on their right flank, dismounted us, and in less time than it takes to tell it we had them whipped and chased them back about two miles toward the railroad, and were bothered by them no more that day. (CV 27: 416)

Forrest lost part of the booty he had captured, because General Smith's men killed the animals pulling the wagons before they retreated. Forrest burned the vehicles he could not bring out, but all his men who needed them acquired new weapons, courtesy of the United States government.

Forrest rested for approximately two weeks. However, periods of inaction were not peaceful for Forrest, because he had poor relations with Van Dorn. The cavalry chief thought Forrest should share the booty he had captured at Thompsons Station and Brentwood, while Forrest was concerned about arming his own command. There was also the usual bickering over who was, and was not, getting credit for the victories in the papers. On one occasion, Forrest found himself challenged to a duel by Van Dorn, although the meeting never came off (Hurst, 117). Van Dorn would soon be removed from the whole drama due to making a foray into the bedroom of another man's wife.

## Streight's Raid

In the meantime, Forrest was dispatched to north Alabama to help Philip D. Roddey protect the Tennessee River route toward Decatur and Huntsville, Alabama, from a force led by Union general Grenville Dodge. Unknown to Forrest, Dodge's move was only a feint to cover the move of some fifteen hundred raiders under Col. Abel Streight, who planned to cut the Western & Atlantic Railroad at Rome, Georgia.

Streight's raid was based on a misunderstanding on the part of the Union forces. The Federal command thought Bragg was being supplied by the Western & Atlantic Railroad, which connected Atlanta with Chattanooga. They believed that supplies flowed from Chattanooga, up the Nashville & Chattanooga, to Bragg's headquarters at Tullahoma, Tennessee. The Federals were wrong. Bragg collected his food from the area from Shelbyville west to Columbia and beyond. Almost nothing was coming up the W&A to supply the Army of Tennessee. Streight could have been successful and the Confederate army would still have been able to stay precisely where it was. The supplies coming up the W&A were bound for Virginia, but the road did provide Bragg with an avenue for troop movements back and forth to Mississippi, via Atlanta and Montgomery.

Streight had a head start, being in position at Tuscumbia, Alabama, before Forrest had even crossed the Tennessee River. While Forrest and Roddey were fighting Dodge around Town

Creek, Streight was heading toward Moulton, Alabama, and the start of his path toward Rome, Georgia. When Forrest learned from a scout that Streight was the real threat, he sent Roddey to make a pursuit until he could ready a force to follow the raiders himself.

Of all the exploits of Forrest's cavalry, the pursuit and capture of Abel Streight is the most amazing, the stuff of which Forrest legends have been made ever since. Knowing just how difficult the pursuit would be, especially since his men had been marching and fighting for the last several weeks, Forrest took only his toughest men. He chose the Fourth and Ninth Tennessee and, of course, his Escort Company. Morton's Battery was left to support the attack at Town Creek and Roddey's battery was taken on the pursuit, but the two rifled guns from Morton were added to the artillery support of Forrest's cavalry (CV 25: 360).

On April 30, 1863, Forrest caught up with Streight at Days Gap near Blountsville. As the Escort rode up the mountain road toward the Yankees holding the head of the gap, two little farm girls appeared in the yard of their cabin. Spontaneously the two children began to sing "Dixie." One of the Escort commented that "such a yell went up that the Yankees must have thought the whole of Bragg's army was coming after them" (CV 3: 363).

A participant in the fight recalled:

Forrest's Escort occupied the extreme left of the line, with instructions to move around the flank and get a position in the rear, while Edmondson took the offensive in the front. At the same moment, two pieces of Ferrell's artillery were pushed forward and opened at a distance of 200 yards from the Federal lines. The enemy promptly answered, but Edmondson's men steadily advanced to within less than a hundred yards of the enemy, under a hot fire. They were a splendid lot of men. The Escort, meanwhile, had charged on the left flank to within fifty yards of the Federal lines, the men of which were lying down concealed; rising, they delivered a withering volley, inflicting considerable loss. Roddy's [sic] men, comparatively raw, gave way, leaving 40 of our 350 either killed or wounded. Ferrell's guns, however, had by this time been bravely pushed to within sixty yards of the Federal position and were throwing a stream of grape and canister into the enemy. When Roddy's command gave way, Col. Streight charged and forced Edmondson back, killing the horses of a section of Morton's Battery, under Lt. A. W. Gould which was abandoned to the enemy. But both

Edmondson and Roddy's men promptly rallied, retook the position previously occupied, and reformed for another struggle. The Federal commander handled his men with decided nerve and ability, and massing them, made a resolute charge that forced the Confederates back to another position, which he likewise attacked with equal vigor, but was this time repulsed. The Federal commander then retired to the position in which he had first awaited battle, and Forrest resumed possession of the ridge in his immediate front. From these two positions an animated skirmish was maintained between the sharpshooters of both forces until 3 p.m. Starnes's and Biffle's regiments, having been meantime ordered up, now appeared upon the scene, they were at once dismounted and deployed to take part in an immediate grapple with the enemy.

In this new attack, Starnes's Regiment was on the extreme right, and Edmondson on the left, Biffle and Roddy in the center. In the road along which Ferrell's Battery of four guns advanced, Forrest's Escort and Capt Forrest's company constituted a small reserve. The enemy did not await the onset. As a matter of fact, they had been gone an hour, leaving a thin line of skirmishers, which gave back without giving the fire to the advancing Confederates. . . .

Biffle and McLemore, the latter leading, with their regiments, were directed to push on by the road taken by the enemy, while Gen. Forrest, heading his Escort and a company of the 4th TN, dashed ahead to overtake and bring the enemy to bay. (CV 35: 453)

The men Forrest was pursuing were proving to be worthy opponents. At Days Gap they had counterattacked after being surprised, had inflicted several casualties, and had captured two pieces of artillery. Among the wounded was William, the general's brother. As the command prepared to move on, men were detailed to stay and deal with the wounded and the Yankee prisoners. Young Willie Forrest, an aide on his father's staff, was among those told to stay in Days Gap, in part to make sure his uncle William received personal attention.

Streight was attempting to gather some of his forage from the countryside, and he badly needed to take all available horses to replenish his own supply of mounts and to deny fresh animals to Forrest. The men sent out on this duty were vulnerable. Two members of the Seventy-third Indiana fell into the hands of the local home guard, who were quite upset over the looting of their farms and barns. "Henry Bird and Shannon Carr had left the command early in the morning as foragers, and about the time of the engagement were captured by Roddey's men who turned them over to a squad of guerrillas, calling themselves Home Guards, and were by them taken to a lonely ravine where they were murdered. This . . . was seen by one of our cavalrymen, a native of Alabama, who was expecting a similar fate" (Willett, 113).

The medical staff of the Seventy-third also had an adventure. As the regiment pulled back, acting as Streight's rear guard, Dr. W. H. Peck and Dr. Henry R. King were busy attending to the Union wounded. By the time they finished their work, the blue troopers were long gone and the two men hurried to catch up. They had ridden for some distance before they began to pass troops they assumed were the rear guard but suddenly noticed they knew none of the soldiers. When they realized they were encountering Confederate troops, they both put spurs to their horses. Dr. Peck was well mounted and made his escape; Dr. King was taken prisoner by a member of the Escort (Willett, 124-25).

As King, and other Union troops, were run down or captured in skirmishes, Capt. Charles Anderson took on a duty familiar to Staff officers. It became his duty to make a list of prisoners, send to the rear all for whom a guard could be spared, and issue paroles to the wounded and any others who would agree to go home until exchanged. The paroles given on this occasion read: "We, the undersigned members of Colonel Streight's Brigade soldiers of the United States Army, hereby pledge our sacred honor, not to take up arms, give aid or information, which could be detrimental to the Confederate States of America, until regularly exchanged, so help us God." On the back of these signed statements Anderson wrote a "pass," allowing the bearer to go through Confederate lines. Sixty captured Yanks and eight who had been working in the field hospital signed such paroles after Days Gap (Willett, 124, 177).

Forrest pursued with only the Escort and one company of the Fourth Tennessee until he reached the village of Blountsville. Charging into the village with pistols blazing, this tiny force brought all of Streight's men into combat. The fight went on for over two hours with neither side gaining an advantage, though the rest of Forrest's command came up to join the fight.

About eight o'clock, Biffle was ordered to move with his reserves around by the left flank, gain the rear of the enemy, and attack the horse holders. At the same time, Forrest sent his Escort on a similar service around by the right flank. The lines were by this time brought to within thirty yards of each other. The Confederates scattered behind trees and other objects that greatly favored them. (CV 35: 454)

The attack from the rear was joined by a frontal assault, which convinced Streight to burn his six supply wagons and begin a running fight toward the Big Black River, also called the Big Fork of the Black Warrior (CV 36: 15). The Escort and the single company from the Fourth Tennessee continued the pursuit of Streight's entire force and drove on across the Big Black.

On May 2, the running fight continued, with the Escort still in the thick of the pursuit. Other units were rotated to the rear for a few hours' rest and then brought back to the front to push the Yankees. This meant Streight's men had to keep moving under the pressure of comparatively fresh men. But the Escort did not rotate back for any rest. Forrest seemed not to feel comfortable unless these men were at the front. Accompanied only by the Escort and fifty additional men, Forrest drove Streight ahead of him for ten miles toward Gadsden, Alabama. At Black Creek, about three miles from Gadsden, the raiders got across the bridge in time to fire the structure, seemingly stopping Forrest. In a much celebrated event, seventeen-year-old Emma Sansom showed Forrest a crossing a few hundred yards downstream, and soon the pursuit was on again (CV 36: 17).

As he passed through Gadsden, Forrest called for volunteers to make a rush to Rome to warn the community. John Wisdom volunteered to leave his mail route and play Paul Revere, a task he completed successfully, so that the Rome home guards and convalescent Confederate soldiers took up the flooring from the bridge over the Oostanaula River and manned the town's defenses. There was no need. Exhausted, and confused by a multiplicity of roads in an area of woods where the trees had been cut for burning charcoal, Streight stopped to rest his men at Lawrence's Plantation, near Gaylesville, Alabama. There the Escort caught up with him, and Capt. Henry Pointer immediately sent in a Forrest-style demand for surrender. Pointer was another supernumerary officer, originally commanding a company in the Third Tennessee Infantry. His unit was captured at Fort Donelson and, on exchange, he found himself without a command when the regiment was reorganized. He promptly joined Forrest (Horn, 2: 181).

Forrest came up before an answer to the surrender demand was received and began the process by which "a bluff beat a straight." In the presence of Colonel Streight, commands were sent to several Confederate regiments that were not even there. Captain Pointer offered Streight a drink of whiskey, commenting it might be the last drink the colonel ever got (CV 35: 18). Artillery was driven across the same opening in the trees until twenty-three guns had been counted. At this point Streight gave up. He surrendered 1,740 men and a battery of mountain howitzers to about 500 men, many of whom had not yet come on the field.

Forrest then told Streight that forage was scarce at Rome, so the Escort and one regiment would march the prisoners to the Georgia town and turn them over to the provost there but the rest of the command would march back to Gadsden. This would keep Streight from knowing Forrest's true numbers. For the Escort, the duty of guarding the prisoners was both a testament to their fighting ability and a recognition of the arduous duty they had performed in capturing Streight. On the way to Rome, the Escort was met by a company of militia from the town, who assisted in guarding the prisoners. This militia unit became a source of new recruits for Forrest.

Lieutenant Hooper, of Stonewall Jackson's Command, was in Rome, Georgia, on May 2, 1863, on recruiting service when a message was received by General Black, who commanded the militia of that district, from General Forrest urging that General Black raise all the forces he could and intercept General Streight, who was headed for Rome. At the request of General Black, Lieutenant Hooper secured a mounted company of old men and boys, numbering less than two hundred. This company crossed the Etowah River at Rome and went to meet General Streight. . . . This militia company at the request of Major Strange, General Forrest's Adjutant General, took charge of the Yankee officers who surrendered, guarded them to Rome, and took care of them until they were paroled.

General Forrest was pleased with the action of this militia company and asked if they would not like to join his command. With some effort eighty-six members were secured who were willing to enlist, six of which were over forty-five, eighty being only fifteen to eighteen years of age. (CV 22: 131)

In 1864 Forrest offered to send this company back to Georgia to defend their home state, but the men felt such an attachment to the general that they held a meeting and wrote a petition asking to remain with him. This they did until the end of the war.

On this occasion, Forrest did receive the sword of his defeated opponent. Forrest later presented the weapon to Gen. John Breckenridge, who gave it to one of his Staff officers, Capt. Charles J. Mastin of Huntsville, Alabama (CV 3: 117).

The Escort were the men of the hour when they marched their captives into Rome. The rest of the command were equally treated as heroes when they arrived. Dinners and speeches were the order of the day, along with a lot of sleep. Before Forrest left to return to Tennessee, the citizens of Rome presented him with a war-horse, soon to be known as "King Philip."

Reaching Gadsden on May 7, Forrest and the Escort spent the night at the estate of R. B. Kyle. Forrest said not one word about the war but passed the time by playing with Kyle's two-year-old son. The next morning the fierce general insisted on carrying the toddler two or three miles with him in the saddle before the father returned the child home. As they parted, Forrest kissed the boy and said, "My God, Kyle, this is worth living for" (CV 4: 43). No doubt the most hard-bitten member of the Escort would have agreed.

On their return to Spring Hill, the Escort and Staff got a new leader, Major General Forrest. Although the Confederate Congress would not confirm the promotion for several months, the Escort was confident it would go through. With Van Dorn dead, the victim of a jealous husband, there was no other leader with the stature or the ability to command the left wing of Braxton Bragg's cavalry. At last Forrest had the recognition many felt he deserved. He in turn gave his Escort and Staff the acclaim they had earned.

Pleased as he was with his promotion and the defeat of Streight's raiders, Forrest had one unpleasant task to perform, which led to a tragedy. Lieutenant Gould, the officer who had lost Morton's two rifled pieces to Streight at Days Gap, was being transferred at Forrest's insistence, but he did not wish to go quietly. The lieutenant felt that the transfer impugned his honor and he demanded to see Forrest. The interview took place in Columbia, Tennessee, on the afternoon of June 12. Before the matter was ended, Forrest was shot with Gould's pistol, and the young officer was fatally wounded by a pocketknife in Forrest's hands. Before Gould died, both men expressed to the other their regret for the anger in which they had acted (Lytle, 181-82).

On June 26, word reached Forrest that the center of the Confederate line along the Duck River was collapsing. Rosecrans had led his Army of the Cumberland in a skillful campaign of feint and maneuver that had turned Bragg's right flank (see, Bradley, *Tullahoma,* for a discussion of this campaign), making it necessary for Forrest to evacuate his position on the left flank. The rainy weather that began on June 26 and lasted until July 3 must have been hard on the general, who was back in the saddle for the first time since being shot by Gould, but he led his command across the Duck River below Shelbyville while Wheeler fought a rear-guard action in the streets of that village. Although the rest of the Army of Tennessee was concentrating at Tullahoma, Forrest's cavalry corps passed through there without stopping and took up blocking positions toward Manchester, where Rosecrans was gathering his forces.

To further threaten Bragg's position, Rosecrans sent the Mounted Infantry Brigade commanded by Col. John Wilder, 1,200 men armed with Spencer repeating rifles, toward Bragg's rail link with Chattanooga. Wilder struck the line at Decherd, but Forrest was soon on his trail, and Wilder withdrew into the mountain ridges nearby. On June 30 Forrest and the Escort Company were riding in advance of the rest of the cavalry, searching for Wilder. Rounding a turn in the road,they found themselves confronting a larger body of Yankees. Both sides were wearing oilcloth slickers and no uniforms were visible, so Forrest coolly engaged the Union officer in conversation as he and the Escort passed. Once around another bend, Forrest waited for more of his troops to come up, but Wilder's men began arriving first. Without another thought, Forrest and the Escort doubled back and charged the larger force, cutting a path through them and scattering the remainder. Wilder immediately packed up his outfit and turned back toward the main Union army (Lytle, 185-86).

The Yanks would have their day soon enough. On July 3 Forrest and the Escort formed the rear guard of the army as the Confederates withdrew toward Chattanooga. They ascended the slopes of the Cumberland Plateau toward the village of University Station, home of the infant University of the South, founded shortly before the war by Bishop (now Lt. Gen.) Leonidas Polk. As Forrest and his men made a fighting retreat through the village of Cowan, the time came to run for the nearby mountains, devil take the hindmost. As the horsemen swept through the dusty streets of

Cowan, an old woman stood on her porch berating them as cowards. She was particularly abusive of Forrest because of his size. "You big ole rascal! You cowardly cur! If Ole Forrest was here he would kick your butt and make you fight!" Forrest, the Escort recalled, laughed heartily at her language (Wyeth, 212).

As the Army of Tennessee withdrew toward Chattanooga, the Escort Company and Staff had the satisfaction of knowing they had won recognition throughout the western Confederacy. Their commander had received the thanks of the Congress for his capture of the Streight raiders, which reflected favorably on them. This satisfaction would have to carry them through several weeks of routine duty, except for Lt. George Cowan, who was sent on duty that was far from routine. As Cowan related the event later:

> I was detailed to go to Pulaski with a message for Major Mason, who had charge of our forage wagons, telling him to move south of the Tennessee River and to rejoin the command at Chattanooga. After delivering this message I was to scout through Rosecrans' army procuring information which I was then to deliver to Chattanooga. I fell in with one of Rosecrans' cavalry regiments and followed it to Shelbyville where General Ormsby Mitchell's division was camped. I made my way into his camps with some butter to sell, wearing Confederate gray clothes, all I had. While selling the butter I was accosted by General Mitchell's adjutant-general with the question "Aren't you a rebel soldier? What are you doing with that uniform?" I replied that while the rebels were here "us boys wore them kind of clothes, but if he would give me one of his nice uniforms i would wear it." After selling the butter at 50 cents a pound I left and went on to where General Rosecrans was camped with his main body. It took two weeks to get all the information I wanted. I was not suspicioned till one night I heard two officers discussing me. One thought I was a spy, the other not. The next day there was a foraging party going out so I joined them and slipped away to Chattanooga. (Burton)

Once Bragg reached Chattanooga, he spread his cavalry along the Tennessee River both north and west of the town. Forrest was sent upriver toward Knoxville, a sector that proved to be rather dull, as the main Federal thrust would come from the direction of Tullahoma to Bridgeport. During the remainder of July and August, the Staff handled the tasks associated with reconnoitering as Forrest carried out the duties associated with close support of the infantry. There had been some question as to whether the general was a raider or whether he could command regular cavalry, but these weeks answered such questions. Forrest was an expert at penetrating the enemy's lines and wreaking havoc on a supply and communications system, but he could also provide the information and screening required by an army. However, these routine duties did not offer opportunities for exploits for the Escort Company or Staff. Also, having to work closely with regulation-bound men such as Bragg seriously tested Forrest's ability to countenance any example of idiocy.

Still, if the Escort and Staff found this to be a time of leisure, it was not unwelcome. The first six months of the year had been rather busy. John Morton recalled:

> Reaching Kingston, where the sparkling Clinch enters the turbid Tennessee, the writer was delighted to find himself in a fruitful and smiling valley of plenty once more. During the long, hot days a great portion of time was spent in water sports. Many of the soldiers swam both streams on wagers. General Forrest, coming to the bank one day, asked: "Who is my best swimmer?" "Captain Morton," was the reply of one of the swimmers. "Then he must prove his right to the championship," declared Forrest. Seating himself on the bank, he called for contest after contest in the various forms of this delightful exercise. The discipline and activities of camp life had changed the writer, to whom, it will be remembered, General Forrest has referred at their first meeting as a "little, tallow-faced boy," to a sun-browned, sturdy, though still slender body, with a great deal of muscle and endurance; and, as has been stated, swimming had been his favorite pastime from early youth, so that it was not difficult to maintain the reputation so kindly pronounced by those who had not had his experience. (Morton, *Artillery*, 112)

During these weeks, before a revolt against Bragg's passivity broke out, Forrest saw his Escort develop a new trick to confuse the enemy. Twice, "deserters" from the Escort were reported to have shown up in Union camps and passed on "valuable information" as to the whereabouts of Forrest's command (Wyeth, 217; OR 30: 563). In both cases, the "valuable information" was totally false. The Escort had found within its ranks natural-born actors who could play the role of "deserter" quite well, passing on misleading information and then fading away to rejoin the command.

Bragg was maneuvered out of Chattanooga and fell back into the mountains of north Georgia. As the Union army divided itself into three columns to follow the Rebels, Forrest and the Escort once more found themselves in the position of scouting the enemy advance, harrying their movements, and slowing any pursuit of the main Confederate army. On September 11 Forrest again found himself facing Wilder, as the Lightning Brigade, armed with their Spencer repeaters, led Crittenden's Union Corps along the railroad south. The fight started at Ringgold, Georgia, with a sharp skirmish that lasted two hours and saw fighting in the streets of the town itself. At Tunnel Hill the Confederate cavalry were dismounted and reinforcements came up. The Union advance was stopped there but not before Dr. J. B. Cowan was called up to treat yet another wound received by Forrest. On this occasion, the doctor reported, Forrest did something he never did unless ordered to do by his surgeon; he took a drink of whiskey (Wyeth, 217-18; Henry, 179).

## Chickamauga

On September 19 and 20 Forrest's command participated in the Battle of Chickamauga, the largest engagement in which the command ever fought. While the Staff performed quite well, few individual deeds stand out from the smoke of that battle. On the first day of the fight, Forrest was in command of a major portion of the Confederate line, pinning the Army of the Cumberland in place. The fighting on September 19 was very confused, with first one side and then the other attacking, pushing back their opponent, becoming disorganized by fighting in the woods, and then being pushed back as the other side received reinforcements. In one of these advances, Forrest had captured a battery only to lose it again to a Union counterattack. As his line fell back, Forrest observed some of his own guns about to be left behind because the battery horses had been shot down. He turned to his Escort and told them to resolve the situation. While a brief stand was made to hold back the Yanks, other members of the group rigged the artillery harness over their saddled mounts and dragged the guns to safety. Later that day, the Escort and Forrest found themselves in a tight place from which they were saved only by quick thinking and excellent discipline. On the night of September 19 Forrest went on a reconnaissance, accompanied only by the Escort. In the smoky woods, with darkness rapidly settling in, the small unit rode into an ambush. A Union brigade observed the horsemen approaching across a small opening and moved to surround them. Forrest was on top of the Union soldiers before he could distinguish the color of their uniforms. Once the troops were known to be Yankees, Forrest shouted for the Escort to form a column four across and to charge a correspondingly narrow segment of the Union line. The horsemen struck like a thunderbolt, breaking the infantry line and escaping with only two men killed (Lindsley 2: 770).

On the second day of the battle, Forrest was stationed on the Confederate right flank and used his artillery to help isolate the Union position on Snodgrass Hill. It was there that Forrest and his men received one of their highest compliments. Gen. D. H. Hill saw Forrest's men going into combat and asked who commanded such a steady brigade of infantry. On being told he was looking at cavalry, he asked to meet the commander. Capt. Charles Anderson of the Staff was asked to take General Hill to meet Forrest. When the two came together, Hill said, in the presence of the Escort:

> General Forrest, I wish to congratulate you and these brave men moving across that field like veteran infantry upon their magnificent behavior. In Virginia I made myself extremely unpopular with the cavalry because I said that, so far, I had not seen a dead man with spurs on. No one can speak disparagingly of such troops as yours. (Morton, *Artillery,* 122-23)

On the day after the Confederate victory, Forrest scouted up to the fortifications of Chattanooga and repeatedly urged Bragg to send forward infantry to capture that town while the Union defenses were still fluid. Bragg's failure to do so brought into the open the friction between the two men, friction that soon became a flame of revolt.

On September 28, while he was still trying to find a way into Chattanooga, Forrest received an order from Bragg saying all Forrest's troops were to be turned over to Wheeler. Captain Anderson wrote the brief reply Forrest sent, which merely noted that he would appear at army headquarters in person to discuss the matter. With most of his men preparing to cross the Tennessee River back into middle Tennessee on a raid led by Wheeler, Forrest asked for ten days' furlough to go to LaGrange, Georgia, to see his wife. While there he received an order placing the rest of his troops under Wheeler. Dr. J. B. Cowan, a relative of Mrs. Forrest, had just closed his hospital on the battlefield of Chickamauga and had reported himself ready for other duty. Forrest asked Dr. Cowan, as an in-law, to accompany him to army headquarters (Henry, 197-98).

During the journey to see Bragg, Cowan later noted, Forrest was strangely quiet. At headquarters both men were shown into Bragg's presence. Forrest refused to shake hands with the commanding general and immediately launched into the worst tongue-lashing Bragg would ever receive. As Cowan recalled the scene, Forrest said:

I am not here to pass civilities or compliments with you, but on other business. You commenced your cowardly and contemptible persecution of me soon after the battle of Shiloh, and you have kept it up ever since. You did it because I reported to Richmond facts, while you reported damned lies. You robbed me of my command in Kentucky, and gave it to one of your favorites—men that I armed and equipped from the enemies of our country. In a spirit of revenge and spite, because I would not fawn upon you as others did, you drove me into west Tennessee in the winter of 1862, with a second brigade I had organized, with improper arms and without sufficient ammunition, although I had made repeated application for the same. You did it to ruin me and my career. When in spite of all this I returned with my command, well equipped without thanks to you or the government, a brigade which has won a reputation for successful fighting second to none in the army, taking advantage of your position as the commanding general in order to further humiliate me, you have taken these brave men from me.

I have stood your meanness as long as I intend to. You have played the part of a damned scoundrel, and are a coward, and if you were any part of a man I would slap your jaws and force you to resent it. You may as well not issue any more orders to me, for I will not obey them, and I will hold you personally responsible for any further indignities you endeavor to inflict upon me. You have threatened to arrest me for not obeying your orders promptly. I dare you to do it, and I say to you that if you ever again try to interfere with me or cross my path it will be at the peril of your life. (Jordan and Pryor, 242-43)

Bragg appears to have believed that Forrest meant every word, for this rebellion went unnoticed and unpunished. A few days later, Forrest was given official orders to proceed with a plan he had himself proposed. Taking the Escort Company of about sixty men, his Staff, McDonald's Battalion, and the Second Kentucky Cavalry, Forrest proposed to operate in north Mississippi and west Tennessee, raising another command and arming them as he had the last. He wanted rifles for these men so he could use them as mounted infantry. He asked that Capt. W. W. Carnes be assigned to command his artillery, to consist of three-inch rifles (Jordan and Pryor, 246). Captain Freeman, the original commander of Forrest's artillery, had been killed by the Fourth U.S. Cavalry at Franklin only a few weeks before, and Forrest's relationship with John Morton had not yet developed into one of complete trust.

Carnes was another of the Memphis connection from which Forrest drew so frequently when looking for subordinates. As the commander of a battery attached to Cheatham's Division, Carnes and his command had distinguished themselves with their performance at Perryville, Stones River, and Chickamauga. In the last battle, Carnes' Battery had taken more casualties than any battery on either side. Militarily, Carnes had an unusual background for an artilleryman—he was an 1857 graduate of the U.S. Naval Academy. Since his battery had suffered so many losses at Chickamauga, Carnes was temporarily assigned to the staff of Lieutenant General Polk when Forrest asked for him. The request was refused, with Carnes being assigned a battalion of artillery at the Battle of Missionary Ridge and then being assigned to the Confederate Naval Service at Savannah beginning January 1, 1864 (CV 1: 264, 6: 178, 384, 515-18).

Forrest was right in telling Bragg that his command was recognized as second to none in fighting ability in the entire army. Recognition had been won, but revolt had taken place. Now would be a renaissance of the Escort and Staff, as Forrest went to new fields to win new laurels. Much of the credit for those laurels would belong to the men who were so closely associated with the general.

## Transfer to Mississippi

In Mississippi, Forrest would be under the command of Gen. S. D. Lee, a man who both valued Forrest's talents and had enough sense to leave him alone to do what he did so well. In late November 1863, Forrest and about 500 men with two guns commanded by Morton, who was assigned to follow the Escort and

Staff to Mississippi, crossed into west Tennessee while S. D. Lee created a diversion. The Escort had already scouted the area and identified for Forrest the crossing point on the Memphis & Charleston Railroad. By December 6 the command arrived in Jackson, Tennessee, and the Staff was dispersed over the surrounding countryside to bring in already organized bands of recruits, which numbered from 25 to 200 men. The people of Jackson greeted Forrest as a deliverer, although he had only 500 armed men, and the new recruits were soon being entertained as if they were visiting royalty. William R. Dyer, a member of the Escort, kept a diary, which includes this period. He notes that the entire command lived well in Jackson, with the Escort being quartered in the livery stable. On December 21 the Escort gave a party, which became "the talk of all the country around Jackson." Dyer also notes that he purchased clothes at the cost of seven dollars for a coat, three dollars for a pair of pants, one dollar for two pairs of drawers, and two shirts for three dollars (Dyer, *Diary*).

Forrest stayed in Jackson, bringing in hundreds of recruits and a great herd of beef cows and hogs. Then, on December 23, the Escort and other scouts told him it was time to leave in order to escape the net the Yankees were throwing out for him (Maness, 187, 189-91).

As the recruits and armed soldiers left Jackson, they moved about eighteen miles southwest to Estenaula and the crossing of the Hatchie River. Colonel Richardson had already taken one Confederate regiment to secure the crossing and had successfully blocked a Union advance under Col. Edward Prince. On Christmas Eve, Forrest got the command across the Hatchie, then took the Escort Company to help Richardson. The day was sharply cold, the roads were wet and muddy, and not a man in Forrest's command experienced a moment of relief from the elements. Work, not a Christmas celebration, was the order of the day. As night fell, Sgt. Sam Boone was sent ahead with ten men from the Escort to scout the Yankees. He later recorded that his orders were to "ride right through everything until I came to something solid" (Lytle, 252). Crossing the Hatchie, Sergeant Boone ran right over a Yankee picket and crashed into their support, some forty strong. Going too fast to stop their horses, the little band simply created chaos until the rest of the Escort arrived. A few hundred yards farther on, Lt. Nathan Boone, commanding the

Escort, topped a rise and saw what the entire command had been dreading all day. Across the line of advance was a chain of bivouac fires. Some men moved around the fires cooking food while others were already rolled in their blankets. Boone estimated there were at least six hundred Yankees in front of him. He led only eighty men.

Between the Escort and the Yanks was a field of dry cornstalks. Boone decided to use the corn to "multiply" his numbers. The eighty men of the Escort were strung out in a line, each man fifteen or twenty feet from his neighbor. Every sergeant was then instructed to repeat Boone's orders, just as if the sergeant commanded a larger unit. When everyone was in place, Boone yelled, "Brigade! Forward!" The sergeants then shouted, "Regiment! Forward!" Next came the order to trot, then gallop, and the bugler was told to sound the charge.

With cornstalks crashing, yells resounding, and pistols beginning to pop, the Yankees took immediate notice. Those who could catch a horse fled at once. Those who were rolled in blankets struggled out and ran off into the dark, some of them not reaching another camp until morning after wandering about the countryside all night in their long-johns. The Escort dismounted, put more wood on the fires, and began a very modest Christmas celebration (OR 31: 613-14; Maness, 192). Perhaps the victory was made sweeter by the arrival of the news that Forrest's promotion to major general had been confirmed.

Intercepted dispatches told Forrest that the Yankees were concentrating near Saulsbury, where he had first crossed the Memphis & Charleston Railroad, so he headed farther west. To confuse the enemy, he used his Staff to guide columns of armed men toward Bolivar in the east and, under Major Strange, the adjutant, to the outskirts of Memphis, while the main body of unarmed recruits and the animal herd crossed the Wolf River at Lafayette Station, now known as Rossville (OR 31: 615-17).

When Forrest moved through middle Tennessee on his way to Mississippi, he left behind a small detachment from his Escort commanded by Lt. George Cowan. This detachment was to scout the country, round up wounded men who had been left behind, and arrest deserters. Being a small unit deep within Union lines, the group saw its share of adventures. Cowan later said:

While on scout duty we stopped at Mr. Dwiggins' farm house about five miles from Shelbyville, thinking we could get young Dwiggins to return to his command. The father met us at the door. I said "You know me, Mr. Dwiggins." He said, "No, there are so many Yankees coming here pretending they are Confederate soldiers that I do not know anybody; but I will tell you how I will recognize you as Confederates. There are three men now in my dining-room whom I think are Yankees. If you will go in there you can soon find out who they are." We drew our weapons and entered the dining-room and ordered the men to hold up their hands, which they did promptly. On demanding who they were they said they were members of Ross' Texan Confederate Brigade and I, recognizing the Lieutenant, was satisfied they were.

Mr. Dwiggins then asked us to have supper. The Texans had failed to put a sentry outside, so we placed one there and then sat down to our supper. While at the table our sentry came running in saying "The Yankees are on us." We rushed to get our arms but before we could do so the enemy surrounded the house and demanded that we surrender, which we did. But I, knowing that I had been outlawed on account of going in and out of the lines so often as a scout knew that my life would be in danger if I surrendered, determined to take my chance and make my escape. While the Yankee detail was searching us and taking our arms away from us, they took two pistols from my overcoat but overlooked two I had under my overcoat. While they were searching the remaining of our men and disarming them I determined to slip away, so unbuttoning my coat I drew one of the pistols from my pocket. The two men who were guarding me called out "Look out, he has a pistol!" On the instant I struck them both with my pistol, one from the right and one from the left, knocking them both down. Then I dashed through the line of Yankees and made a break for the pike five hundred yards distant, on the opposite side of which I knew was a corn-field in which I could hide, but on reaching the corn-field a ball from the enemy struck me on the heel, but having a large spur on it saved the ball from entering my foot but caused me to fall, and disabled me from walking. While lying there two other Confederates ran by trying to make their escape, followed by five Yankees. As they passed me, seeing me lying in a little ditch they said "Damn him, there he lies. We've got him!"

After they passed on I found that I was not so badly wounded as I thought and was able to crawl to some weeds where I found some logs which I crawled under and examined my wound. I found the spur had saved the ball from entering the foot and found that I could hobble to where my mother was staying about three miles away. I arrived about day-break. Mother tended my wound, gave me something to eat, and filled my haversack. That night I was able to make my escape and later returned to my command in Mississippi. (Burton)

"Young Dwiggins" was H. C. Dwiggins. He was born in Alabama on October 8, 1844, and went into business with his father, R. S. Dwiggins, running mills in and around Shelbyville, Tennessee. In the fall of 1862, H. C. enlisted as a private in Company D, Fourth Tennessee Cavalry. Apparently he took an "unofficial leave" in late 1863 and was listed as a deserter. He returned to his unit, however, and served until the end of the war (MCHQ 30, no. 1 [spring 1999]).

Forrest moved to Como, Mississippi, and organized his recruits into four small brigades. While drilling began, Forrest went looking for weapons for his new men. He wanted rifles, not carbines, for he planned to do a lot of fighting dismounted. The Staff took an important role in this organization of new men, and the Escort provided a shield of scouts and spies to keep the developing unit informed about Federal intentions.

Rations were scarce at Como, so Lt. George Cowan organized some of the Escort to go on a bear hunt. The men brought in a wagon loaded with fresh bear meat, but the skinned carcasses looked suspiciously like sheep. For thirty years, tales about the "Como bear hunt" were told at reunions of the Escort.

By the time camp was established at Como, something that had happened before had been repeated. Out of the mud and cold of west Tennessee, a new cavalry corps had been born, a renaissance for Forrest, his Escort, and the Staff.

# CHAPTER 4

# Trial by Fire: 1864-65

Forrest was not given much time to get his new command in condition to fight. On February 3, 1864, Gen. William Sherman left Vicksburg with over 20,000 infantry and artillery to march on Meridian, Mississippi. The purpose of this maneuver was to destroy the agricultural productivity of the area and the communications net that supported the Confederate effort both locally and in the larger war. At the same time, Gen. Sooy Smith was to leave Memphis with 7,000 cavalry to bring destruction to another swath of Mississippi and to divert Confederate forces away from Sherman. The area targeted by Sherman was, as yet, largely untouched by war, as one of Forrest's Escort testified. Johnston S. Ryall wrote to his parents, "Can't you send Lizzie out here to school? There is an excellent school at Sommerfield, Alabama, and there they do not know there is any war, have plenty of everything" (Ryall, December 9, 1863).

## The 1864 Mississippi Campaign

Sherman's expedition to Meridian was successful in capturing and destroying vast amounts of public property and burning hundreds of private dwellings and farm buildings. Smith did not leave Memphis on time and was not so successful. It was February 14 before Smith was well under way, and by the eighteenth, Forrest's scouts had located his column and deduced his intentions. On February 21, Smith decided to withdraw north, but he first sent out a unit to make a diversionary attack on a handful of Confederates at Ellis Bridge on Sakatanchee Creek, some three miles south of West Point, Mississippi. Forrest heard of this move and took steps to counter it. The engagement became the Battle of Okolona.

Of all the battles fought by Forrest's cavalry, this was the Escort's fight more than any other unit's. Most of Forrest's command was new recruits who had never faced the enemy unless in a minor skirmish. While confident in the ability of these men, Forrest had reason to be cautious of their skills in combat. No wonder he turned to his "shock troops," the men who never failed to stand by him in the tightest of places, who never failed to attack when ordered, and who never failed to drive the enemy before them. Again and again in this engagement, it would be the Escort Company who broke the Yankee line, although they numbered only about sixty men.

In technical terms, Okolona would be a "meeting engagement," as both sides fed men into the battle as reinforcements came up. Forrest began by sending the Escort with some support from Faulkner's Twelfth Kentucky to charge the Yankee troops at Ellis Bridge. The result of the attack was dramatic.

Just as the Escort struck the Yankee line, McCulloch's Brigade and a section of guns from Morton's Battery arrived on the field (Maness, 206; OR 32: 260, 352-53). Soon Forrest noted that the Yankees were falling back for no apparent reason. Sensing this meant a retreat, he ordered up two companies from Chalmers' Brigade. The request was met by two companies of Kentucky troopers. The Escort was rather disgusted with this choice of troops, since they professed to believe that the Kentucky men were only guerrillas who would not stand up to the work in a real fight. Hearing this criticism, Colonel McCulloch challenged the Escort: "Ride into the fight with them one time and see what they will do" (Lytle, 263). The Escort soon found they were not the only fighters in Forrest's cavalry, and the two units pursued the Yankees for several miles. As night fell, the pursuit had to slow and was halted when Confederate troops, in confusion as to who was whom, fired into the Escort, with a bullet passing through Forrest's clothes. One man of the Escort was killed by this "friendly fire." With that near-miss, the Escort settled into an abandoned Union camp and enjoyed the food and fires left by the recently departed Yanks (Lytle, 264).

Not one to sleep when a successful fight needed to be finished, Forrest led his men onward again at 4:00 A.M. While drowsy Rebel cavalrymen were saddling up, Forrest led the Escort toward the Union position, and soon this little band had outrun the rest of the command and attacked the Yankee rear guard about four miles from the town of Okolona. Bell's Brigade, currently commanded by Barteau, was east of the town, so Forrest left the Escort to pin down the entire Union force while he and the Staff rode to join Barteau and bring his men into the fight (Maness, 207). An attack that flanked the Northern line soon sent the whole force into retreat. The Escort led the pursuit, with the rest of Forrest's command just beginning to reach the field.

At Ivey's Farm, some five miles from Okolona, there was a naturally strong defensive position, and the Union soldiers made a stand there. The flanks of the position were covered with scrub oak brush and the only feasible approach was across open fields, while the Yankees had cover behind the buildings and fences of the farm. The Confederate attack carried the first line but faltered before the second when Jeffrey Forrest was shot from his horse. The general rushed to the side of his stricken brother, who died in his arms.

Jeffrey was the youngest child of the family, born four months after the death of his father, and Nathan was the oldest. For all Jeffrey's life, Nathan had been both his brother and "father." Forrest was relatively wealthy by the time Jeffrey reached his middle teen years and sent his younger brother to college to secure the education Nathan never had (CV 33: 371). The general felt keenly the death of his favorite sibling.

Dr. J. B. Cowan had been called forward to attempt to help Jeffrey, and he described what happened next.

> The rough soldier kissed his dead brother tenderly, with tears streaming from his eyes, laid him gently on the ground, took one last look, and then his expression of grief gave way to one of almost ferocity; he sprang to his horse, shouting to Goss, his bugler, "Blow the charge!" and swept ahead of his men in the direction of the retreating enemy. I followed as close behind as I could and I and most of the Escort stayed near to him. Half a mile down the road we suddenly came upon the enemy who was making a stand. Artillery had been placed so as to sweep the approaches to their lines and they opened fire on us as soon as they saw us. I remonstrated with the General for exposing himself and Forrest said "Doctor, if you are uneasy here you may ride out of range." A minute later his horse was killed under him and he mounted one belonging to Private J.B. Long of the Escort only to have that horse shot a short time later. By then someone had brought up King Philip. Mounted on his favorite horse the charge was again ordered and the sixty men of the Escort went again at the Yankees. (CV 4: 42)

Knowing the attacking party would be badly outnumbered, Cowan rode back for help and soon encountered McCulloch's men. This body dashed around a bend in the road only to see

Forrest and the Escort nearly overrun but fighting like furies. By the time McCulloch had charged home, Forrest had personally killed three men (CV 23: 450), and his Escort had proven themselves the equal of a brigade of the enemy. Ten miles from Pontotoc, a final stand of Sooy Smith's cavalry was broken and Forrest turned the pursuit over to Mississippi state troops.

During the final fight, Lt. Thomas T. Tate of the Escort found himself in combat with a Union officer. Tate had only an empty carbine while his opponent had a loaded revolver. While the Union officer was in the act of cocking his pistol, Forrest swung his saber left-handed and practically severed the man's head from his body. Tate took the revolver from the man's hand before he fell and went on with the attack (Maness, 210-11).

Col. George E. Waring, commander of the Fourth U.S. Missouri, summed up the results of the battle when he wrote, "The Escort and part of the 12th Kentucky drove our 7,000 men without difficulty. This expedition filled every Union man with burning shame, while it gave Forrest the most glorious achievement of his career" (Johnson 4: 418). In his report, Forrest summarized the nature of his Escort: "I determined, therefore, to rely upon the bravery and courage of the few men I had with me, so I advanced to the attack" (OR 32: 354). The Escort was being tried in the refiner's fire and was coming out pure gold.

## Second West Tennessee Raid

After some days of rest, Forrest looked over the strategic situation and realized that the Union forces in west Tennessee were all off balance and that he held the advantage. He decided to move once again into the area to gather supplies, bring in recruits, and rid the country of bushwhackers, outlaws, and other unsavory types that the war was producing in abundance. In particular he had his eye on the Sixth U.S. Tennessee and Thirteenth U.S. Tennessee. These units had made reputations as looters and rapists, and Forrest was determined to put an end to their hellish work. Yet even under this provocation, he maintained a degree of restraint. Capt. Charles Anderson, the only Staff officer to be with Forrest during the entire raid, recounts what happened when the Escort entered Purdy, Tennessee, the hometown of Col. Fielding Hurst, commander of the Sixth Tennessee.

The 6th Tennessee had evacuated Purdy but before leaving had laid in ashes the homes of all Confederate soldiers. Two of our regiments were from McNairy and adjoining counties, and Forrest knew there would be trouble unless timely steps were taken to prevent it. When within a few miles of that place he directed me to take a sergeant and five men from the Escort, dash on into Purdy, and place a guard around the residence of Colonel Hurst.

On entering the town blackened walls, lone chimneys, and charred remains of buildings gave abundant evidence of Hurst's cowardly vandalism. Learning from a citizen that his residence was in the suburbs and directly on our line of march to Jackson, we were soon at its front. Dismounting and entering the portico of his dwelling, I tapped lightly on the door with the hilt of my saber. In a moment or so it was opened by a lady; and when I asked, "Is this Mrs. Colonel Hurst?" she, trembling, answered, "Yes, Sir."

I noticed her agitation, also that on opening the door her countenance quickly changed, manifesting on the instant both surprise and alarm. Hastening to relieve her apprehensions, I said, "We are not here to harm you, but have been sent for your protection. Although General Forrest has not reached Purdy, he is aware of the ruin and devastation caused by your husband's regiment and has sent me in advance of his troops to place a guard around your house. This guard is from his own Escort and will remain with you until all of our command has passed, and I assure you that neither your family nor anything about your premises will be disturbed or molested."

Giving the officer of the guard instructions, I turned to her and was in the act of raising my cap before mounting my horse when, brushing away tears she could no longer repress, she said, "Please, sir, say to General Forrest for me that this guard is more than I had any right to expect of him and that I thank him from my heart for this unexpected kindness. I shall gratefully remember it and shall always think him to be as generous as he is brave."

Returning to the town, I rejoined the General as he was entering the public square, where he halted and was soon surrounded by citizens of the place, among them the venerable father of Col. D.M. Wilson, of our command, who said, "You see, General, the marks of Colonel Hurst's last visit to our town, and you are also aware that a large number of our citizens are Union people, and they are greatly alarmed for fear of retaliation on the part of your command."

Forrest's reply was characteristic and stripped of his habitual way of emphasizing matters. "I do not blame any man for being exasperated and, especially those whose homes have been laid in ashes, for desiring to revenge such cowardly wrongs; but I have placed a guard around the home of Hurst, and others need feel no uneasiness. Orders have been issued to my command that no Union citizen of this town must be insulted, much less harmed, and this order was accompanied by my personal request that it be obeyed to the letter; and I am sure no soldier of my command will disobey the one or disregard the other. Of one thing, however, the Union friends of Colonel Hurst and his cowardly regiment may rely upon; if we ever are so fortunate as to find them in our front, I will wipe them off the face of the earth." (CV 23: 451)

The move into west Tennessee had begun in mid-March 1864, and soon Forrest had recruiting agents at work at Jackson and Trenton while small parties of men moved about the countryside gathering up horses and supplies. Since this was mostly routine duty that involved very small confrontations with the Yankees, there is no special mention in any records of the activities of the Escort and Staff; however, it was the sort of duty in which they excelled. Units did capture the Federal garrison at Union City, and a raid on Paducah took control of the town for several hours while Forrest carried off all the military valuables he could load in his wagons. It was at Paducah that Captain Anderson of the Staff had a memorable adventure.

On orders from General Forrest, Anderson took nineteen of the Escort and made a dash through the streets of the city to the wharf in an attempt to capture a supply of clothing. The gunboat *Paw Paw* opened fire on the squad with shell. Taking shelter behind houses, the Escort members returned fire, putting several shots from their rifles through the portholes of the boat. While the Escort members set fire to several bales of cotton and looked for clothes, a messenger arrived from Forrest with a peremptory order to retreat, as they were nearly cut off. As the group poured back down the streets, Anderson was separated from the rest of the men and found himself facing two Union cavalrymen. One of the men Anderson shot while still several yards away, but he had close to hand-to-hand combat with the remaining Yank. Anderson fired his last pistol shot at the man, missing. The man had had enough and turned his horse to flee, so Anderson threw the empty weapon at his retreating foe, drawing another pistol that had two rounds remaining. Suddenly the Yankee wheeled his horse and charged back toward Anderson. Firing on the run, Anderson missed with both remaining shots. The Yankee fired five times, missing Anderson with every round. Then both men drew their sabers, a weapon Anderson seldom used. A lucky stroke unhorsed the Yank and Anderson made his retreat. The next day, Anderson was sent to the fort where the main body of the Union troops was stationed. His negotiations were a ruse to cover the retreat of the main body of Forrest's command, but while engaged in the parley, one of the Union offices asked, "Are you the man who fought two of our boys in the street yesterday?" Anderson said that was the case. "Are all of Forrest's men like you?" was the next query. Anderson claimed that he was about the worst fighter in all the command. The questioner then said that he was the man Anderson had wounded with his saber and that he did not understand how he had missed Anderson with his pistol five times at such close range. Anderson just smiled and never told the man that he had put four of the five shots through Anderson's coat (CV 4: 359).

The focal point of this expedition was the capture of Fort Pillow on April 12, an event that gave birth to a controversy that still captures the attention of anyone who studies the Civil War in the West. The fighting and its aftermath are described in all the biographies of Forrest and in several monographs on Fort Pillow. The name of the location was taken from a fortification that was constructed by Tennessee in 1861 but that was abandoned when Federal gunboats ran past it and captured Memphis in June 1862. The 1864 engagement did not actually involve a "fort" but was the capture of a Union position protected by a breastwork facing inland and open on the flanks and rear.

Theodore F. Brewer, who served under Forrest at Fort Pillow, felt that Forrest had a personal reason for attacking the position. He wrote:

After Forrest captured Union City and destroyed the supplies at Paducah, he returned to Eaton, Tenn., and was on his way back to Mississippi. At Eaton he was met by many of the citizens of West Tennessee, principally ladies, who besought him not to fail to take Fort Pillow before he left the state. The troops at Fort Pillow were principally negroes who formerly belonged to people that lived in West Tennessee. They had terrorized their old masters's families until they did not know what to expect next. The Rev. G.W.D. Harris, D.D., was held as a prisoner in the fort, and suffered many indignities at the hands of the negroes, and was released only a few days before Forrest's arrival. Dr. Harris was one of the most distinguished ministers in the Southern Methodist Church.

General Forrest was a man of great sympathy, and when he heard the pathetic stories told by the ladies, he changed his plans and decided to capture Fort Pillow. (CV 33: 459)

It is clear that west Tennessee Confederates looked on Fort Pillow as a symbol of Yankee oppression, as a center of the "hard war" policy that had been adopted in stages across the South beginning in 1863. Citizens from across west Tennessee had been arrested by Union provosts and imprisoned at Fort Pillow while parties of scouts and foragers fanned out from there, taking livestock, food supplies, and any personal items that struck their fancy. The infantry commander at Fort Pillow, Maj. William F. Bradford, was a native of Virginia who had lived in west Tennessee for several years prior to the war. The overall garrison commander, Maj. Lionel Booth, was in charge of the black artillerymen at the fort, but his commission was dated earlier than that of Bradford.

These officers, and the troops they commanded, received no respect from Forrest and his troopers. The Union troops assigned to provost duty dealt with unarmed civilians and only an occasional guerrilla and were not thought to deserve the consideration given to seasoned fighters. Those who rode with Forrest thought of themselves, correctly so, as elite combat troops.

The details of the attack on Fort Pillow are already available in the numerous biographies of Forrest. In general terms, when the second-rate troops manning the works of Fort Pillow jeered at the surrounding Confederates, refused to surrender, and forced the delivery of a frontal assault, the stage was set for a disaster. When one adds in that a number of the defenders were drunk, that many who ran from the parapet retained their weapons, and that ammunition in opened boxes was positioned on the river face of the bluff, then it is no wonder that only a small amount of animosity would be needed to achieve the results that history records. (Nathaniel C. Hughes, Jr., in *Brigadier General Tyree H. Bell*, has an excellent discussion of the Fort Pillow affair. In his treatment of the subject, the author is fair and judicious and maintains historical perspective.)

Capt. Charles Anderson of the Staff played a significant role in the events there. His account speaks, probably, for all the Staff in presenting their understanding of what happened at Fort Pillow.

# Anderson's Account

After the return of General Forrest's command from his expedition to Paducah his Adjutant General, Major Strange, was attacked with hemorrhage of the lungs, and when ready for the move against Fort Pillow his condition was so critical that General Forrest thought it best to leave Colonel Galloway and his son, Willie Forrest, at Jackson with him, hence, I was the only staff officer with General Forrest in his expedition against that fort.

General Chalmers, with Bell's and McCulloch's brigades, and four small pieces of artillery, moved out from Jackson on the morning of the 10th of April, 1864. General Forrest, with Escort, and a detachment under Lieutenant Colonel Wisdom, followed later. On reaching Brownsville he directed General Chalmers to make a forced march on the night of the 11th and if possible to reach Fort Pillow by or before day on the morning of the 12th (in order to take the garrison by surprise), and to attack at once on arrival.

General Forrest rested a few hours at Brownsville, and followed Chalmers. When within eight or ten miles of the river we heard the first cannon firing at the fort, and knew then that General Chalmers was at work. Our march was quickened, and some three or four miles from the fort we were met by a courier with a dispatch from General Chalmers stating that he had driven the enemy into their works and the rifle pits around the fort, and, as I now remember, expressing the opinion that they could not be assaulted and captured except with heavy cost. This dispatch put us in a trot, and General Forrest was soon on the ground and in command.

As everything was comparatively quiet, our jaded horses were rested for a few moments, while the General held a short conference with General Chalmers. After which, unaccompanied except by myself, he made a rapid circuit around the land face of the fort from the Federal horse lot to Coal Creek above, returning to our starting point over a diminished distance from the works. In returning we were subjected to a constant and dangerous fire from the parapets. The General's horse was wounded, and my own pulled up dead lame after leaping a small ditch. I supposed him shot also, but it proved a strain. Going at once to the Escort's position in rear of the Federal horse lot, I dismounted Private Lucas of that company, took his horse, and rejoined the General as he was returning alone from a reexamination of the ground over which we had ridden, and as we galloped rapidly around and down toward the river, a second horse was shot under him and killed.

In these examinations he found a ravine almost encircling the fort, and that from the high ground over which we had ridden sharpshooters could command most of the area inside the fort, and could enfilade its retreating angles, and render them untenable or the occupation exceedingly hazardous. He also discovered that the ravine once gained by our troops, they would be just as well fortified as were the enemy, one party being inside and the other just outside the same earthworks. His plan of action was quickly determined, and was speedily communicated to General Chalmers, and by him to his brigade commanders, and preparations and dispositions made at once for its execution.

Under signals from the fort, the gunboat "New Era" lay abreast of the mouth of the ravine below the fort, and was constantly shelling us. By the General's directions, I moved a section of artillery to the high bluff below the mouth of the ravine, where a plunging fire would necessarily drive her from her position. Of this movement she was doubtless advised by signal from the fort, as she steamed up the river and out of range before we could open fire on her.

While absent on this duty, strong lines of sharpshooters had been thrown forward to the high ground previously referred to, and when I rejoined the General our whole force, under a terrific fire from the artillery and small arms of the garrison, was closing rapidly around the works. Bell's Brigade was on the right, extending from the mouth of Coal Creek southward; McCulloch's Brigade on the left, extending from the ravine below the fort northward, his right joining with the left of Bell's line abreast of the fort.

When General Chalmers had gained the desired position, which was done rapidly and handsomely, but with the loss of some brave officers and men, General Forrest determined, in order to save further loss of life, to demand a surrender. He knew the place was practically in his possession, as the enemy could not depress their artillery so as to rake the slopes around the fort with grape and canister, and the constant and fatal fire of our sharpshooters forced the besieged to keep down behind their parapets. He believed the Federal commander fully recognized the situation, and that he would accept an offer to surrender in preference to an assault by a force much larger than his own, and in full view. Bugles were sounded for a truce and a parley and a white flag sent forward with a demand for the immediate and unconditional surrender of all the Federal troops at Fort Pillow.

The smoke of approaching steamers ascending the river had been visible for some time. Three of them were now nearing the fort. General Forrest ordered me to take a detachment from McCulloch's brigade and move to the bluff, and prevent them from landing. I at once detached three companies (about one hundred and fifty men) and moved them rapidly to a position within sixty yards of the south entrance of the fort, descending by a path and occupying some old rifle pits on the face of the bluff, which were built by the Confederates in 1861 for protecting their water battery. These pits were washed out, broken, and in many places filled in by caving banks from above, yet afforded some protection.

The channel of the Mississippi River at Fort Pillow runs close under the bluff, and as the foremost steamer neared our position I directed one of the men to fire at her pilot house. A second shot from another secured attention at once, and she sheared off toward the bar across the river. This steamer was the "Olive Branch," crowded from forecastle to hurricane deck with Federal soldiers. She was closely followed by the "Hope," and the "M.R. Cheek," both of which adopted the course of the leading steamer, making for the bar on the west side of the river, and all of them passing up to the position of the gunboat "New Era," which lay midstream just above the fort.

The bugler of the Thirteenth Tennessee Federal Cavalry had taken advantage of the truce to recover his trappings from his horse, which he had left tied in a small gulch or ravine leading from the fort toward the river. As I rode to the head of it I discovered him, with his back to me, busily engaged in securing his gum cloth and coat. I waited quietly until he turned to regain the fort. His astonishment and trepidation can well be imagined at finding a six shooter leveled at his face and an able bodied "Reb" behind it. Ordering him to hand me his carbine butt end foremost and then to untie his horse and lead him out ahead of me, I rode down, and around to the General's position, who was then with much impatience awaiting an answer to his final demand for a surrender.

As there were no steamers in sight coming from below, I remained with him until the final and emphatic refusal of the garrison to surrender was received.

I had in the meantime communicated to him the position of the gunboat, also that two large empty barges were cabled to the shore in rear of the fort, which might be utilized by the garrison, under her protecting fire, as a means of escape. I was equally particular in impressing upon him the hazardous position of the detachment on the face of the bluff, (out of sight of, and entirely separated from, the balance of the command), and that in the event of any failure to carry the works by assault, a sortie from the south entrance of the fort in their rear, with the gunboat and its cannon and marines in their front, their destruction or capture would certainly follow.

He fully recognized their isolated and exposed position, but, ignoring the contingency, he directed me to return to my position at once—to take no part in the assault, but to prevent any escape from the garrison by barges or otherwise—to pour rifle balls into the open ports of the "New Era" when she went into action, and, to use his last expression, "fight everything 'blue' between wind and water until yonder flag comes down."

Returning at once, all necessary orders were given to the senior officer of the detachment, and by him they were passed along the trenches. I took a position in speaking distance of him, and where, by remaining mounted, I could see the fort flag; preferring to expose myself and horse to the expected fire of the "New Era" to that from the parapets of the fort; from which I was not fifty yards distant, but fully protected by an intervening ridge, around the head of which I had intercepted the bugler.

From this position I had a full view of the entire water line in rear of the fort, and much of the sloping bank above it. Owing to the conformation of the bluff, its brow in the rear of the fort was not visible, but nearly all the slope from the water line to within twenty or thirty feet of the top of the bluff in the rear of the fort was in plain view.

This was the situation as taken in while anxiously awaiting the sound of Gaus' well-known bugle. It soon came; was repeated along the line, and at once followed by the yells of our men, and a terrific discharge of the batteries and small arms of the fort. In a few moments a portion of the garrison rushed down toward the river and upon them we opened a destructive fire. The yells of our troops as they mounted the parapets could be plainly heard above the din and rattle of musketry, and in a moment more the whole force of the garrison came rushing down the bluff toward the water with arms in hand, but only to fall thick and fast from the short range fire of the detachment temporarily under my command, which threw them into unutterable dismay and confusion. This fire, with that of the whole assaulting line, was, for the few moments it lasted, most destructive and deadly. The moment the Federal colors came down, I ordered the firing to cease at once, and it was promptly done. Directing the commanding officer to bring his men up out of the pits and report to his regiment, I dashed into the south entrance of the fort. Everything was in confusion and the dead and wounded were lying thick around, but there was no firing anywhere.

I met the General between the flag staff and the entrance and his first words were,: "Major, we drove them right to you, and I cut their flag down as soon as I could get to it."

No one under such circumstances could accurately give the time of these transactions, but I am satisfied in my own mind that it was less than fifteen minutes from the time our bugles sounded until their colors came down, and less than two minutes from the time they were lowered until firing had ceased, and I had joined the General inside the works.

Every soldier who has ever participated in work of this kind knows that such actions must be short, sharp and desperate, to be successful.

Gen. Forrest's first order was to wheel around and move out the cannon of the fort so as to command the river. He could have opened fire at long range upon the "New Era," as she steamed away up the river, but instead of doing so, directed me to take Capt. Young, the Federal provost marshal, and a white flag, and endeavor to open communication with her, with a view of delivering the Federal wounded and securing surgical aid for them until they could be removed.

With a flag we followed her up the river bank, waving her to stop and send a boat ashore. She paid no attention whatever to our signals. Doubtless her commander thought our flag a ruse to effect his capture, and his vessel soon disappeared around the point above the fort.

Returning and reporting to the General our failure to communicate with the "New Era," he at once caused details to be made of all the unwounded Federals, under their own officers, to first bring into the huts and houses on the hill all their wounded comrades, and then to proceed at once to bury their dead.

When the wounded and dead had been removed from the face of the bluff, a detail of our own men was sent down to gather up all the small arms thrown down by the garrison. I went with this detail myself, and inspected and handed over to our ordnance officer two hundred and sixty-nine rifles and six cases of rifle ammunition, all of which were gathered up on the face of the slope from the fort to the water's edge. The six cases of cartridges were piled against the upturned roots of an old tree, with their tops removed, ready for immediate distribution and use.

Gen. Forrest remained on the ground until late in the evening, hoping to be able to deliver the wounded to some steamer, should any approach the fort; but as none ventured to come in sight, he gave full directions to and turned over the command to Gen. Chalmers, and, moving out on the Brownsville road with his Escort, we encamped at a farm house about seven or eight miles from Fort Pillow.

As we were mounting our horses next morning (the 13th) en route to Jackson, a heavy cannonading began at the fort. The General at once directed me to take ten men from the Escort and, with Captain Young (who was still with us), to proceed back to Fort Pillow and again attempt negotiation with the Federal fleet for the removal of their wounded.

On arrival I caused all of Gen. Chalmers' details, at whom the gunboats were firing, to be at once withdrawn, and accompanied by Capt. Young only, with a white flag, rode down to the water's edge. The gunboat "Silver Cloud" discovered us and our flag, ceased firing, and steamed slowly in shore. When within hailing distance her engines were stopped, and her commander, through his trumpet, asked, "What was wanted?" I asked him to send an officer ashore, and I would deliver my communications in writing. Seeing him run out and launch a small boat into the river, I dismounted from my horse, and wrote briefly what was desired; but, on turning around, found the small boat nearing our position with the United States flag at its bow and six armed marines and an officer aboard. Waving him back, and calling his attention to our white flag, I told him that I could hold no parley with him until he returned to his vessel, hoisted a white flag, and returned with his oarsmen unarmed. This he readily did, and on his return a communication was given him, requesting the landing of the "Silver Cloud" in order to negotiate for a truce, and for the delivery of all the wounded of the garrison, and assuring the commander of his safety in landing under a white flag; but, if unwilling to land, to send a boat back and I would go on board to complete the desired arrangements.

As soon as my message was delivered, Capt. Ferguson lowered his colors, ran up a white flag, and landed his vessel. Going on board, I was furnished by the purser with pen and paper, and in a short time an agreement was made for a truce from 9 o'clock A.M. to 5 o'clock P.M. All the conditions named were accepted by Capt. Ferguson, and the articles drawn up in duplicate and signed by both parties; after which I went ashore, sending a dispatch at once to Gen. Chalmers' headquarters, notifying him of the truce, and that, for fear of a collision, none of his troops must be allowed to come within the old Confederate rifle entrenchments, but suggesting that he and his staff come down whenever his duties would permit. I then sent four of my men to clear the fort and its surroundings of all stragglers, and to allow no one to remain on the grounds but surgeons and their assistants.

Allowing time for the men to carry out these orders, I notified Capt. Ferguson to run out his stagings, and that the fort and all its surroundings were now in his possession. Several steamers were in sight awaiting developments and signals. They were signaled to drop down and land, and in a short time the removal of the wounded to the steamer "Platte Valley" began.

I remained at her gangways, taking a full and complete list of the wounded as they were carried on board, placing a guard at the stage planks of the other steamers to insure the delivery of all the wounded upon one vessel.

Capt. Young, left ashore in charge of Sergt. Eaton, of the Escort, learned that his wife was on one of the steamers just landed, that she was in great stress of mind as to his fate, and asked permission (under guard) to go on board, assure her of his safety, give some instructions as to his private affairs, and bid her farewell. I placed him under parole of honor to report back to me at 2:30 P.M., and allowed him to go at once. He accepted the parole, with many thanks for my kindness, and reporting promptly at the designated hour, was sent out to Gen. Chalmers' headquarters to join his comrades as a prisoner of war.

Permission was given to all the passengers on the three steamers to visit the fort, and all of them did so, many of them bringing back in their hands buckles, belts, balls, buttons, etc., picked up on the grounds which they requested permission to carry with them as relics or mementos of Fort Pillow. All such requests were cheerfully and pleasantly granted.

Gen. Chalmers and staff came down and remained an hour or more, and notified me that he was withdrawing his command to Brownsville, and offering to leave a detachment to accompany me after the truce, which I declined, because I thought we could soon overtake them. With the prisoners and fort artillery I thought they could not move very rapidly. I did not know then that one brigade and the prisoners and artillery were already half way to Brownsville, or I would most certainly have accepted a stronger escort.

Before the expiration of the truce all the wounded had been placed on the "Platte Valley," and a receipt in duplicate taken from them, signed by Capt. Ferguson, of the "Silver Cloud." I was, as may well be imagined, worn down and exhausted and when my duties were over a couple of lieutenants of the Federal army on the "Platte Valley" insisted on my taking a parting glass with them at the bar of that steamer, which I, of course, did little thinking at the time that my acceptance of their hospitality and their courtesy would cost them their commissions. For this courtesy and kindness, one officer was cashiered and the other reduced to the ranks.

A while before five o'clock I suggested to Capt. Ferguson the departure of the passenger steamers yet at the landing, and stated to him that at the expiration of the truce I should proceed to burn all the buildings at Fort Pillow; that they had been preserved for the accommodation of the Federal wounded, and their existence was no longer necessary or desirable. When the steamers had all left, I assured Capt. Ferguson that there was no Confederate force within two miles of the fort, and that he could let go his lines and depart at his leisure, and without fear of molestation.

I then saluted him an adieu, and with my little squad rode slowly up the bluff.

The men with me were dismounted, and set to work scattering and distributing loose straw, hospital beds and bunks through all the buildings. We waited until the "Silver Cloud" let go her lines and swung out into the river. As she lowered her white flag the torch was applied, and as she ran up her colors the last buildings left at Fort Pillow burst into flames. We then mounted our horses and bade Fort Pillow a lasting adieu.

The fearful loss of life at Fort Pillow is alone chargeable to the total incapacity of its commanding officer, and to the fatal and delusive promise of or agreement made by Capt. Marshall, of the gunboat "New Era" with Maj. Bradford—that is, that when whipped the garrison was to drop down under the bluff, and the "New Era" would give the rebels canister and protect and succor them. Maj. Booth, who commanded Fort Pillow, was killed early in the morning by a bullet through the brain. His death placed the command in the hands of Maj. W.F. Bradford, of the Thirteenth Tennessee Federal Cavalry, a man without any military capacity whatever; and, if reports were true of him, his conduct as a soldier, as well as the violation of his parole after capture, show him as destitute of honor as wanting in military skill and ability.

When he found himself surrounded by a force thrice his own, and knew that his works were no longer defensible against an assault by such numbers, his plain duty was to surrender the fort and save further loss of life. Nor can he be excused for relying upon the promise of Capt. Marshall, after seeing and knowing that the movement of two howitzers to the low bluff had driven the "New Era" from the only position in which her promised aid could have been at all available.

Marshall did know, and Maj. Bradford ought to have known, that with the channel of the river right under the bluff, and a broad bar with shallow water right opposite the fort, the "New Era" could not get sufficient "offing" to elevate her guns and do any damage to parties on top of a bluff at least eighty feet above the water line.

Yet, with all this, the sequel shows that Maj. Bradford, relying upon the promise of Capt. Marshall, refused the third and last demand of Gen. Forrest for his surrender; and when assaulted and driven from the works, he retreated with arms in hands, and ammunition provided and placed under the bluff, only to find that the "New Era," instead of dropping down and giving the Rebels grape and canister, steamed quickly out of harm's way, leaving the duped commander and the deluded garrison to their fate.

How far Capt. Marshall could have aided the garrison no one can say, but it would have been far better for his name and fame had he moved his vessel promptly into action, and perished in attempting to do as he promised, than live and know that his violated promise, and his abandonment of the garrison, first led and then left hundreds of his countrymen and comrades to a swift and sweeping destruction.

I have never hesitated to assert, as I do now, that, numbers considered, the detachment temporarily under my command did, by far, the most fatal and destructive, as well as the very last firing done at Fort Pillow. It was enfilading, a terribly short rifle range, and began with the retreat of the very first troops that left the fort, and continued steadily and rapidly until the Federal flag came down. In our position under, or on the face of the bluff, one could only know when the fort was in our possession by the falling of its colors or a special messenger. The former was the quicker, and under my orders, as soon as it fell, firing was promptly stopped, and, ordering the detachment to report back at once to its regiment, I was with the General in less than two minutes after the flag came down.

The charges against Gen. Forrest and his men of massacre and butchery at Fort Pillow are outrageously unjust and unfounded. He did every thing in his power to induce a surrender and avoid an assault. Thrice was a surrender demanded, and as often refused. There never was no surrender, therefore no massacre after surrender, as has been so erroneously and widely charged.

I take occasion here to say that in my long service with Gen. Forrest, his kindness to the vanquished, the unarmed and unresisting foe, was a marked characteristic of the man. He believed and always said and dealt, that "war meant fight, and fight meant to kill," but never in all his career did a Federal soldier throw down his arms and surrender, that did not receive at once his consideration and protection. He captured many thousand Federals, and there is not one living today who can truthfully say that he was ever mistreated or ever insulted by Nathan Bedford Forrest (CV 3: 322-26).

## Brices Crossroads and Tupelo

Upon returning to Jackson, the Escort and Staff took time to perform a sad duty, one with which they had become all too familiar. Among the Confederate dead from Fort Pillow was Col. Wiley Reed, former pastor of the First Cumberland Presbyterian Church of Nashville, Tennessee. He had served as an officer in the Fifty-fifth Tennessee Infantry until that regiment was consolidated with another unit, at which time he requested service under Forrest. He had only joined Forrest in March 1864 and was killed while commanding the Fifth Mississippi Cavalry. He was a good friend of Capt. Charles Anderson and Col. D. C. Kelley. Reed had been mortally wounded at Fort Pillow and died on May 1 at Jackson. On May 2, Colonel Kelley read the funeral service of the Methodist Church, South, over his coffin, and the local Masonic Lodge joined the Escort in bearing the body to the cemetery where it was interred (CV 5: 101-2).

While his fellows were raiding into Kentucky, Staff member Mercer Otey was having an adventure of his own. Forrest, as noted, had vowed destruction on Fielding Hurst and his "Galvanized Yankees" and sent Otey under a flag of truce to Memphis to protest some of Hurst's actions there. While riding along the road toward Memphis, Otey suddenly found himself abreast a column of blue troopers. When asked their identity, they stated they were in Hurst's regiment. Otey, of course, kept silent about his mission. After delivering his message to the Union commander at Memphis and visiting his sisters for a few hours, Otey returned to Jackson in the company of a Union officer carrying a flag of truce with a message for Forrest (CV 9: 108).

As the weather improved, Forrest decided to withdraw from his exposed position in west Tennessee, taking his booty and recruits back to Mississippi. Before he left the area, he made a suggestion that might have affected the outcome of the war had it been taken. Forrest suggested that his command be combined with the rest of the cavalry under the command of Gen. S. D. Lee and that the entire force be sent to middle Tennessee to operate against Sherman's supply line.

While falling back toward Mississippi, L. H. Russ, "the baby of the Escort," found himself in a great deal of trouble. Maj. Solomon Street had served under General Chalmers earlier in the war and had then been attached to Forrest's command. In the winter of 1862 Street had become involved in a dispute with William Galloway, a citizen of Saulsbury, Tennessee. The affair ended with Street shooting Galloway. The son of the dead man, Robert Galloway, swore vengeance and joined the Confederate army for the purpose of finding Major Street. At Bolivar, Tennessee, on the withdrawal from west Tennessee, young Robert encountered the major and killed him. Of course, he was arrested, with Russ being one of the men assigned to guard him.

Russ and the other guards were sympathetic to Robert Galloway and what he had done. They said loudly in the presence of the prisoner that he ought to escape and that they probably would not be able to hit a running figure in the dark. Galloway soon understood the drift of their talk and made a break for his horse. Russ and the other guards held their fire until Galloway was well under way and only belatedly raised the alarm.

Forrest was furious that the killer of one of his officers had escaped, and he was most suspicious of the circumstances under which it had happened. After cursing all the men assigned to the guard detail, Forrest had the entire squad arrested and announced his intention of "shooting every damn one of 'em as soon as the command reached Tupelo."

Russ maintained his composure during the entire march to Tupelo. He repeatedly assured his companions that Forrest had no men to spare, much less men from the Escort. Good men were too hard to find to waste them in such a manner. On reaching Tupelo, the group was locked up in a goat shed, but Russ soon pried up a corner of the roof, squeezed his slender body out through the hole, and went to Capt. John Jackson to explain why the escape had been allowed. Jackson intervened on behalf of the men, and Forrest decided there was no real evidence of how Galloway had gotten away, so the matter was dropped. In 1903 Galloway met Russ by chance at a Masonic convention, the first time the two had met since 1864 (Tippah County Papers).

With the opening of the Atlanta Campaign, the Nashville & Chattanooga Railroad became the most strategically important piece of real estate in the Western Theater of the war. Every day ten freight trains, each consisting of ten cars, left Nashville to make the all-day trip to Chattanooga. These cars carried the ordnance supplies Sherman required for his campaign. Severing the rail line would have forced Sherman to fight with limited supplies of ammunition or to retreat. Sherman was concerned for his supply line and gave specific orders that Forrest was to be kept away from the Nashville & Chattanooga at all costs (Maness, 262-64; Bradley, *With Blood and Fire*, 12-13).

Forrest had made some preliminary moves toward concentrating his men in north Alabama, but any nascent move into Tennessee was interrupted by the beginning of the Union advance that would culminate in the Battle at Brices Crossroads. Gen. Samuel D. Sturgis was leading over 8,500 men and twenty-two guns from Collierville, Tennessee, toward the fertile farmlands of east-central Mississippi, an area he was to devastate so Confederates could draw no supplies from there. In addition, Sturgis was to defeat Forrest and so damage his command that a raid into Tennessee against Sherman's rail lines would be impossible. Beginning on June 1 Sturgis slowly moved forward, taking nine days to cover ninety miles. On June 10 he was nearing a rural crossroads named for the Brice family, just a short distance from the crossing of Tishomingo Creek.

The entire Federal force was forced to advance over a single road that was in poor condition because of recent heavy rains. Forrest decided to concentrate his more mobile force, all of it cavalry and artillery, around Brices Crossroads and defeat the Yankees "in detail" as they came up to the battlefield. He knew the blue cavalry would arrive first and that the infantry would be slower to arrive and would come to the field tired from a march through a swamp in hot weather. Forrest had at the crossroads only a small brigade under Hylan Lyon and the indefatigable Escort. On this occasion the Escort was reinforced by a Georgia company commanded by Capt. Henry Gartrell (Henry, 288). As a former mayor of Rome, Georgia, a town Forrest had saved from destruction at the hands of Abel Streight in 1863, Gartrell and his men had a special debt to repay. On this day they balanced their account of gratitude with Forrest. It is interesting to note that Gartrell was also a newspaper publisher and the uncle of Henry W. Grady, the "New South" advocate of later years. He was also a friend of Joel Chandler Harris, the author of the "Uncle Remus" stories, and wrote a story about General Forrest, "The Shadow Between His Shoulderblades" (see Appendix D). On June 10, 1864, Captain Gartrell was simply a hard fighter. It was well that he was. The outnumbered Confederates were planning to defeat successive waves of Yankees, some of them armed with repeating weapons.

As Sturgis's men came up from the creek bottom onto the plateau around Brices Crossroads, Forrest sent the Escort in a mock charge through the scrub oaks to make the Yankees think a large group was confronting them. At the same time Lyon's men were piling up fence rails, brush, logs, and whatever they could lay hands on to provide breastworks. Throughout the morning the Escort was in a severe skirmish with the blue cavalry. Both sides greeted the arrival of reinforcements, which were immediately fed into the growing battle. During this phase of the battle, Capt. John Jackson took overall command of Gartrell's Georgia Company and two Kentucky companies, while Lt. George Cowan took immediate command of the Escort (Morton, "Brices Crossroads," 367). About one o'clock, the last of the Confederate forces arrived, Bell's Brigade and Morton's artillery, and Forrest ordered an attack that saw the last of the Union cavalry begin to fall back just as the first of the Northern infantry was arriving, puffing from a rapid march of five miles on a hot Mississippi morning.

The Staff was active in placing the troops for this carefully coordinated advance of the entire Confederate line. Capt. Charles Anderson was detailed to work with Morton to bring up all the guns under the artilleryman's command and run them forward to within a hundred yards of the Yankee line. Forrest himself came to inspect the placing of the cannon, and Morton risked a thorough "cussing" by suggesting that the general move to a less exposed position. Much to the captain's surprise, Forrest did not lash out at him but quietly moved down the hill a short way and sat down at the base of a tree to rest a moment.

While Forrest was taking his short rest, Lt. George Cowan was riding for the extreme left flank with orders for the Escort to slip around the end of the Federal line and attack from the rear. Similar orders had been sent to the Second Tennessee on the right flank. At the signal, the entire Confederate line rolled forward, including Morton's guns. This, Morton would later comment, was the first and perhaps only time an artillery battery charged an infantry line, and it was done without supporting troops for the guns. Morton was acting as chief of artillery, commanding a four-battery battalion, and the guns in the center of Forrest's lines were actually under the command of Captain Rice. As Morton recalled the moment, just after receiving the order to charge the Union line, Captain Rice approached him and asked, "Captain Morton, do you reckon the general meant for us to charge sure enough without support?" Morton replied:

> You heard the order. Be ready. I am more afraid of Forrest than I am of the Yankees. (Morton, *Artillery*, 178-79)

At the order, the guns moved forward, and at a range of sixty yards Morton fired double canister and tore great holes in the Union line. With the Confederate attack on the Union front in full sway the Escort made its way around the Union flank, routing the Seventh Illinois and the Tenth Missouri cavalry (Bearss, 97). Spotting the unprotected wagon train across an open field,

Lieutenant Cowan immediately ordered a charge, and quickly the wolves were among the sheep. Wagons full of ammunition and food were soon in Confederate hands, but the Escort still had to pay a price. Morton's artillery saw the confusion among the wagons and, thinking they were attempting to escape, opened fire on them. Cowan, after the war, wrote to Morton, "I can assure you your range was good. One of your shells took off the rear end of one of the wagons in our possession, but General Forrest, recognizing his own colors through his field glasses, soon changed your fire from us to the enemy; this was a great relief, as your fire worried us more than that of the enemy" (Morton, "Brices Crossroads," 372). Hand-to-hand fighting ensued as Forrest's men charged home on the Union front line, and, in such an encounter, Yankee bayonets were no match for Rebel six-shooters (Bearss, 91).

The Federal infantry did not stand but ran back the way they had come as fast as the road conditions would allow. Every stream crossing was clogged with wagons, ambulances, and artillery from which the horses had been detached so the teamsters could get away faster. Heat exhaustion began to fell dozens of Yankees, and panic soon set in. Forrest, meanwhile, had given an order that most of his men should rest for two hours while the Escort followed the retreat and kept the pressure on. As Forrest would say later that day, he believed in "get 'em skeered, then keep the skeer on."

All the way into the morning of June 12, the pursuit continued. There was fighting at Llewellyn Church, and the Escort confronted hard-fighting members of the United States Colored Troops for a time before the Yankees pulled back (Bearss, 121). Mack Watson, a private in the Escort, rode close to Forrest all that time until, sometime in the early hours of the twelfth, Private Watson noticed that the general was asleep in the saddle. Reporting the fact to Captain Jackson, Escort commander, Watson was told, "Go wake him up, Mack."

> Watson had seen the famous Forrest temper before so he politely declined the order. "No, sir, you go wake him up."
>
> "Well, go tell Colonel Bell. Let the Colonel wake him up." As Watson started for the Colonel the horse Forrest was riding settled the matter by wandering off the road and running into a tree. Suddenly awake, Forrest saw Watson nearby and ordered him to ride back and tell General Buford to close up with the head of the column, coming on "at a gallop."

When he delivered the order General Buford exploded in a fit of temper himself. "Private, you go back up yonder and tell that madman that my men and my horses are not capable of galloping anywhere and neither the devil nor Bedford Forrest can make them."

"Sir," said Watson, "I will tell General Forrest precisely what you have said."

"Oh, hell, no," said Buford, "I'll tell the bugler to sound 'Gallop.'" (Henry, 299-300)

On June 12, when the battered survivors of Sturgis's expedition finally got back to Memphis, Forrest had won possibly his most complete victory. In his official report, Forrest wrote:

On the night of the 9th I received dispatches reporting the enemy, in full force, encamped twelve miles east of Ripley on the Guntown road, having abandoned the upper route as impracticable. Orders were issued to move at 4 o'clock on the following morning (10th instant). The wagon train of my entire command, in charge of Maj. C. S. Severson, chief quartermaster, was ordered to the rear. . . .

After describing the opening maneuvering and skirmishing, Forrest continued.

It was now 1 o'clock, and as all my forces were up I prepared to attack him at once. Taking with me my Escort and Bell's brigade I moved rapidly around to the Guntown and Ripley road, and advancing on that road, dismounting the brigade, and forming Russell's and Wilson's regiments on the right, extending to Colonel Rucker's left, and placing Newsom's regiment on the left of the road, Duffy's regiment, of Rucker's brigade, and my Escort were placed on the left of Newsom's and formed the extreme left of my line of battle. . . . The enemy having three lines of battle, the left was being heavily pressed. . . . Colonel Duffy and my Escort, dismounted, were ordered to charge the enemy's position in front of Newsom's regiment, and succeeded in driving the enemy to his second line, . . . I directed my aide-de-camp, Captain Anderson, to bring up all the artillery.

Under Morton's assault and another charge by the dismounted cavalrymen, the Union line gave way and a pursuit ensued for the rest of the day. Halting for a brief rest at 1:00 A.M., the pursuit resumed at 3:00.

We came upon them again about four miles east of Ripley, where they had prepared to dispute our advance, but made only a feeble and ineffectual resistance, the Seventh Tennessee and my Escort driving him from his position. He made another stand two miles east of Ripley, but it was followed by another characteristic retreat.

On reaching the town of Ripley, about 8 A. M., the enemy was found in line of battle and seemingly prepared for determined resistance, occupying all favorable positions for that purpose. I had but few troops present. My Escort was sent to the left and engaged the enemy, and Colonel Wilson's regiment was thrown forward, dismounted, as skirmishers, expecting they would be driven until the balance of my forces came up. The advance of Colonel Wilson and the Escort was spirited and determined, and at the first appearance of additional force he again retreated, leaving 21 killed and 70 wounded, another piece of artillery, 2 caissons, and 2 ambulances. . . . Taking with me my Escort and Colonel Bell, with . . . his brigade, we endeavored by taking another road to cut them off at Salem, but reached there an hour after their rear had passed.

Maj. G. V. Rambaut, commissary of subsistence, was highly serviceable. Capt. John W. Morton, chief of artillery, moved with great promptness, and did admirable execution with his guns. My medical staff, under the direction of Chief Surg. J. B. Cowan, were assiduous in attention to the wounded on the field and in their removal to comfortable hospitals.

The Escort and Staff had played their part in Forrest's complete victory. Of the Escort Company, Forrest wrote, "It would be unjust to close my report without referring to the gallant and meritorious conduct of my Escort Company, commanded by Capt. J.C. Jackson. Owing to drill, discipline, and materiel its services were to me on this occasion, as on many other fields, invaluable, and I consider it to-day the best body of men in my command—dashing, daring, and unflinching in the execution of orders given, and as scouts, for reliability and effectiveness, they are without an equal." Of the members of his Staff, Forrest commented, "My acknowledgments are also due to Maj. Charles W. Anderson, acting assistant adjutant-general, and to Lieutenants Donelson and Galloway, my aides-de-camp. Fully alive to the emergencies of the occasion and the odds against us, they were prompt and faithful in the execution of all orders and untiring in the discharge of every duty devolving upon them from the commencement of the battle until pursuit was ended" (OR 39: 226). Anderson had by then been promoted to major.

In his address read to all his troops, Forrest added some names.

> Nor can the general commanding forget to mention the efficient aid rendered by the artillery, commanded by Capt. John W. Morton. He moved rapidly over the roughest ground and was always in action at the right time, and his well-directed fire dealt destruction in the masses of the enemy. The general commanding also takes pleasure in noticing the intelligent alacrity with which Maj. C.W. Anderson, Capt. W.H. Brand, Lieutenants Otey, Donelson, Titus, and Galloway, of my Staff, conveyed orders to all parts of the field. They were ever near my person, and were prompt in the discharge of every duty. (OR 39: 229)

The victory at Brices Crossroads did not buy much time for rest and recruitment. Two weeks later, on June 26, Union general A. J. Smith moved out of Memphis at the head of 14,000 men on a route that would bring them to battle with the forces of Forrest and S. D. Lee at Tupelo. On July 12, the advance guards of both Union and Confederate forces were engaged near Pontotoc.

The strategy Forrest adopted was one that had worked well before. He decided to allow Smith to advance until he could be caught in a pocket and then harassed on all sides by the Confederate cavalry. Smith, however, did not cooperate. On July 13 he turned off the road from Pontotoc to Okolona and moved toward Tupelo, catching Forrest out of position to block the move immediately. On that day, Forrest used his Escort in its now-familiar role as shock troops to drive the last Union troops out of Pontotoc and pursue the Yankee column toward Tupelo. The Escort was on the heels of the blue troops all day but never managed to stampede them or get ahead of a large part of the column to cut it off (Wills, 222).

That night, Forrest and Staff lieutenant Samuel Donelson had a close encounter with Yankee pickets. Forrest was suffering from an outbreak of boils, and, as anyone who has ever had such a malady knows, many of them erupted on his buttocks. This made riding a painful matter, but Dr. J. B. Cowan could do nothing to relieve the discomfort until the boils had collected the infection into a head that he then could lance. After an uncomfortable day in the saddle, debilitated by the heat and the pain of the boils, Forrest had taken off his coat and weapons belt and had lain down under a tree. As twilight faded to dark, he called to Lieutenant Donelson to mount and join him on a reconnaissance. As the two passed through the forward Confederate pickets Forrest noted that he had left his pistols lying on the ground under the tree. Donelson offered Forrest his own weapon but Forrest declined, saying he did not think they would need arms. After riding through the Union wagon park and turning back toward their own lines, Forrest and Donelson stumbled on two Union pickets. When challenged for the password, Forrest asked, "What do you mean challenging your own commanding officer?" and rode away in the darkness. A few seconds later, the Union soldiers recovered from their surprise and fired down the road in the direction in which the two men had ridden. Forrest and Donelson, expecting such a result, were hunched far forward over the necks of their mounts. Forrest later quipped that a bullet in the butt would not have been a bad thing if it had opened one of the boils (Henry, 316).

The next day, Forrest, following orders from S. D. Lee, led his men in an attack on the fortified Union position. Maj. Charles Anderson later said that Forrest did not favor an attack but wanted to wait for Smith to retreat and then to attack him from the flank and rear. General Buford recalled that Forrest was optimistic about whipping the Yankees as usual. At any rate, the usual luck of his command was not present that day, the attacks were uncoordinated, the Union position was unusually strong, and the Yanks held their post until dark. One of casualties of this attack was Felix Hicks. He was a lieutenant in the quartermaster department and asked permission to fight with the Escort on this occasion. He was killed less than fifteen minutes after joining the battle. Another casualty was Pleasant Arnold, an African-American who had enlisted with the original Escort in October 1862. Private Arnold had always been carried on the roll as a combat soldier, not as a member of a support service.

On July 15, Smith decided to retreat and Forrest sent the Escort after him. The pursuit was not as vigorous as the earlier chases, because Forrest was wounded in the foot a few miles from Tupelo and Dr. J. B. Cowan had to order the general to stay off his feet for a time, an order that Forrest did not follow even though the wound was extremely painful. Forrest would be forced to ride with only one foot in the stirrups for several weeks.

The battles at Brices Crossroads and Tupelo resulted in tactical Confederate victories but they still extracted a price. Numerous horses had been worn out or killed; men had become casualties. The available resources could no longer replace these losses. As Union forces again moved south in July and August, it became obvious that Forrest would have to counter their advance with deception and cunning instead of confrontation on the battlefield. Out of this need was born the legendary raid on Memphis, a daring ride on which the Escort and Staff accompanied their general. On August 18, 1864, the plans for the move coalesced.

Moving rapidly through heavy rain, passing over muddy roads, and turning his cavalrymen into engineers to bridge swollen streams, Forrest led his men into Memphis before dawn on August 21, a Sunday morning. Once in the city the 1,500, raiders split into several groups, some attempting to capture Union generals while others pinned down the defenders. The Escort participated in the latter duty. In a brush with the Third Illinois Cavalry, the Escort charged their camp, capturing it along with 28 men and most of the blue troopers' horses (Bearss, 290).

By 9:00 A.M., Forrest and his raiders were on their way back out of town, with Col. Matthew Starr's Sixth Illinois Cavalry in pursuit. James Dinkins was a teenage Confederate in this fight. As the Yankee horsemen thundered down on the defending Rebel line, one of Dinkins' comrades went dashing toward the rear, loudly shouting he could not hold his horse. Dinkins recalled one wag in his unit calling equally loudly that he would "give a thousand dollars for one of them horses a feller can't hold" (CV 2: 27).

Forrest and Starr met in personal combat during the melee, and Starr became another of those dispatched by Forrest. The death of their commander ended the Union pursuit. Later that afternoon, Maj. Charles Anderson was sent back toward Memphis with a flag of truce to get shoes and clothes for the 400 prisoners Forrest had captured in their underwear while they were asleep (Henry, 340).

## Attacking Sherman's Supply Line

Using the momentum gained by his thrust into the heart of the Union command structure, Forrest moved east to begin his much-anticipated but long-delayed raid against the Nashville & Chattanooga Railroad, Sherman's main line of supply for the Atlanta Campaign, and the Tennessee & Alabama Railroad, a secondary supply line for the Yankees moving into Georgia. Maj.

Charles Anderson was given the responsibility of moving the artillery, ordnance trains, and other vehicles to a crossing on the Tennessee River, where the rest of the command would meet them.

Shortly after the cavalry had crossed the river, Forrest surrounded a strong Union earthwork at Athens, Alabama, on August 24, 1864. The Escort, supervised by Major Anderson, was sent to block the train tracks north of town, trapping a locomotive and train of cars. Morton and the artillery were placed so as to shell the fortification, and the cavalry were dismounted and placed to act as infantry if an assault became necessary. Major Strange carried to the fort the usual demand for surrender. Col. W. Campbell, the Union commander, refused unless he could be convinced he was facing superior numbers. Forrest was an old hand at this game, having convinced Col. Abel Streight to surrender to "superior" forces in April 1863. As Forrest showed Campbell his position, the Yankee officer counted twenty-four pieces of artillery and about 9,000 men. In reality, Forrest had eight cannon and 3,500 men. Remembering the bloodshed that had accompanied the rejected demand for surrender at Fort Pillow, Campbell surrendered. Reinforcements for the Union garrison were coming from Decatur, twenty-five miles to the south, but these were stopped by Forrest on the outskirts of Athens, and Campbell surrendered without ever knowing help was on the way.

Now Forrest and his command faced a new target. The Tennessee & Alabama Railroad had been provided with blockhouses to protect culverts and small bridges against guerrilla attacks. These blockhouses were built of heavy timbers, up to twenty-four inches square, with an earthen berm to protect the lower courses of logs. Loopholes were provided for infantry, and some of the blockhouses had one or two howitzers mounted to fire through embrasures. Several of the more important locations had blockhouses that were "double cased," built with two layers of logs with a layer of dirt between the wooden walls. Morton would find the blockhouses easy targets for his artillery, however. Two blockhouses a short distance north of Athens surrendered quickly when Morton opened on them with his three-inch rifled cannon (OR 39: 544). Morton described the taking of one of the works.

I sent in a demand to surrender before opening fire but the officer in command, a Dutchman [German] profanely refused. This refusal angered General Forrest who said "if the damned fool wants to be blowed up, I will blow him up." The first round from one of the "Bull Pups" tore a large log off the top of the blockhouse and the second round penetrated between two logs, killing five and wounding nine of the garrison. Immediately a white cloth was thrust out a porthole and I ordered the gunners to cease firing. Forrest would have none of it. "Keep on firing, Morton. After the way that fool has behaved it will take a bed sheet to attract my attention." Soon a much larger flag appeared over the blockhouse. After that, whenever we approached a blockhouse we sent the Dutchman in with our demand for surrender. (Morton, *Artillery*, 232)

The next day, Forrest arrived at Sulphur Creek trestle and surrounded the earthwork there and the blockhouses that helped guard the lengthy trestle. Again the Staff carried in a demand for surrender, and again Morton placed his guns to enfilade the interior of the work. This time the Union commander was stubborn and Morton wreaked havoc on the buildings inside the fort, and on the garrison, before they surrendered. About two hundred Union soldiers became casualties, with no losses to the Confederates, since all the fighting was done by Morton's artillery.

According to one Staff officer, a captured Union sergeant asked who commanded the Confederate forces. On being told it was Forrest, he said, "Hell, we thought it was Roddey. If we had known it was Forrest we would have quit before the guns opened up" (CV 8: 489).

Pushing on north, the raiders captured an abandoned Union earthwork at Elk River and burned the railroad bridge there. At the crossing of Richland Creek, near Pulaski, Forrest and the Staff found another blockhouse. By this time the capture of such strongpoints had become routine, so Forrest and a few of his Staff calmly rode to the rear of the blockhouse and then called on the 40 Yankees inside to surrender, the alternative being to call up Morton and the Bull Pups. The men marched out and laid down their rifles (OR 39: 546). As the Confederates neared Pulaski, resistance became stiffer and Forrest yet again called on his Escort. Early on August 27, the Union forces took up a strong position along Richland Creek, blocking both the road and the railroad. Forrest had only about 3,300 men on the field, but he sent the 60 members of the Escort in on foot. Charging the hill at the center of the Yankee position, these men carried the hill and broke the Northern line. The horse holders brought up their mounts and the Escort, joined by the Staff, pursued the enemy until they withdrew into their earthworks around the town of Pulaski (Jordan and Pryor, 571-72).

At this same engagement, J. P. Young of the Seventh Tennessee volunteered to fight with the Escort, as their numbers were dwindling due to wounds and loss of horses. He was assigned to stay with Forrest as a courier. Young and Forrest found themselves facing the hill the Escort would soon charge but with, as Young put it, "shells flying around us like marbles." Forrest took cover behind the only sizable tree around. One of the Escort said, "General, that isn't fair. We don't have trees." Forrest replied, "But you wish you did, don't you. You just want to get me out of my place" (CV 5: 277-78). A little later that same day, Young and Forrest came under fire while observing the Yankees from a hilltop. Both men dismounted, but Young moved to place his horse between him and the hostile fire. Forrest had pulled some blades of grass and was feeding them to his mount. Seeing what Young had done he said, "Soldier, better get on the other side and see if you can stop the bullets. Horses are scarcer than men right now." Young declined to move (CV 5: 278).

Forrest wanted to make sure that Pulaski was strongly held, so he took his Escort and moved to his right until he reached the northern part of the little town. There he observed that the Northern troops were numerous and held strong fortifications. Leaving a small group of men to keep campfires burning, Forrest led his command toward the Nashville & Chattanooga Railroad.

The Confederate column made a rapid march east from Pulaski toward Fayetteville, passed north of that town, and hoped to strike the Nashville & Chattanooga at the bridge across the Duck River, but on the night of the 28th the weather turned rainy and roads quickly became quagmires. Progress through the darkness and downpours slowed to a crawl.

As Forrest and the Staff rode down a hill, they came upon a caisson mired in the muck. As usual, when he was frustrated, Forrest turned the air blue, demanding to know who was in charge of the detail trying to move the ammunition carrier. Capt. Andrew McGregor, Company G, Fourth Tennessee, answered that he was "and that he did not intend to be cursed by anyone, including his commanding officer." While saying this, Captain McGregor picked up a torch that had been lit to illuminate the scene and plunged it deep into one of the ammunition chests on the caisson. Forrest spurred his horse and splattered mud all about as he rode rapidly up the road. The Staff could barely keep their saddles for laughing because they knew the caisson had been emptied of powder long before. Forrest joined in the laughter but, it was noted, he never again cursed Captain McGregor (Wills, 256-57; Morton, *Artillery,* 240-41).

That same night Forrest ordered Lt. Nathan Boone of the Escort to take twenty men and cut the Nashville & Chattanooga line at some point north of Tullahoma (OR 39: 547) while another group from the Twelfth Kentucky was sent to do the same south of the town. Tullahoma was the headquarters for the force defending a seventy-five-mile stretch of the Nashville & Chattanooga and had the largest garrison between Murfreesboro and Chattanooga. If that garrison could be isolated, it might be possible to do real damage to the rail line before Union reinforcements could arrive from Chattanooga or Nashville. But Boone and the Escort inflicted only slight damage, and this proved to be all Forrest could accomplish against the Nashville & Chattanooga, Sherman's major supply line. The Union forces were closing in too quickly, so Forrest fell back.

Damage had been done to a secondary Union supply line, but the real goal of the expedition could not be accomplished. Forrest, however, had no complaints about the efforts of his Escort and Staff. In his report of the raid, he concluded that his Staff— Maj. J. P. Strange; Maj. Charles Anderson; Col. R. W. Pitman, who was serving as assistant inspector general, having been declared supernumerary in his former command of the 154th Tennessee Infantry; Maj. G. V. Rambaut, and Col. M. C. Galloway—had "cheerfully and promptly executed my orders and their bearing throughout was highly commendable" (OR 39: 550).

Not satisfied with the results of his raid into middle Tennessee, Forrest again turned his attention to the western part of the state, specifically, the Union supply depot at Johnsonville on the Tennessee River. This depot had been developed to supplement the flow of supplies brought into Nashville by river and rail and had been connected to Nashville by a railroad constructed under Union military authority. Forrest decided to set up a "rolling blockade" on the Tennessee River by posting men and artillery at various points. As the fortunes of war would have it, he also captured a couple of boats and for several hours was commander of "Forrest's Navy," manned by "horse marines." Abandoning his "navy," Forrest turned his attention to the Union supply base at

Johnsonville. The young Rebel, James Dinkins, describes what happened there.

Johnsonville itself, independent of the depot buildings, was a hamlet at the mouth of a creek and was built upon the slope of the river bank, which rises gently from the water some three hundred yards, making an elevation of about fifty feet. Upon this eminence an extensive redoubt had been built that overlooked and commanded the western bank. The works were garnished with large cannon. There was also a long line of rifle pits surrounding the depot.

General Lyons with about four hundred men arrived. He had been an artillery officer in the old army and stood high with General Forrest for his skill in the use of artillery.

Losing no time, he ordered Lyons to place Thrall's Battery of 12-pounder howitzers as near the desired point as possible without risk of discovery, where the guns were sunk in "chambers" (big pits) and cut embrasures through the solid bank in front. . . . Colonel Rucker also had much experience as an artillery officer, and General Chalmers likewise ordered him to establish Morton's Battery directly opposite Johnsonville; and he posted two guns of Walton's Battery about four hundred yards to the northwest.

All the guns were sunk as described. . . . By noon, everything in readiness, the enemy, satisfied the Confederates had departed, were moving about unconcerned. General Forrest had the watches of all the commanders uniformly set and ordered that the batteries would open fire precisely at two o'clock. The five gunboats had withdrawn out of sight, but the three at Johnsonville were moored at the landing, with steam up and their decks covered with officers and crews. The crews were scrubbing the decks and washing their clothes. The troops of the garrison were sauntering about on the hillsides, and laborers were at work unloading stores from transports and barges. . . .

Precisely at two o'clock all the guns were discharged with such harmony that it sounded like one report, one heavy gun.

Immediately steam and smoke poured forth from the boats, while their crews were jumping into the river, swimming to shore. . . . Only one of the gunboats returned the fire, but the guns in the redoubts burst forth with such a storm of shells thrown with much precision, though they could not reach the Confederate guns in the chambers.

Every gunboat was perforated. . . . The conflict was maintained for an hour. The gunboats, now wrapped in flames, deserted by the crews, floated down against the transports and barges and set them on fire. By four o'clock every vessel was on fire. General Forrest now directed that all the batteries turn their fire on the warehouses and supplies on shore. There was a vast heap of corn, hay, and bacon, covering several acres, and higher up the slope, a large pile of barrels under tarpaulins. Several well-directed shells were thrown with the happiest effect, for a blue blaze was quickly seen to dart from under the tarpaulin.

Instantly a loud shout burst forth from our men, but doubtless they would have been glad to save a few barrels of the liquor. Soon the barrels began to burst with loud explosions, sending the burning liquor high in the air and flowing down the hillside, spreading the flame in its course toward the river and filling the air with fumes of burning spirits, sugar, coffee, and meat. . . .

When the Confederates retired after night, the river was lurid with red and blue lights as it floated down the stream, and the vicinity was almost as light as day. (CV 34: 178-79)

Capt. John Morton recalled the delight with which Forrest himself, with Generals Bell and Buford, served as a gun crew, with Forrest as the gunner. When a shot fell short, Forrest would exclaim, "Ricekty-shay, I'll get 'em the next time" (Morton, *Artillery*, 256). Indeed, by dark some three million dollars worth of supplies had been reduced to ashes, and the supply base that helped feed Nashville would be out of commission for weeks.

Forrest recognized Morton's contribution in his report on the expedition.

To Capt. John W. Morton, acting chief of artillery, and the brave troops under his command my thanks are especially due for their efficiency and gallantry on this expedition. They fired with a rapidity and accuracy which extorted the commendations of even the enemy. The rammers were shot from the hands of the cannoneers, some of whom were nearly buried amid the dirt which was thrown upon them by the storm of shell which rained upon them by the enemy's batteries. (OR 39: 872-73)

## Hood's Tennessee Campaign

Sterner work was awaiting the Escort and Staff. John Bell Hood and the Army of Tennessee were waiting for the horsemen to come lead them back into middle Tennessee. Forrest took twenty men from his Escort and marched them to meet Hood near Florence, Alabama. George Cowan remembered an incident on this march. On the way to Florence, the group approached a farm-house, looking for a place to spend the night.

On approaching the house we passed an old deserted cabin occu-pied by a lot of hogs. It was a dark, rainy night. General Forrest struck a match and looked in. He told the boys it was a good place for them to spend the night. I was the officer commanding the Escort with him, and I insisted it was not clean enough for them to sleep in, but the General ordered them to do so. We all then approached the farm house and procured quarters for the General and his staff, about six in number. After supper two of the men from the cabin came up and asked me if I could procure a pot and some salt for them to cook their meat in. I should have been down with the men at the cabin at that time, but the General insisted on my staying for supper with them. The lady of the house very kind-ly complied with my request. The General looked around the room and winked at his Adjutant-General, Major Strange. After supper I again proposed going to the cabin and staying with the men for the night, but General Forrest objected and said for me to stay right in the room with him as the men were able to take care of themselves. I then suspected why he did not wish me to go.

Shortly afterward we heard the report of a gun, followed by the squealing of a hog. The General looked slyly over at his Adjutant and winked once more. On our march toward Corinth the next day about noontime the General suggested that if we had anything to eat we could stop at a spring by the roadside and have our lunch. The spread the boys put before us consisted of cornbread and fresh boiled pork. The General took a shank of the fresh meat and, cutting off a slice, remarked to his Adjutant, "Do you reckon this is the old man's brood sow the boys killed last night? But it eats fine." (Burton)

At Florence, Forrest assumed command of all the cavalry with the Army of Tennessee, a total of about five thousand men. These he divided into three columns, one advancing toward Waynesboro, Tennessee; one toward Lawrenceburg, Tennessee; and one east then north toward Pulaski, Tennessee. Forrest and his Staff and Escort accompanied the middle column, which was commanded by Rucker. As the troops crossed the line from Alabama into Tennessee, they saw a sign some of their fellows had erected. It read, "A free home or a grave." For many in the Army of Tennessee, it would be the latter. Forward movement began on November 21, and by the twenty-third the Escort was in combat.

Rucker had occupied Lawrenceburg, routing the small Federal

force there and capturing 35,000 rounds of small-arms ammunition. Moving toward Pulaski to join the Confederate force approaching that place from the south, Rucker found his path blocked at Fouche Springs, some nine miles west of Pulaski. Forrest ordered Rucker to attack in front while Kelley's regiment went around the Union left and Forrest led his Escort around the right.

The advance of the Escort was so rapid that the eighty men soon found themselves three miles behind the line where Rucker was fighting. Overtaking some Union stragglers, they learned that only one regiment faced Rucker while another had gone into bivouac in the direction of Mount Pleasant. Forrest determined to attack this camp, although he had only the Escort with him. Several elements favored this attack. The Escort were all wearing rubber slickers to protect them from the rain and were thus indistinguishable from Union cavalrymen. Second, it was rapidly growing dark and the attacked party would not be able to see their small numbers. Third, Forrest had armed his Escort with Spencer repeaters, so their firepower would be far greater than their numbers would indicate. All these factors, coupled with surprise, made the move the success that Forrest anticipated. Sweeping into the camp, the Escort scattered the larger Union numbers but not before taking casualties of three dead and five wounded. With some sixty prisoners and even more horses, Forrest led his Escort back toward Rucker's position but decided to turn off onto a lesser-used road to avoid a collision in the darkness with the Yankees Rucker was driving back.

While they rode down this grassy track, a group of soldiers suddenly loomed out of the darkness. Before this party could be identified, one of them pointed his pistol at Forrest and, with the muzzle only inches from Forrest's chest, ordered him to surrender. Forrest began to draw his own weapon, and as the Yank fired, Major Strange struck his arm so that the ball missed Forrest entirely. Quick work was then made of the stray Union detachment. One of the casualties taken by the Escort on this occasion was William Lipscomb, the eighteen-year-old son of a prominent Shelbyville physician. The father was notified about his mortally wounded son and came from his nearby home to attend him during his last hours. When the young man died, the grieving father took him home and laid him to rest in the Willow Mount Cemetery. There the family erected a stone that reads:

Willie E. Son of Dr. T. and R. Lipscomb
Born April 11, 1846
Died Nov. 26, 1864
From a Mortal Wound received in a charge made by Forrests Escort
of which he was a beloved member.
Gently we heap the turf above thee
With gushing tears beneath the sod,
And in our heart of hearts enshrine thee
Submissive trusting thee to God

Forrest moved on to set up an ambush on the road that the force retreating from Rucker would follow, and this move twice brought in prisoners and horses. Rucker soon moved up to the position held by the Escort, and the engagement in which the Escort whipped two regiments ended (Jordan and Pryor, 614-16; OR 49: 499-500). Moving on to Columbia, Forrest maneuvered against that place until the main infantry force of the Army of Tennessee could come up. By the time the foot soldiers arrived, the Yankees had withdrawn to the north bank of the Duck River, so Forrest began to find fords by which he could cross the river and turn their flanks. At the same time, the Escort was sent toward Shelbyville to cut the Nashville & Chattanooga Railroad to prevent the withdrawal of several small Union garrisons to their stronghold at Murfreesboro (OR 45: 752; Wills, 281).

The Escort was not in time to stop the withdrawal of the garrisons at Shelbyville, Tullahoma, Cowan, and other places, nor did they have artillery to compel the surrender of the blockhouses that were left garrisoned to protect bridges along the railroad. However, this deployment did keep the Escort out of the fighting at Spring Hill, Franklin, and Nashville. The Escort rejoined Forrest when he was dispatched, with Bate's infantry, to confront the Union position at Murfreesboro. Since many of the members of the Escort were from the country around Shelbyville, no doubt many men enjoyed a quick visit home. For one of these men, the visit took on an unexpected element of danger.

W. E. McClain had left LaGrange College to join Forrest when he was sixteen years old. In 1906 he related:

After the fight at Pulaski I was sent with a detachment on the right to Boons Hill where the Federals were said to be robbing the stores and houses. [This activity was actually being carried out by Union "home guard" units and Tennessee units in the Union army. Booneshill, in Lincoln County, was in an area of divided loyalties.] After a little fight we captured some and scattered the rest. We then decided to camp on Swan Creek for the night.

As we passed through the little town the girls allowed their appreciation by bringing us apples to the gate and thanking us for driving the enemy from their town. Then some of them said that they were several miles to go home and that they were afraid to go alone. What could we do but be gallant enough to offer to escort them home.

The one that fell to my lot was no beauty, but a finer looking country lass you never met—the brightest eyed, bravest little lady I ever saw. Her name was Lydia West. She said she was a good reb, but that she was visiting an uncle up the creek who was a strong Union Man.

Well, boys, I certainly enjoyed that ride. When I got to her gate she called a boy to take my horse saying I must stay to supper. What poor, hungry soldier would have refused a good, hot supper? I didn't.

Then the country lassies began to gather in for a good, old-fashioned dance. Miss Lydia said just the neighbors would be there, so sweet sixteen was green enough to lay his pistols aside and go to dancing with the girls. Boy, my face grew long when there walked into the room five big Tories with pistols buckled around them.

They were a tough looking lot and would have weighed two hundred pounds each, while I weighed only ninety and my pistols were gone. I tell you I felt small when one of them slapped me on the back and said in a friendly way, "Buddy, what command do you belong to?"

"My own," I said. "Where do you come from?"

"From up the creek."

"Well, I come from down the creek."

I danced around and around and so we watched out at each other, but all the time I was wondering how I would ever get my belt of pistols out and my good horse under me once more. Well, I knew that they would hang me that night if I did not make my escape. But say, they watched me like hawks, one at each door. And my pistols! Where were they? They had disappeared from where I had put them, and among all that gang of enemies I had just one little friend. She came to me and said, "Mr. McClain, this is our dance" and then she whispered.

"They are after you, and the Tories intend to hang you tonight, if they can. But trust me to help you." Then in a loud voice she added, "Let's go get a drink of water."

But at our back came one of the Tories, saying he wanted some water too. Quickly picking up the bucket the girl said, "There's none here. Come, Mr. McClain, let's go to the well for some."

The moon was shining like day, and the scamp stood in the door and watched us. My horse was about a hundred yards from the house. One of the Tories said to another one, "I've seen his horse, it's a d——d good one."

She whispered to me, "When we get back, you go to dancing with some girl and I'll slip out your pistols, saddle your horse, and lead it to the house, and hide it behind the chimney. But promise me, if they shoot at you, you will not return the fire, for if you do they will burn us out, and hang my grandfather."

Of course, I promised, and so we went back, I to dancing with her friend, and she slipped out. One of the Tories came up and asked, "When are you going down the creek?"

I began singing, "I'm going to dance all night till broad daylight, And go home with the girls in the morning."

Miss Lydia came back after a short time, and we danced another set together, and she stopped near a side door, and while laughing and talking passed me through and out. Handing me my pistols she said, "Go." There stood my horse. Oh, how good it seemed when I buckled that belt of pistols around me and felt my faithful horse under me once more. I had to go around the house and by the front door to get out of the yard. The pounding of my horse's feet sounded to me like thunder and brought the whole pack after me with the cry "He's gone!" The bullets cut the timber around my head, and seemed to sing out "I'll get you if I can." But I kept my promise to Miss Lydia and the next day when we marched by with the command, Miss Lydia said, "The Tories that came to catch and hang you last night wanted your horse, and were puzzled to know how you got away. They accused grandfather of helping you, and started to hang him and burn the house but I said I was the guilty one, that I caught and saddled the horse, brought it to you, and stole the pistols wrapped up in the folds of my dress. They made a lot of threats but they left." (*Fayetteville Observer,* October 3, 1906)

Such was life for the boys of the Escort.

## The Final Battles

By December 4, Forrest had detached Chalmers' Division to assist in the attack on Nashville and had taken his other forces, as ordered by Hood, to operate against the railroad between

Nashville and Murfreesboro. Forrest was also charged to keep an eye on the Union forces gathered in Fortress Rosecrans at Murfreesboro, some seven thousand men commanded by Gen. Lovell Rousseau with Gen. Robert Milroy as second in command. Most of these men had been in garrison along the railroad and had been withdrawn to the security of the fortifications at Murfreesboro.

Fortress Rosecrans covered 200 acres and was composed of lunettes, or half-moon-shaped works, connected by zigzag walls with four inner redoubts, which provided further security within the outer walls. These lines of earthworks could provide powerful crossfires and direct fires of both artillery and infantry on all the approaches. The slopes near the works could be swept by artillery emplacements, while long-range artillery was sited in the sur-rounding country (OR 49: 503). The Union army estimated that the fortress could be taken only by siege. Forrest, on seeing it, agreed it was not a target for his cavalry, though he had been rein-forced by the small division of infantry commanded by William B. Bate. On December 7, Forrest fell back on the Wilkinson Pike in an attempt to draw some part of the Union force out of their stronghold to fight in open country. His plan was to have the infantry hold in front while his cavalry swept around the Yankee flanks, a tactic that frequently worked. Yet much to Forrest's dis-tress and disgust, the infantry broke and ran when the Yanks advanced. Bate's men had just been through the bloodletting at Franklin a week before and were not ready to fight again that day. Forrest may have shot a retreating Confederate color bearer in order to stop him taking his flag off the field, with the rest of the unit following. The evidence is not clear. At any rate, Maj. John Strange carried a frantic message to Jackson's Division to charge the enemy or all would be lost. Jackson made the charge with Strange in his company, and his success was aided by Buford, who got into the town of Murfreesboro, in rear of the Yankee advance. Morton, who was with Buford, soon found himself at the scene of an earlier fight. In Forrest's first raid on Murfreesboro, in July 1862, the Union garrison in the courthouse had run for the cupo-la and Forrest had built a fire on the stone floor of the building, literally smoking the men out. This time the garrison went to the basement and continued fighting, but the distraction Morton caused forced the Union troops in front of Forrest to withdraw (Morton, *Artillery,* 281).

More minor operations around Murfreesboro filled the next week until, on December 14, Forrest received news of the fighting around Nashville and was ordered to move cross-country to protect the rear of Hood's retreating army. There is no more pitiful chapter in the history of the Army of Tennessee than that of the retreat from Tennessee to Tupelo, Mississippi, but there is no more shining chapter in the history of Forrest's cavalry than that of the same retreat. Forrest covered the rear of the army and held back the overwhelming numbers of the Union force at Anthony Hill, Sugar Creek, and the crossing of the Tennessee River. The Escort and Staff evidently played a role in this defense because names of their members are found in the casualty lists, but no individual exploits have been recorded.

Once the battered remnants of the Confederate force reached Mississippi, Forrest allowed most of his men to return home to rest, gather additional clothing, and acquire remounts. After three weeks most of them returned, a testament to the morale instilled by their commander, but the end was fast approaching. On March 22, 1865, Gen. James Wilson led three columns of Federal cavalry across the Tennessee River into the last pocket of Confederate control. Forrest moved to counter, but he commanded fewer than 3,000 men (Maness, 358) to confront Wilson, who commanded a total of 22,000, with some 13,000 armed with Spencer repeating carbines. Among the Confederates, only the Escort was armed with repeaters. In addition, Forrest had to guard against potential Union moves from Baton Rouge and the Gulf Coast. In such circumstances, the services of the Escort would be more valuable than ever.

Wilson reached and destroyed the ironworks at Elyton, Alabama, now called Birmingham, without opposition on March 30. That same day, his main force moved south toward Confederates near Montevallo, while one of Wilson's divisions was sent to Tuscaloosa to burn the state university. Reaching Montevallo, Wilson found P. D. Roddey's command along Six Mile Creek and opened an engagement with them there. Forrest and the Escort joined the fight on April 1, when it centered around Ebenezer Church, north of Plantersville.

Forrest, as usual, decided to attack, and the Escort followed their leader to the flank of the Union column, cut in behind the advance guard, and charged it from the rear. This surprise attack had the expected results, and the Yankee troopers broke for cover.

The Escort could not hold its ground, however, in the face of the superior numbers coming up against it (CV, 40: 425). The four saber companies of the Seventeenth Indiana Mounted Infantry charged the Escort and Staff, and soon a hand-to-hand fight swirled across the road and adjoining field. With fewer than one hundred men at hand, the Confederates were badly outnumbered, and the Federal charge came into their line hard. The momentum of the Union horsemen was so great that one Yankee's horse rammed the wheel of a Confederate cannon, shattering the wheel and killing the horse. Forrest made a conspicuous figure on his favorite horse, King Philip, and soon half a dozen Union soldiers swarmed around him, hacking with their sabers. The Escort crowded toward the general as best they could, but each man had from two to four opponents. Forrest had been using his pistol, as was the Escort, and he tried to parry saber blows with his revolver. Soon the weapon was damaged and could not be fired. Wheeling King Philip, Forrest dashed for the rear, but the road was blocked by a two-horse wagon. Without a pause, Forrest's war-horse made the jump, clearing the wagon and landing some distance beyond. Drawing his sword, Forrest turned, only to be confronted by Capt. James D. Taylor of the Seventeenth Indiana. Taylor slashed Forrest on the right arm but was himself run clear through the body by a return thrust from Forrest. Taylor probably did not see the blow coming, since Forrest was left-handed and so struck from Taylor's "blind" side (CV 26: 152). This was one of the most ferocious fights in which the Escort engaged. One of the casualties was Lt. Nath Boone, temporarily commanding the Escort, who was severely cut above his left ear (Henry, 432). In this fight, the Escort killed fifty-four Union cavalrymen and suffered no deaths and only two wounded—Forrest and Boone.

At Selma, the Confederate defenses were a mere skirmish line that included old men and boys from the town. A single Union attack broke that line, though, at a cost of 300 casualties to the attackers. A counterattack by the Escort bought a little time and allowed many Southern men to escape across the Alabama River on the Montgomery road (Maness, 366). As the Escort and Forrest rode out of Selma, they met Union troops near Burnsville and fighting erupted. The Escort witnessed Forrest kill a Union soldier, the thirtieth he had killed since the beginning of the war.

As night fell, the Escort was looking for a place to bivouac when they heard the screams of women. Rushing to the scene, they found a group of Union soldiers attempting to rape three women whose house the Yankees had just looted. The Escort took no prisoners (CV 35: 177).

A local woman remembered how glad they were to have some Confederates in the area, since the Union soldiers were engaging in widespread rape and looting. Mary A. Hamner was sitting on her front porch at about 11:00 P.M. fearing the arrival of the Yankees when she heard horsemen riding up to her gate. When the officer in charge called, "Hello, the house," she relaxed, for it was an unmistakable Southern voice. It proved to be Nathan Boone and the Escort, Boone with his head wrapped in a towel because of his recent wound. Ironically, Mrs. Hamner lost contact with Boone until she read his obituary in the *Confederate Veteran* in 1899 (CV 7: 358).

There was one other encounter that night. Capturing a picket of the Fourth U.S. Cavalry, the Escort learned that more men of that regiment occupied a house nearby. The Escort, led by Lt. George Cowan, moved to attack the house but only after convincing Forrest to stay behind. At the house, the old score of the Fourth U.S.'s murder of Capt. Sam Freeman was settled. Thirty-five Union soldiers were killed and wounded and five captured (Wills, 310-11; Henry, 433).

While Wilson moved on Montgomery, the Escort followed Forrest's command to Gainesville, Alabama, where several peaceful days ensued as Forrest and the remnant of his command contemplated their next move. In long rides with Maj. Charles Anderson, Forrest discussed his plan of leaving the country to go to Mexico, a proposal that was being adopted by several Confederates, including the governor of Tennessee, Isham Harris. Anderson convinced Forrest that his men and the South needed him to stay and work for recovery (Wills, 314-15). Forrest agreed and then sketched out the outline of ideas he wanted to pass on to his men before they parted. Anderson then wrote the farewell address to the men of Forrest's Cavalry Corps, including the Escort. The address was a model of moderation and urged Forrest's soldiers to be as good citizens as they had been fighters.

During this interval, Forrest also found time to contemplate his personal fate. Because of the hysteria fomented by a congressional committee that had investigated the Fort Pillow attack and that had spread many unfounded atrocity stories, Forrest was uncertain if he would be arrested and imprisoned or even executed. He was also concerned about the plans of his youngest son, William, to marry. Forrest prepared a letter to his son that addressed these concerns and he had the letter delivered to William. The style and vocabulary of the letter deviate so strongly from Forrest's other correspondence that it is almost certain Major Anderson took the sentiment Forrest expressed and put it into his own words. The letter says:

Gainesville, Alabama

Lieut. W.M. Forrest
My Dear Son,
Loving you with all the affection which a fond father can bestow upon a dutiful son, I deem it my duty to give you a few words of advice. Life is you know at best uncertain, and occupying the position I do it is exceedingly hazardous. I may fall at any time, or I may at no distant day be an exile in a foreign land, and I desire to address you a few words which I trust you will remember through life. You have heretofore been an obedient dutiful son, you have given your parents but little pain or trouble and I hope you will strive to profit by using suggestions I may make.

I have had a full understanding with your mother as to our future operations in the event the enemy overruns this country. She will acquaint you with our plans and will look to you in the hour of trouble. Be to her a prop and support. She is worthy of all the love you bestow upon her. I know how devoted you are to her, but study her happiness above and beyond all things, give her no cause for unhappiness. Try to [emulate] her noble virtues and to practice her blameless life. If I have been wicked and sinful myself, it would rejoice my heart to see you leading the Christian life which has adorned your Mother's.

I have heard with pain and astonishment of your matrimonial engagement. My dear son, let me beg you to dismiss all such thoughts for the present. You are entirely too young to form an alliance of this sort and the young lady upon whom you seem disposed to lavish your affections is unworthy of you. There are insuperable objections to her, which I would name if I thought it necessary to induce you to change your mind. Take the advice of a father and abandon all thought of marrying. You must wait until your character is formed and you are able to take a proper position in society. You will then be the better prepared to select a suitable partner. At the proper time you will have my consent to marry and my blessing on the union.

What I must desire of you my son is never to gamble or swear. These are baneful vices and I trust you will never practice either. As I grow older I see the folly of these two vices and beg you will never engage in them. Your life has heretofore been elevated and characterized by a high-toned morality, and I trust your name will never be stained by the practice of those vices which blighted the prospects of some of the most promising youth of our country. Be honest, be truthful, in all your dealings with the world. Be cautious in the selection of your friends. Shun the society of the low and vulgar. Strive to elevate your character and to take a high and honorable position in society. You are my only child, the pride and hope of my life. You have fine intellect, talent of the highest order. I have watched your entrance upon the threshold of manhood and life with all the admiration of a proud father, and I trust your future career will be an honor to yourself and a solace to my declining years. If we meet no more on earth I hope you will keep this letter prominently before you and remember it as coming from

Your Affectionate Father

N.B.Forrest (Author's Collection)

The men of the Escort and Staff felt as if they shared in the parental concern Forrest showed for William. The fire of war had forged bonds of comradeship that would not be broken.

On May 9, 1865, a formal surrender to Union forces took place and then they all went home, the Escort proudly proclaiming they had more men in their ranks at the end than they had at the organization of the unit (see Appendix A and B). One hundred five enlisted men had left Shelbyville in October 1862; 110 surrendered with Forrest at Gainesville, Alabama.

# CHAPTER 5

# Years of Turmoil, Days of Peace: 1877-1909

"Reconstruction" is a curious name to apply to the period following the war. Indeed, the war had left widespread destruction, but the government in Washington had no policy of reconstruction. The South was left to its own economic devices, which largely amounted to being exploited by Northern interests who took advantage of cheap land, cheap labor, and readily available natural resources. This exploitation and neglect created an economic morass, the results of which endure into the twenty-first century. In 1860, the majority of the ten wealthiest states were Southern; since 1865, no Southern state has been at the national average of per-capita income. The devastated economy affected ex-Confederate, ex-Unionist, and ex-slave alike. There was an equality of poverty.

The only problem the national government attempted to address was a reconstruction of state and local governments in the South. This was initially done on a basis that excluded all ex-Confederates. Not surprisingly, governments based on the leadership of carpetbaggers, scalawags, and freedmen, groups that represented a minority of the population, met widespread and violent opposition. This attempt to create a government based on racial equality was made even more ludicrous when many of Northern states rejected the Fourteenth and Fifteenth amendments to the U.S. Constitution, creating a situation where the states that said they had worked to free the slaves failed to grant equality to people of color. Since racial equality was the goal of the radicals, their leadership in Congress decreed that the Southern states would have to approve the amendments before reentering the Union. Racial equality was not accepted in the North, so it would be forced on the South. This policy was doomed to failure not only because racial equality was an extreme idea in 1865; it would be resisted because it was being enforced by coercion. Given the depth of feeling the men of the Escort and Staff had expressed for the cause of an independent Confederacy, it is not a surprise that these men opposed the Reconstruction-era governments in the Southern states.

That Forrest was active in the Ku Klux Klan and became its first Grand Dragon is a matter of historical record. His former Staff members were themselves active in the organization. John Morton was head of the Klan in the Nashville area and he says he inducted Forrest into the Klan in late 1867. By 1869, Forrest, acting as Grand Dragon, notified the Klan that the organization had largely fulfilled its objective of seeing the control of the state government returned to conservative Democrats and he ordered the Klan to disband (Morton, *Artillery*, 341-42).

The problem facing the members of the Staff and Escort at the end of the war was how to make a living from the devastated economy that was the major residue of the war. For the next decade, most of these men seem to have lived hand to mouth, including Forrest. By 1877, Reconstruction was over. The last of the "carpet-bagger" governments, that of South Carolina, was defeated at the polls, and the new president of the United States, Rutherford B. Hayes, let it be known he had no intention of continuing to promote enforcement of the Fourteenth and Fifteenth amendments to the Constitution, thus abandoning the attempt to create a society reflecting racial equality. By that time a degree of economic stability was returning to the South, though the region was far from the prosperity it had enjoyed in antebellum days.

In 1877 Forrest was in poor health. Given all that is known of his personality, one could surmise that the general suffered from a variety of health problems associated with high blood pressure. Seeking relief, he decided to spend some days at Hurricane Springs, a health resort near Tullahoma. From there Forrest wrote Charles Anderson, inviting him to come for a visit. Anderson took the cars of the Nashville & Chattanooga to Tullahoma and a stage from the station for several miles out to the hotel. More than twenty years later, Anderson recalled the reunion with his old commander.

> When the stage arrived, I found the General waiting for me. As I waited for ladies to alight, Gen. Forrest went to the opposite side of the coach, gave me a hearty handshake, and expressed his pleasure at my visit. There was a mildness in his manner, a softness of expression, and a gentleness in his words that appeared to me strange and unnatural. At first I thought his bad health had brought about this change, but then I remembered that when sick or wounded he was the most restless and impatient man I ever saw.

Soon I told him that there was something about him that I couldn't understand; that he didn't appear to me to be the same man I used to know so well. He was silent for a moment, then seemed to divine my trouble, and halting suddenly, he took hold of the lapel of my coat and turned me squarely in front of him, and raising his right hand with that long index finger (his emphasizer) extended, he said, "Major, I am not the man you were with so long and knew so well—I hope I am a better man. I've joined the Church and am trying to live a Christian life." Said I, "General, that's it, and you are indebted to 'Old Mistess' (as we called Mrs. Forrest), and to no one else, for this great change." "Yes, you are right," he replied, "Mary has prayed for me night and day for many years, and I feel now that through her prayers my life has been spared, and to them am I indebted for passing safely through so many dangers." (CV 5: 387)

## Organization of the Veterans Association

The next day Forrest expressed a desire to see as many of his Escort and Staff as might be able to assemble at Hurricane Springs over the next few days, so notices went out to area newspapers and, on the appointed day, men began to gather. George L. Cowan was among those present and was selected as secretary to make a record of the event. The record is provided below as Cowan wrote it.

The first reunion of Lieut. Gel. N.B. Forrest's Escort & Staff was held at Hurricane Springs on Friday, July 27, 1877. The attendance was large considering the short notice given but many ex-confederates of different commands with the large number of guests at the Springs made the crowd very large. Many of the old Escort and Staff came in from the adjoining counties, mounted, and many of them clad in the gray jeans the same as worn in service. Genl. Forrest met, and shook hands, with each one as he rode up, and was able to call most of them by name.

The meeting was called to order by Chief Surgen J.B. Cowan and Maj. Chas. Anderson was made chairman and Lieut. Geo. L. Cowan Secretary. The Roll being called the following were found present.
Lieut Genl N.B. Forrest
Maj. Charles W. Anderson Act Assist AG
Dr. Jas. B. Cowan Chief Surgeon
Capt. Samuel Donelson Aid.De.Camp

Escort
Capt. Nathan Boone

1st Lieut. Mathew Cortner    2nd Lieut. Geo.L. Cowan
3 Lieut. John Eaton          Orderly Sarg M.S. Parks
2nd Sgt. W.E. Sims           3rd. Sgt W.L. Shofner
4th Sgt. C.C. Arnold         Com. Sgt Wm. H. Matthews
Quartermaster Sgt. B.B. Ingle    Corporal L.H. Russ

Privates

| A.D. Adair | F.F. Arnold | D.R. Bedford | H. L. W. Boone |
| O.F. Blackwell | W.C. Cooper | H.F. Dusenberry | M.A.L. Enochs |
| F.R. Evans | T.J. Eaton | S.W. Edens | G.W. Felps |
| Geo. Hastings | Joshua Huffman | C.S. Massey | J.S. McFarland |
| K.M. Pybas | F.M. Reeves | E.W. Rainey | R.W. Shofner |
| H.C. Troxler | J.N. Taylor | J.H. Womack | |

The following resolution was offered by Lieut. Geo. L. Cowan and unanimously adopted.

Resolved, That we now be formed into an Association to be known and designated as the Association of Lieut. Genl N.B. Forrest Escort and Staff, and that all honorably discharged members of Genl. Forrests Escort and Staff are entitled to Membership.

Resolved, That the officers shall be one President, three Vice Presidents one Treasurer, one correspondent Secretary one Rec. Sec.

Resolved, That in the absence of Capt. John C. Jackson and many other familiar faces who were always seen in times of danger are sincerely regretted.

Resolved That the thanks of this association are hereby tendered to Messers Miller Brothers proprietors of Hurricane Springs for the elegant manner in which we have been entertained today.

Resolved that we go into the election of officers for the ensuing twelve months.

PERMANENT ORGANIZATION

| President | Capt. Nathan Boone |
| 1 Vice President | Capt John C. Jackson |
| 2nd Vice President | Private A.D. Adair |
| 3rd Vice President | Sgt. W.C. Cooper |
| Treasurer | Lieut. Geo. L. Cowan |
| Cor. Sect. | Lieut. Jno Eaton |
| Rect. Sect. | Corp. L.H. Russ |

Short addresses were made by Dr. J.B. Cowan, Sam Donaldson, Judge A.S. Marks, Maj. C.W. Anderson, Jno C. Burch, Frank P. Cahill, W.P. Tolley, and Lieut. G.L. Cowan, after which Genl. Forrest addressed the association as follows.

Ladies Gentlemen and Comrades,

It is useless for me to speak after what has been said. You all know my physical condition. I am unable to speak. I simply desire to return my sincere thanks to my Escort. No one can express the feelings which have passed through my breast today. I love the members of my Escort. I love the memories. I feel greatful that I have been spaired to meet so many of them, after an absence of twelve years. When I left them, I was a strong, hearty, and robust man, but I am different now. I may not live long but I hope we may all meet in heaven.

Resolved that we now adjourn to meet at Shelbyville Tenn on (no date appears in the minutes).

N. Boone Pres

L.H. Russ Rec. Sec.

Judge Albert S. Marks was a man well known to the Escort and Staff though he had no wartime connection with them. Marks had studied law with the firm of Colyar and Frizzell in Winchester, Tennessee, and was admitted to the bar in 1858. In 1861 he stood as a candidate for the Constitutional Union party in opposition to secession, but when the war began he was chosen captain of what would become Company E, Seventeenth Tennessee Infantry. The men comprising this company were from Franklin County and Marble Hill, now in Moore County. In June 1862 Marks became colonel of the regiment. At Murfreesboro, Colonel Marks suffered a wound to his right leg, which required amputation. He married four months after losing his leg (Speer, 74). Due to losses, the regiment was consolidated with other units a number of times, was attached to Longstreet's command during the 1863 East Tennessee Campaign, and finished the war in Virginia (Horn, 2: 210-11). Marks served several terms as chancellor for the district around his home and was elected governor in 1878.

The Veterans Association did not meet the next year in Shelbyville; in fact, it did not meet at all until 1883. Only two months after the meeting at Hurricane Springs, members of the new Veterans Association would have read the following announcement in the *Memphis Avalanche,* dated October 30, 1877.

Gen. N.B. Forrest died at 7 1/2 o'clock last night at the residence of Col. Jesse Forrest on Union Street. His disease was chronic diarrhea and malarial fever. He had been in ill health for a year or more, and for several months past his condition had been deemed critical. In August he was reported dying at Hurricane Springs; but he rallied, and was a few weeks afterward able to return to Memphis. . . . About two years ago Gen. Forrest made a profession of religion and became a member of the Cumberland Presbyterian Church. He died in this faith, and met his death with Christian calmness and resignation.

## Early Years

Forrest's death, along with continuing financial problems throughout the South, seems to have disrupted activities of the Veterans Association, so that the minutes do not record a second reunion until September 1883. The meeting took place at Pylant Springs, a health resort located between Tullahoma and Winchester, Tennessee.

The Association was called to order by President N. Boone and on calling of the roll the following members were found present
Capt. N. Boone      President
Capt. J.C. Jackson   1st Vice President
Sargent L.H. Russ   Rec. Secretary
and Lt. M. Courtner, Lt. Jno. Eaton, Sgt. M.L. Parks, Bugler W.A. Bailey, H.L.W. H. L. W. Boone, T.G. Cheairs, Jas Cumings, J.H.C. Duff, Sgt. B.B. Ingle, Jas Newsom, Sgt. W.E. Sims, W.L. Shofner, and J.N. Taylor. Dr. J.B. Cowan
    On motion the Association adjourned until 1 oclock P.M.
    On assembling at 2 oclock P.M. the Association was entertained by an address from Capt. W.P. Tolley in his happy and characteristic style, adjourned until 7:30 P.M.
    On assembling at 7:30 P.M. in Capt. Boones Room Dr. J.B. Cowan was called to the Chair and J.H.C. Duff to act as Secretary.
    On motion of Corp. L.H. Russ Mrs. Genl. N.B. Forrest was made an honorary member of this Association. Dr. J.B. Cowan in Seconding the motion paid a glowing tribute to Mrs. Forrests many Christian qualities and graces, to her devotion to her husband our beloved commander and her love and devotion to the men who had followed him through so many trying scenes, and to the cause we espoused, carried by a unanimous rising vote.
    On motion the chairman appointed the following committees on
CONSTITUTION AND BY LAWS
Lt. M. Courtner, Chm Sgt.   L.H. Russ      J.N. Taylor
ON FINANCE
Sgt. B.B. Ingle                   W.L. Shofner   W.E. Sims
ON HISTORY
Lt. Geo. L. Cowan Chm.      W.L.H. Boone  Capt. N. Boone

Capt. J.C. Jackson            John Eaton      W.T.H. Wharton

On motion of L.H. Russ the association will meet at Tullahoma Tenn next Sept 18th 1884. Dr. J.B. Cowan on seconding the motion guaranteed the hospitality of his mountain city.

On Motion the following honerary members was elected

Capt. Jno W. Harton & Lieut. Jas. M. Travis of Tullahoma

Dr. J.T. McFarland and Evand Bennett of Lavergne

T.W. H. Johnson and Charles Williams of Old Jefferson and John Holt, son of our late Lieut. Josh Holt of Shelbyville, Tennessee, also Jessie Forrest of Memphis, Dick Blakemore, Colonel D.C. Kelly of Nashville.

The chairman appointed the following committee on arrangements for the reunion at Tullahoma.

Dr. J.B. Cowan, Chm      Lt. J.T. Travis and Capt. J.W. Harton Honorary Members.

Letters were read by the Secretary from Lieut. Geo. L. Cowan of Nashville, Tennessee, Private Geo. Simmons of Terrell Texas, and W.J. Biggs of Jackson, Tennessee.

On motion a very happy and feeling address was delivered by Dr. J.B. Cowan as only Dr. Cowan can talk on such occasions to his old Comrads. Lt. Travis of Tullahoma was next called for and responded in a well timed earnest and patriotic address.

On motion the thanks of the Association was voted Messers L.H. Russ, W.E. Sims, and Wm. H. Matthews of Shelbyville, the committee of arrangement, also to the host of the Springs, R.S. Stewart.

An assessment of (50) fifty cents be made on each member to pay the current expenses of the Association. While the members promptly responded the Treasurer Capt. Boone who begged off from a Speach seemed to be quite happy.

On motion Col. D.C. Kelley was elected to deliver the address at the next meeting in 1884.

The following officers were elected to serve the next twelve months:

| | |
|---|---|
| President | Capt. John C. Jackson |
| 1st Vice President | Capt. N. Boone |
| 2nd Vice President | Dr. J.B. Cowan |
| Recording Sect. | L.H. Russ |
| Cor Sect | J.H.C. Duff |
| Treas | Capt. N. Boone |

Thomas Gorum Cheairs is the member listed as T.G. Cheairs. Thomas was from Spring Hill and was a part of the well-known Cheairs family of that area, his family home being Rippa Villa plantation.

Lt. James M. Travis was a local man who had served in Company

C, Thirty-fourth Tennessee Infantry. His company was originally called "The Ridgeville Guards" and was from what became Moore County (Horn, 2: 247). Travis had become a successful businessman in Tullahoma and was a trustee of the local Confederate Cemetery.

R. M. ("Dick") Blakemore had served with one of Forrest's favorite units, the Fourth Tennessee. This unit was originally commanded by James W. Starnes, a physician, until Starnes was killed near Tullahoma in June 1863. The command then passed to W. S. McLemore (Horn, 2: 62). During the war this unit saw as much fighting with Forrest as any in the army.

Jesse Forrest was the younger brother of the general and had commanded a regiment under him.

On September 18, 1884, the Veterans Association met in Tullahoma, Tennessee. The meeting saw more business conducted than usual but also revealed that the association's committee structure was not working well. Many of the committees had done little or nothing toward fulfilling their assigned responsibilities. This would be a problem for the rest of the life of the association.

## Minutes of the 1884 Reunion

The Association met in the Hall of Montgomery & Davis and was called to order by Vice Pres J.B. Cowan and on call of the roll the following officers and members were present.

Capt. Jno. C. Jackson Psd, Capt. N. Boone, VP, Dr. J.B. Cowan VP, Lt. M. Cortner, Lt. Jno. Eaton, Sgt. M.L. Parks, Sgt. W.L. Shofner, Sgt. W.E. Sims, W.A. Bailey, Jas, Newsom, T.J. Eaton, T.N. McCord, B.B. Ingle, E. Clark, T.G. Cheairs, T.R. Evans, J.K. Cunningham, H.L.W. Boone, R.E. Fay, F.M. Adkinson, G.W. Felps, W.R. Shofner, Frank Arnold, J.A. Taylor.

Honorary Members        Capt. Jno. W. Harton, Lt. Jas. M. Travis.

On Motion, All ex-Confederate soldiers present were cordially invited to seats with the Association. Thereupon M.B. Sims, H.T. Smart, Dr. Buckner & Robert Harris came forward.

The committee consisting of Lieut. Cortner, Russ, & Taylor on Constitution and By-Laws reported nothing done and asked to be discharged which was done and a new committee composed of J.N. Taylor, Jno. Eaton and M.L. Parks.

The Finance committee reported that fifty cents annual dues would be sufficient for current expenses adopted and committee continues.

The Committee on reminiscences had no report to make and were discharged.

Letters of regret were read from Maj. G.V. Rambant, Capt. Jno. W. Morton, W.C. Cooper, L.H. Russ, and Geo. L. Cowan.

On Motion, the letter of L.H. Russ was ordered spread on the minutes:

Shelbyville Tenn   Sept 11th 1884

To the Officers and members of Association Forrests Escort & Staff

Old Comrads, To one who has looked forward to the 18th day of Sept. 1884 the day named for our reunion, with a degree of pride and pleasure, bordering on happiness, it is hard to forgo the pleasure anticipated of again meeting and clasping by the hands many of the bearded and bronzed old Troopers I knew some twenty years ago. My health has been bad for some two weeks, though not sick in bed, but under the treatment of a physian, and he advises against my going to Tullahoma thinking it may possibly do me more harm than good. [Author's Note: The distance from Shelbyville to Tullahoma is sixteen miles by road and about twenty-five miles by rail.] But while deprived of the pleasure of meeting you in person, my heart is with you and will even still at meeting Forrest and his Cavalry. While writing my memory runs back till I again see the company line. I can picture each familiar face distinctly. Why, I even know the horses, for there about the center of the line is "Crellendur" with feet stuck out on either side of "Old Roan" and next to him is Snell on "Rat" and farther down I see Keen Pint on the yellow Roan and Mack Watson on the little white pony and Carpenter on big footed Charly and just off to the right of the line is Matthews preparing to mount old "Jack," noble old horse that had to forage for himself, though he bore upon his back as brave a soldier as ever rose in his stirrups at Sound of Bugle and that big harted Lieu Cowan on "Big Dick" ever ready with a smile for a march, charge, or a Bivouac. The fact is, boys, I know you all, know your horses, know the mules that Newsom drove, and if I could hear the rattle of the Sabers and Spurs I would be ready to obey the command "Mount your horses" and move at a moments warning. Wishing you much joy and happiness and hoping the organization will be perfect and substantially officered, to the end that the reunion will recur each year, and that some steps will be taken for the purpose of giving to the World at no distant day an impartial and unbiast history of Forrest Escort in the Field. I am truly and Fraternally yours

Lee H. Russ

On Motion Dr. J.B. Cowan read the farewell address of Genl. Forrest to his corps as follows

Headquarters Forrests Cavalry Corps

Gainesville Ala    May 9th 1865

Soldiers! By an agreement made between Lieut. Genl. Taylor, commanding the department of Alabama and Mississippi and Eastern Louisiana, and Maj. Genl. Canby commanding United States forces, the troops of this department have been surrendered. I do not think it proper or necessary at this time, to refer to the causes which reduced us to this extremity. Nor is it now a matter of material consequence to us how such results were brought about. That we are beaten is a self evident fact and any farther resistance on our part would be justly regarded in us as the height of folly and rashness. The armies of Generals Lee & Johnston, having surrendered, you are the last of all the Confederate States Army East of the Mississippi to lay down your arms. The cause for which you have braved dangers, endured privations and sufferings, and made so many sacrifices, is today hopeless. The Government which we sought to establish and perpetuate is at an end. Reason dictates and humanity demands that no more blood be shed. Fully realizing and feeling that such is the case, it is your duty, and mine, to lay down our arms, submit to the 'powers that be,' and to aid in restoring peace and establishing law and order throughout the land.

The terms upon which you were surrendered are favorable, and should be satisfactory and acceptable to all; they manifest a spirit of magnanimity and liberality on the part of the Federal authorities, which should be met on our part, with a faithful compliance with all the stipulations and conditions there in expressed. As a commander I sincerely hope that every officer and soldier of my command will cheerfully obey the orders given and carry out in good faith the terms of the cartel. Those who neglect the terms and refuse to be paroled may assumably expect, when arrested, to be sent north and imprisoned. Let those who are absent from this command, for whatever cause, report at once to this place, or to Jackson, Mississippi, of if too remote from either, to the nearest United States Garrison for parole.

Civil war, such as you just passed through, naturally engenders feelings and animosities, hatred and revenge. It is our duty to divest ourselves of all such feelings and, as far as in our power to do so, to cultivate friendly feelings towards those with whom we have so long contended and heretofore so widely and honestly differed; neighborhood feuds, personal animosities, and private differences should be blotted out; and when you return home a manly straightforward course of conduct will secure for you the respect even of your enemies. Whatever your responsibilities may be to Government, to society, or to individuals, meet them like men.

The attempt made to establish a separate and independent Confederacy has failed; but the conscientiousness of having done your duty faithfully and to the end will in some measure repay for the hardships you have undergone.

In bidding you farewell, rest assured that you carry with you my best wishes for your future welfare and happiness. Without in any way referring to the merits of the cause in which you have been engaged, your courage and determination as exhibited on many hard fought fields has elicited the respect and admiration of friend and foe, and I now cheerfully and gratefully acknowledge my indebtedness to the officers and men of my command whose zeal, fidelity, and unflinching bravery have been the great source of my past successes in arms.

I have never on the field of battle sent you where I was unwilling to go myself; nor would I now advise you to a course which felt myself unwilling to pursue. You have made good soldiers; you can make good citizens. Obey the laws, preserve your honor, and the government to which you have surrendered can afford to be, and will be, magnanimous.

N.B. Forrest
Lieut. Genl

On Motion, the corresponding Secretary was ordered to have printed two hundred copies of the above address for distribution among the members of the Association.

The orator of the day, Dr. D.C. Kelley, being absent Dr. J.B. Cowan was called upon and as he is ever ready to talk on war subjects, entertained the boys with many remanicsances of the Battle field and Bivouac, which times brought laughter to the face, and tears to the eyes of his hearers.

The following officers were elected as follows for the next twelve months:

| President | Thos. N. McCord |
| 1st V. Pres | Capt. N. Boone |
| 2nd V.P. | Dr. J.B. Cowan |
| Rec. Sect | Lee H. Russ |
| Coro. Sect | J.N. Taylor |
| Chaplain | Elder T.C. Little |
| Commissary | Lt. Jno. Eaton |

On Motion of J.N. Taylor Mrs. J.B. Cowan was elected an Honery Member of the Ass.

On Motion of Dr. Cowan Genl G.G. Dibbrell and Genl A.W. Campbell were also elected Honery Members.

On Motion Dr. D.C. Kelley and Genl A.W. Campbell were elected orators for the next reunion.

On Motion, W.L. Shofner, F.M. Adkisson, and J.N. Taylor were appointed to confer with the orators. The President was added to the committee.

On Motion of the Pres. T.N. McCord Shelbyville was selected as the next place of meeting which would take place the first Thursday in September 1885 at 12 oclock M.

On Motion the Cor Sect was instructed to make a complete roll of the Escort and Staff.

On Motion a vote of thanks was tendered the committee of Reception

Dr. J.B. Cowan, Capt. J.W. Harton & Lt. J.M. Travis and to the Messers Davis & Montgomery for the use of the beautiful Hall and to the citizens of Tullahoma for this kind and generous and unexcelled hospitality.

Committee on arrangement for 1885 was appointed as follows

L.H. Russ, Chm, W.C. Cooper, W.H. Matthews, M.M. Adkinson & W.E. Sims.

On Motion the Association adjourned to meet at Shelbyville Tenn on the first Thursday of Sept. 1885 at 12 ocl M.

Oct. 30th 1884    J.N. Taylor, Corresponding Secretary
Lynchburg, Tennessee

## The 1884 Honorary Members

Gen. Alexander William Campbell is one of the lesser known Confederates but he did have an association with Forrest's Staff and with the cavalry that earned him an honorary membership in the Veterans Association. Enlisting as a private, Campbell was soon promoted to major, assigned to staff duty, then sent to command the Thirty-third Tennessee Infantry. Severely wounded at Shiloh, Campbell was on sick leave for several months. On returning he was assigned as assistant adjutant and inspector on the staff of General Polk, from which post he volunteered to work under Gideon Pillow in the Conscription Bureau. In July 1863 Campbell was captured at Lexington, Tennessee, while on a secret mission behind Union lines on behalf of Gov. Isham Harris. Exchanged in February 1865, he became acting inspector general on Forrest's Staff and then briefly commanded a brigade in Jackson's Division under Forrest. He was made a brigadier on March 1, 1865 (Warner, 42).

George Gibbs Dibrell was another "old hand" from the early command of Forrest. He had also begun his military career as a private before recruiting the Eighth Tennessee Cavalry in 1862. This unit served under Forrest until detached to join the forces under Johnston at Dalton, Georgia. Dibrell provided the escort for Jefferson Davis as the president fled Richmond and moved south, only to be captured near Washington, Georgia (Warner, 72-73).

## Height of Membership

At the assigned time, but on September 8, 1885, the Veterans Association met at Shelbyville, Tennessee. The minutes do not record the building in which they met. This must have been a poignant meeting for the members of the Escort since it was just twenty-three years earlier that 105 of them had ridden out of Shelbyville toward Murfreesboro as the newly organized bodyguard for General Forrest.

> The Association was called to order by the President T.N. McCord and on the call of the roll the following were found present.
> Pres. T.N. McCord, VP J.B. Cowan, Maj. C.W. Anderson, Col. D.C. Kelley, T.J. Eaton, B.B. Ingle, T.G. Cheairs, F.R. Evans, Jo Cunningham, H.L.W. Boone, R.E. Fry, Geo. C. Gillespie, F.M. Adkinson, W.R. Shofner, F.F. Arnold, E. Clark, W.E. Sims, W.A. Bailey, M.L. Parks, W.L. Shofner, Jas. Newsom, Lt. Jno. Eaton, VP N. Boone, J.W. Horton, Jas. Duff, M. Cortner, J.M. Travis, T.C. Little, L.H. Russ5z, Geo. L. Cowan, W.H. Matthews, Jno. C. Jackson, Davy Crocket Jackson, J.N. Taylor.

The minutes of the last meeting was read and approved.

On Motion of the President the officers for the ensuing 12 months was elected so that the new president could preside.

Geo. L. Cowan      President
B.B. Ingle              1st V President
J.N. Taylor            Cor. Sect.
W.H. Matthews      Rec. Sect.
C.H. Russ              Treas.

The anuel address was now delivered by Dr. D.C. Kelley in a very touching manner.

Other addresses were delivered during the afternoon.

Announcement of the death at Dallas Texas of our comrad R.C. Kibble was read. After dinner we were entertained by Capt. Boone with his military experience and numerous anicdontes that are only good when told by himself.

Lynchburg was Selected as the next place of meeting and the first Tuesday in September 1886 the time at noon.

Geo. L. Cowan      Pres
W.H. Matthews      Rec. Sect.


Death of R.C. Keeble
Dallas Evening Mail

At five o'clock this morning the spirit of Mr. Richard C. Keeble took its flight. To-day a strange feeling of mingled pride and sorrow is in our city. Some are rejoicing at the pleasure of meeting again, after many years of trials, joys and sorrows, others are filled with unspeakable sadness at the death of one of the purest, best and most talented men within our borders. Tall in stature, he was as towering in his commercial life and his Christian walk. Genial and wholesouled, he had the three crowning virtues deep written upon the tablets of his heart. As a business man he had no peer in the State, and the Baptist Church will miss his unfailing devotion in everything that could advance and sustain it.

Mr. Keeble was born in Columbia, Tenn., and at the time of his death he was about 45 years of age. He went from Nashville in Company B, Rock City Guards, First Tennessee Regiment, and served in the Virginia campaign and through the battle of Shiloh. Being in failing health he was given an honorable discharge. After a stay in Mississippi he partially regained his health and returned to his home in Middle Tennessee for a few days.

While there the battle of Murfreesboro was imminent, and taking up his gun he joined as a volunteer, and fought bravely in the battle. After this he was assigned to duty as escort to Gen. Forrest, and continued with him to the close of the war.

His success as a wholesale dealer in the grocery business has reached mammoth proportions. He has been deacon in the Baptist Church for sixteen years and a Christian from boyhood up. As an example to young men, he pointed the way to the highest type—Christian manhood.

He leaves a noble, devoted wife to look in vain for his coming. No more the dear friends will have his presence and counsel. Truly may we say, "death loves a shining mark", and this instance the lightning has riven a tower of strength in our business and Christian walks.

The following year, the Veterans Association met in the village of Lynchburg, which was home to a number of the members of the Escort. The minutes state:

The fifth annuel reunion of Forrests Escort and Staff was called to order by the Pres. G.L. Cowan at 12 oclock m. and an address of welcome on behalf of the citizens of Lynchburg was delivered by Dr. E. Y. Salmons and was responded to in behalf of the association by Capt. Sam Donalson.

On Motion, the association adjourned to 1:30 oclock P.M.

On reassembling at one thirty P.M. the Sect being absent the reading of the minutes and calling of the Roll was dispensed with.

The following committee was appointed to draft suitable resolution on the death of our comrad Henry C. Berry were C.W. Anderson, L.H. Russ, and W.E. Sims.

On Motion of Judge Carmack an Historical committee was appointed to collect facts and history relating to the Staff and Escort while in the field composed of Maj Chas W. Anderson, Lt G.L. Cowan, Capt. Saml Donaldson, Lt. Jno Eaton, Sgt W.C. Cooper.

Moved by Capt. Donaldson that a committee be appointed to correspond with the different monument associations for the purpose of arranging to erect a monument to the memory of Genl N.B. Forrest. Committee, Capt Sam. Donaldson, S.W. Carmack and W.C. Cooper.

On Motion, the committee on constitution and By-laws was discharged.

On Motion of Dr. Cowan the next place of meeting was selected. Fayetteville, Tenn being put in nomination by W.L. Shofner, seconded by Judge Carmack who appealed to the Boys not to put any other place in nomination, assuring them that they would be received with out stretched arms. No other place being put in nomination Fayetteville was selected unanimously.

On Motion of W.C. Cooper the following committee on arrangements was appointed: Judge S.W. Carmack, W.L. Shofner, H.L.W.

Boone, T.C. Little, J.C. Shofner, J.W. Newsom, T.C. Gillespie, John Johnston.

Motion to elect officers for the ensuing year being in order the following were elected:

President      S.W. Carmack
1st V Pres     L.H. Russ
2nd V Pres     Jno Eaton
Cor Sect       J.N. Taylor
Rec Sect       W. L. Shofner
Treas          N. Boone

On Motion, a committee was selected to select oritors for the next reunion. Committee: J.N. Taylor & T.J. Eaton, the President was added to the Committee.

Lt. Geo L. Cowan was selected to read a paper on the history of the Escort at the next meeting.

Letters of regret were read from Capt. John C. Jackson, Capt. J.W. Morton, and W.T.F. Wharton.

On Motion of T.N. McCord Dr. Thos Lipscomb was elected an honorery member.

A recess was taken to hear an address from Dr. J.B. Cowan in his happiest mood after which Capt Doughty, a Federal Soldier who in a fine, happy, and well timed remarks, expressed his thanks for the courtisies and kindnesses shown him. After which Maj Chas W. Anderson then told of the only speach he ever made in his life and proceeded to pay a glowing tribute to the memory of Maj. J.P. Strange, than whom no braver soldier or more perfect gentleman followed the flag of the Lost Cause. Capt Boone was also called upon but his modesty as usuel kept him back.

At 7 oclock P.M. Judge Carmack the orator for the occasion delivered a very able address which was listened to with rapt attention by all after which by request Miss Nannie Salmonds recited "the prayer of the South."

On Motion the thanks of the Association was tendered Miss Nannie Salmonds and to the citizens of Lynchburg for their kindness and hospitality. Adjourned to meet at Fayetteville Tenn Sept 1887.

W. L. Shofner    Recording Sect.

On September 14, 1886, the *Fayetteville Observer* copied an account of the reunion from the *Nashville American*. The Fayetteville paper noted that, while the Escort had numbered as many as 150, only 40 were present for the reunion. The meeting was held at the Lynchburg courthouse, which is still in use today. The speech made by Dr. J. B. Cowan was described as "rich, racy, and in a happy style and abounded in amusing incidents of the war." Judge Carmack delivered a "deep, logical address on the causes of the war," according to the Fayetteville paper. "He discussed the question in a spirit of fairness, doing injustice to nobody, and received the approbation of all in the audience on both sides." "The Prayer of the South" was a well-known poem of that day, written by Fr. Abram Ryan, the poet laureate of the Confederacy and a Catholic priest. Father Ryan High School in Nashville is named for this Confederate chaplain. As with most of Father Ryan's poems, Southern schoolchildren committed "The Prayer" to memory. The first stanza reads:

> My Brow is bent beneath a heavy rod;
> My face is wan and white with many woes;
> But I will lift my poor chained hands to God
> And for my children pray, and for my foes.
> Beside the graves where thousands lowly lie
> I kneel, and, weeping for each slaughtered son,
> I turn my gaze to my own sunny sky,
> And pray, O Father, may thy will be done. (CV 1: 83)

The little girl who recited the poem for the meeting was Nannie Salmon, the daughter of the man who welcomed the Veterans Association to Lynchburg in the opening session. He was Ezekiel Young Salmon, captain of Company A, the "Lynchburg Rangers," of Peter Turney's First Tennessee Infantry, a unit that fought for four years with Lee's Army of Northern Virginia. Dr. Salmon practiced medicine in Lynchburg beginning in 1857. He also owned Salmon & Taylor's Drug Store with his brother-in-law, Dr. J. N. Taylor, and Salmon & Spencers Dry Goods. In 1867 he built a two-story Greek Revival addition on the front of his home, which was also used as a hotel. That hotel was later sold to Miss Mary Bobo and is still in business as a restaurant, Miss Bobo's Boarding House, under the ownership of the Jack Daniels Distillery.

Judge S. W. Carmack was a member of the Escort during the war and is listed as serving as a private in Jackson's Cavalry Company, the name of record for the Escort (Horn, 1).

Jasper Newton Taylor, named to the committee to select orators for the 1887 reunion, had been a member of Peter Turney's First Tennessee Infantry, Company D. He was discharged after one year's duty and returned to Lynchburg only to join Forrest's Escort later in the war.

His brother, William Ford Taylor, was a veteran of the Mexican War and had also served in the First Tennessee Infantry before returning home at the end of his enlistment. While living in Lynchburg in 1862 he was arrested by Union soldiers of the Fifth Tennessee Cavalry and was ordered to be taken to Shelbyville, where the Fifth Tennessee had its headquarters. While on the road to Shelbyville, Taylor's guards shot him three times. He escaped into the woods, survived his wounds, and joined Forrest's Escort in October 1862.

Dr. Thomas Lipscomb was a wealthy physician and farmer in the area of Shelbyville. He apprenticed in medicine with his father in Winchester, Tennessee, and moved to Shelbyville in 1831. He proved himself to be a skilled surgeon as well as a physician and soon had a wide practice. He served as president of the Shelbyville branch of the Bank of Tennessee, purchased a plantation in 1854, and acquired fourteen slaves at the same time. One of his sons, William E. Lipscomb, served under Forrest and was killed during the Tennessee Campaign of 1864 (Speer, 102). During the war years, Dr. Lipscomb was frequently harassed by the Union provost marshal's troops because of his pro-Southern stance.

On the first day of September 1887, the Veterans Association assembled in Fayetteville. The seat of Lincoln County was home to many of Forrest's men and strongly pro-Confederate. The Escort and Staff were, as promised, welcomed with open arms.

The Association was called to order by President S. W. Carmack and prayer was invoked by the Chaplin T.C. Little after which the address of welcome on behalf of the citizens of Fayetteville and vicinity was delivered by Judge S.W. Carmack.

On Motion of J.B. Cowan all ex-Confederate soldiers present were asked to come forward and be seated with the Association. Mr. Chick of Forrest's Old Regiment, McDonald's Battalion was introduced and entertained for a time the Association with reminiscences of our gallant old leader and the different commands.

On Motion a committee composed of Dr. J.B. Cowan, Lt. Geo L. Cowan and H.L.W. Boone was appointed to formulate resolutions asking McDonald's Battalion, Freemans & Mortons Batteries to join our Association.

Adjourned until 2:30 oclock P.M.

On reassembling the minutes of last meeting were read and approved. Letters were read from the following absent comrads: A.W. Key, Sam Donalson, J.W. Morton, M. Cortner, H.D. Lipscomb, J.C. Jackson, T.N. McCord, Chas. W. Anderson, & J.O. Crump.

Lt. Geo L. Cowan was called on for his Historical paper but

instead gave some interesting sketches and anecdotes of the company which was not only interesting but Historical.

Dr. J.B. Cowan Chm of Special Report Committee reported the following resolutions:

Whereas, the intimate associations that existed during the late war between Mortons and Freemans Batteries and the part of Forrest's old Regiment known as McDonald's Battalion and the Escort and Staff, being so close and of such long duration resulting in a mutual attachment and respect, therefore, be it resolved, that we cordially invite these commands to unite with us in our Annuel Reunions, for the purpose of keeping fresh in our memories the pleasant association of former years, furthermore Resolved, that a committee be appointed whose duty it shall be to confer with these commands in reference to these subjects, and that the Corresponding Secretary be required to furnish a copy of these resolutions to the said Commands.

Submitted: J.B. Cowan, Hugh Boone, Geo. L. Cowan, committee. Unanimously adopted.

Moved by Lt. Geo. L. Cowan that the sect get up as complete a roll of the company as possible.

On Motion a committee as follows was appointed to confer with Mortons & Freemans Battery:

Lt. Geo. L. Cowan, W.A. Baily, O. McKissick, Maj. C.W. Anderson & J.B. Cowan.

The following officers were elected for the following 12 months:

| | |
|---|---|
| President | Dr. J.B. Cowan |
| 1st V Pres | Geo W. Foster |
| 2nd V Pres | B.B. Ingle |
| Recoding Sect | W.L. Shofner |
| Cor. Sect | J.N. Taylor |
| Chaplin | T.C. Little |
| Treasurer | N Boone |
| Buglar | W.A. Bailey |

On Motion the former Historical and Monumental Committees are continued.

On Motion of J.B. Cowan, Lt. Geo. L. Cowan was appointed custodian of all Historical matter of the Escort and Staff.

On Motion of G.C. Gillespie the Sect. was instructed to procure badges containing the Portrait of Genl Forrest for the use of the Association.

On Motion of J.N. Taylor a committee was appointed composed of J.N. Taylor, Orville McKissack, & Dr. J.B. Cowan to carry out the motion to secure the badges.

On Motion, Petersburg Lincoln County Tennessee was selected as the next place of meeting. The following committee was appointed on arrangements: Geo. C. Gillespie, A .A. McEwen, Geo. W. Foster, and James Pearson. The committee on orators were J.N. Taylor and W.L. Shofner.

Adjourned until 7:30 P.M.

The Association was called to order at 7:30 oclock and was addressed by Genl John M. Bright who presented in a very able and forcible manner the Confederate views of the causes of the war. He was followed by Col. A.S. Marks in a very chaste and eloquent address in which he paid a glowing tribute to the bravery and gallantry of the Confederate Soldier and the loyalty and devotion of the southern woman. There was a very large attendance of citizens in addition to the old soldiers present who were highly entertained.

On Motion, a vote of thanks was given to the good people of Fayetteville for their many kind acts of hospitality.

On Motion, the Association adjourned to meet at Petersburg on the sixth day of Sept. 1888.

J.B. Cowan       Pres
W.L. Shofner     Sect

The meeting of the Veterans Association was held in Bright's Hall, a theater located on the south side of the courthouse square in Fayetteville. The theater, or opera house, occupied the top floor of a two-story building; businesses filled the bottom floor. On September 8, the *Fayetteville Observer* noted that twenty-four members of the Escort and Staff had attended. The reporter opined, "General Forrest was the greatest of all cavalry leaders, but, left to himself his genius could not accomplish anything. These are the men who carried out his plans and wrote his name high in the annals of warfare." In his oration, "General" Bright (there is no military record for a Gen. John Bright) noted that Forrest "moved with his Invincibles as on the wings of a tempest, struck like a thunderbolt, and eluded pursuit like a phantom."

Old men are susceptible to flattery and flirtation, however. One of the veterans commented that he went through the entire war without being taken prisoner but that he was immediately captured by one of the young ladies of Fayetteville.

George W. Foster was a good example of the sort of man who joined the Escort. Foster had originally enlisted in the Eightth Tennessee Infantry, serving until he was severely wounded in the neck at Murfreesboro, a wound from which he never recovered. Offered a medical discharge, he chose instead to enlist in the Escort and served the remainder of the war.

The meeting at Fayetteville was followed in 1888 by an assembly in the nearby village of Petersburg, a pleasant and prosperous place in the closing years of the nineteenth century. It was a marketing center for a large area of fertile countryside and boasted hotels, a private school, and several churches. It made a good place for the seventh meeting of the Escort and Staff Veterans Association.

> The Association was called to order at 10 A.M. by the president in the Town Hall with a good attendance of the Association but with very bad behavior on the part of the weather. The Cock being offended at the discourtesy of the committee gave us a bad rainey day, almost all day. The morning was spent in exchanging greetings and hand shaking. Capt Boone was at his best and kept the boys in laughter until the dinner was announced which was served in an elegant and bountiful style at the Russel House.
>
> After dinner the Association was called to order by the President and opened by prayer by the Rev W. L. Blanton who also addressed us in a few well timed and appropriate words, reminding us that life was itself a battle and we were yet all Soldiers, that we should gird our loins and press forward with strong wills and high purposes to an assured victory by the help of him who never refused those who sought him in meekness and faith.
>
> The Minutes of the last meeting were read and approved.
>
> On the call of committee Maj. Anderson from the committee on History and Judge Carmack from committee on monuments made a verbal report that those respective committees had not been called together for which they were criticized severely for their neglect of duty. The President, Dr. J.B. Cowan, was called on for a report of his committee and not being able to do any better than the others. The committee on Badges having done nothing they were discharged and Capt Jno W. Morton was appointed a committee of one to get up and have made a suitable badge for the Association.
>
> The following officers were elected for twelve months:
> President      Maj. Chas W. Anderson
> 1 Vi Pres      H.L.W. Boone
> 2 Vi Pres      M.L. Parks
> Rec Sect       W.L. Shofner

```
Cor Sect    J.N. Taylor
Treas       Capt N Boone
```

Dr Cowan, in retiring from the chair, presented the President-Elect, Maj C.W. Anderson, who upon taking the chair thanked the Association for the enthusiastic and unanimous manner of his election and assured them of his fidelity to them and the cause for which they had suffered.

On Motion, Tullahoma, Tenn, was selected as the next place of meeting. Dr. Cowan thanked them for selecting his town and hoped it would be the largest and most successful meeting we ever had. He thought we should carry over the solid consolidated organization of the Association and we should gather in to it every soldier who had at anytime served under Forrest. That so far, at least as we were concerned, our hero rested in an unmarked grave and that by bringing all of the associations together we might hope to erect a monument to his memory worthy of his deeds of chivalry. Remarks were made by Maj Anderson, Capt Morton, G.C. Gillespie, and others, and the following committee to carry out the above sentiments was appointed:

Dr. J.B. Cowan, Maj C.W. Anderson, and Judge S.W. Carmack.

On Motion, Capt Morton was asked to lend a helping hand, Dr. D.C. Kelley was asked to help also.

On Motion, Dr. Cowan was appointed a committee on arrangements for next meeting with power to select his own committee.

On Motion, S.W. Carmack, J.B. Cowan, and G.C. Gillespie were selected a committee on orators for the next reunion.

On Motion, Burrell Buchanan, colored, was elected a member of the Association and on thanking the Association for electing him a member said that he had been faithful during the trying scenes of the war and his heart had never changed since.

Adjourned until 7 oclock at the Presbyterian Church.

Promptly at 7 P.M. the Association was opened with prayer and song. The orator of the occasion, Col J.D. Tilman, being absent Capt John W. Morton addressed the Association. He gave a thrilling account of the Battle of Brices Cross Roads, showing from his maps the different positions of each command. He held his audience spell bound and as one of the audience expressed it, he had been through the hard contested battle all over without firing a gun or being shot at.

At the request of the Ladies, Dr. J.B. Cowan and Maj. Chas W. Anderson addressed the audience and related many thrilling incidents of camp and field.

On Motion, the thanks of the Association were tendered the good people of Petersburg for the good time had.

On Motion, the Association adjourned to meet in Tullahoma, Tenn, on Sept 5th 1889.

Chas W. Anderson, President

W.L. Shofner, Sect.

The Petersburg town hall, in which the group met, was located upstairs over the bank. In order to accommodate a larger number of visitors, the evening meeting, with featured speakers, was scheduled at the Presbyterian Church. The *Petersburg News,* in an article copied by the *Fayetteville Observer* on September 13, 1888, noted as present C. W. Anderson, J. W. Morton, Dr. J. B. Cowan, Nath Boone, T. G. Cheairs, M. L. Parks, E. Clark, H. L. W. Boone, B. B. Ingle, S. W. Carmack, Joel Reese, A. A. McEwen, G. C. Gillespie, James Pearson, and Burl Buchanan.

Two events set this meeting apart from those that had gone before. Dissatisfaction with the lack of performance of committees resulted in an open rebuke to some of the leading members of the group. Obviously, a number of the men were growing impatient with the failure of committees to carry out more than the simplest of tasks. As they grew older, they were anxious to see a monument erected to Forrest and to leave some permanent record of their wartime deeds.

The second notable event is the admission to membership of a black Confederate. At a time when the Grand Army of the Republic was strictly segregated by race, the United Confederate Veterans often had meeting with them the black men who had served with and by them during the war. Numerous photographs of Confederate veterans reunions show a sprinkling of black faces. In this case, Burrell Buchanan was not a guest; he became a full member of the group. He had served during the war as a cook and had remained with the unit until the end, although he must have had numerous opportunities to run away. The issue of race in the nation during the nineteenth century is much more complex than public opinion acknowledges, and the South was not the source of all problems concerning the issue. As this event shows, good relations often existed between individuals of different races and even among groups (see Appendix E).

The orator for this meeting was a man much after the hearts of the Escort and Staff Veterans Association members, a dyed-in-the-wool Rebel. James D. Tillman served as lieutenant colonel and, later, as colonel of the Forty-first Tennessee Infantry. This regiment was captured at Fort Donelson, paroled in time to fight in the Vicksburg Campaign, but not in Vicksburg at the surrender, so it took part in the fighting at Chickamauga as well. In 1864, the regiment served throughout the Atlanta Campaign and Nashville Campaign and sent its pitifully small band of survivors on to North Carolina, where they surrendered with the rest of Joseph Johnston's forces (Horn, 2: 262-63). Tillman represented the tragic way in which the war split families. His father supported the Union while the son went with the Confederacy. It was many years after the war before the two were reconciled.

On the morning of September 5, 1889, the Veterans Association met in Aydelott Hall in Tullahoma, Tennessee. As was customary, once the meeting had been called to order the rest of the morning was spent in greetings and casual conversations.

After a sumpious dinner at Hurrican Hall the association again assembled at Aydelotts Hall the Pres Maj C.W. Anderson in the chair. Despite the rain and unclement weather a goodly number of citizens were present. An address of welcome was delivered by Dr. Buckner on behalf of the citizens and one by Lt. Travis in behalf of the ex-Confederates of Tullahoma, responded to in behalf of the Association by Maj. Anderson.

On the roll being called there were more than an average attendance.

The following officers were elected for the ensuing 12 months:
Pres          Col. D.C. Kelley
1st V.P.    Rev Jos Irvine
2nd V.P.   Lt Jno Eaton
Rec Sect   S.W. Carmack
Cor Sect   J.N. Taylor
On call of committees it was found that Capt Morton on Badges, Lt Geo L. Cowan on History and Dr. D.C. Kelley on monuments were absent which called forth a flight of eloquent tirade and criticism for the absence and neglect of so many chairmen of important committees by Dr. Cowan, Judge Carmack, and Maj. Anderson. But they were ably defended by comrad G.C.

Gillespie who reminded Dr. Cowan and Judge Carmack that people in Glass houses should not throw stones as both of them being present and on very important committees had made no report.

Resolutions commemorative of the love we bore our Departed comrad Lt Mat Cortner were introduced and unanimously adopted and coppies ordered sent to his family and to the papers at Shelbyville, Tullahoma, and Fayetteville. Appropriate remarks were made by many of the association about Life, Character, and Soldierly qualities.

On Motion, the following honerary members were elected: Maj. Jesse Sparks, ———— Crump, J.D. Buckner, and J.G. Aydelott.

On Motion, the election of the next place of meeting was taken up and a letter from Lieut Geo L. Cowan asking the Association to meet in his home at Franklin, Tenn, which was part of the historic Battle Field of Franklin. Other places were put in nomination but owing to the eloquence of Maj Sparks Murfreesboro, Tenn, was selected by the Major promising to turn the keys of the city and furnish the paint to paint it red.

The following was appointed a committee on arrangements. Maj. Jesse Sparks and Maj C.W. Anderson.

On Motion, Maj. Anderson and J.N. Taylor were selected as a committee on orators. The remainder of the Standing Committees were continued.

Addressed were made by Col. Baxter Smith, Rev. J.B. Irvine, Dr. J.B. Cowan, and Burrill Buchanan, colored.

On Motion, the Association adjourned to meet in Murfreesboro, Tenn, on Sept 4th, 1890.

Again, the Veterans Association expressed its frustration at committees being unable to complete their work. In hindsight, it may be surmised that the difficulty of communication and travel, the continuing poor economy of the South, and the lack of money for much beyond necessities prevented many of the goals from being accomplished. Even the compilation of a history of the Escort and Staff would have taken time that could scarcely be spared from necessary work, although the contemporary historian fumes that it was not done. A modern student of history would be fascinated to know what Burrell Buchanan had to say to the old veterans.

J. G. Aydelott was a member of the Eighth Tennessee Cavalry

and was a Tullahoma businessman. His old commander, Col. Baxter Smith, was one of the orators. Baxter Smith was the original commander of the Eighth Tennessee Cavalry, which was formed in January 1863 from companies that had been on detached duty. Smith had a short war. On May 9, 1863, he was captured while scouting along the Caney Fork River and was not exchanged until February 1865 (Horn, 2: 72).

Maj. Jesse Sparks was a man with an unusual war record. After graduating from Union University in Murfreesboro, he went to Texas. When the war broke out, he joined the Eighth Texas, Terry's Texas Rangers. This unit came under the command of Forrest, and Sparks had an association with the Escort for a time until he was made a major on the staff of Gen. P. O. Herbert. He rejoined Forrest for the last campaign of the war and was on his way to Texas to take up his civilian life when he was arrested and sent to Camp Douglas. After the war, Sparks became a U.S. consul in Mexico and was a member of the Tennessee General Assembly when he attended this reunion (McBride and Robinson, 853).

> The Association was called to order by 2nd Vice President John Eaton in the opera house in Murfreesboro, Tennessee, at 10 oclock A.M. Thursday Sept 3rd 1890. The morning was spent as is the custom of the Association in hand shaking and mutual greetings and general exchange of anicdotes, after which an adjournment was taken for dinner.
>
> On reassembling at 2 oclock the following officers were elected:
>
> President        John Eaton
> 1st Vice Pres    W. T. H. Horton
> 2nd Vice Pres    F. M. Adimson
> Rec Sect         S. W. Carmack
> Cor Sect         J. N. Taylor
> Treas            N. Boone
> Chaplin          Dr. J. B. Cowan
> Sgt at Arms      Burrell Buchanan, colored
>
> On Motion of Dr. Cowan an invitation was extended the Association to attend the reunion of exConfederate soldiers at Tullahoma on Sept 11th, which was accepted.
>
> On Motion of Lieut Geo L Cowan the following resolution was adopted:
>
> Whereas there is an earnest movement being made in many parts of our beloved Southland, looking to the perinal relief of

the disabled exConfederate soldiers and whereas we believe that these disabled vetrens are a heritage left to us. And that we have a sacred duty to perform in Smoothing their pathway down the hill of life. Therefore resolved that we bring this question before our Bivouacks and exConfederate Associations at our homes and enlist the sympathy of the ladies of our beloved South. After remarks on the subject by different members it was unanimously adopted.

On call of committees none reported. After a discussion of some length in regard to the interest we should take in these anuel reunions the Association proceeded to elect the next place of meeting. Thereupon Lt Geo L. Cowan in glowing terms invited them to meet on the Historic battle field of Franklin, assuring them that he would have good tents, and as Bear was plentiful in the adjoining corn field, the boys would not suffer as they did at Como, Mississippi, but could kill every one that would attempt to bite. Unanimously selected.

On Motion, Col J. B. Palmer was elected an honery member.

On Motion, the Association adjourned to meet at Franklin, Tenn on Thursday Sept. 3rd 1891.

Col. Joseph B. Palmer served as commander of the Eighteenth Tennessee Infantry until his promotion to brigadier in November 1864. His unit had fought with Forrest at Murfreesboro during the Nashville Campaign of 1864 and had formed part of the rear guard under Forrest's command during the retreat that closed that campaign. Palmer's men were the last infantry across the Tennessee River when the army returned to Mississippi (Horn, 2: 213-14). Given the shared miseries and glories of that fabled retreat, Palmer must have been welcomed at the reunion as an old comrade in arms indeed.

## Return to an Old Battlefield

"Windermere," the home of George L. Cowan, stands adjacent to Carnton, the McGavock home that was used as a hospital following the Battle of Franklin. Between Winderemere and Carnton lies the Confederate Cemetery, containing the Confederate dead from the struggle. The grove where the 1891 reunion took place overlooks the cemetery and part of the field where the Army of Tennessee fought so bravely, if foolishly ordered to do so, on

November 30, 1864. Carnton is today open to the public under the name "Historic Carnton Plantation."

Pursuent to adjournment the Association met in Lt Cowans grove where he had some large tents stretched and plenty of wood piled up and a commissary well stored with Barbecued Pigs, Lambs, Chickens, Bread, Coffee, and an abundance of Buttermilk. On account of the absence of the President Jno Eaton the Association was called to order by Rec Sect S. W. Carmack and the morning hour was spent as usual in hand shaking and mutual greetings and as most of them had spent the night around the campfires anicdotes were at a discount. After a sumptious dinner reinforced from the kitchen of Mrs. Cowan the Association went into the elections of officers as follows:

| | |
|---|---|
| President | Geo L. Cowan |
| 1st Vice President | W.A. Bailey |
| 2nd Vice President | H.L.W. Boone |
| Rec Sect | S. W. Carmack |
| Cor Sect | J. N. Taylor |
| Chaplain | Dr. J. B. Cowan |
| Treas | Thos Cheairs |

The committee having made a report on motion of Capt Morton this committee was requested to make a complete roll of the Escort and Staff. The following were added to the committee: J. B. Cowan, J. W. Morton, S. W. Carmack, and J. N. Taylor.

A committee on Badges being selected as follows: S. W. Carmack, J. N. Taylor, and J. B. Cowan.

On Motion, the following Honerary Members were elected: Col John McGavock, Dr. Wat Gentry, Capt E. H. Douglas, Maj Nat Cheairs.

Col McGavock in accepting the honor spoke in a touching manner of the pleasure it gave him to see so many brave men present who had risked their life for a cause they thought just, and that they were very near to his heart and that he had a constant reminder of their deeds of valer and heroism in the graves of those who rested just over beyond you a little ways. Capt. Douglas also spoke in a very feeling manner. Maj Cheairs spoke in glowing terms of our old chieftan.

Letters of regret were read from Sam Donalson, Maj C. W. Anderson, and H. C. Lipscomb.

On Motion, Spring Hill was selected as the next place of meeting and a committee appointed of Thos Cheairs, Orville McKissack, W.A. Bailey, and Lim Padget.

On Motion, the thanks of the Association was voted Lieut Cowan and his good lady for their untiring efforts to make our meeting a success most especially Mrs. Cowan for the good things she kept us on hand to eat.

On Motion, the Association adjourned to meet at Spring Hill the first Thursday in Sept 1892.

Geo L. Cowan, President      S. W. Carmack Rec Sect

John McGavock was an appropriate choice as an honorary member. His house, Carnton, had been used as a field hospital after the Battle of Franklin and had been crammed with Confederate wounded. Several of the five generals killed on that sanguine evening had been laid out for burial on the back porch of the house, and McGavock's wife, Hattie, had earned the life-long respect of the wounded men she helped tend. In 1866, the family set aside a piece of land for the burial of Confederates whose battlefield graves were being disturbed as the lands around Franklin returned to peacetime uses. George L. Cowan was McGavock's son-in-law.

Dr. Wat Gentry was a surgeon of the Seventeenth Tennessee and had been with the Escort and Staff at Murfreesboro in December 1864 as well as on the retreat to Alabama. He was from Bedford County (Horn, 1: 210).

E. H. Douglas was from Freeman's Battery, a unit with a long association with the Escort, and the surviving battery members had been especially invited to join the ranks of the Veterans Association at an earlier meeting (Horn 2: 133).

Maj. Nathaniel Cheairs had joined the army in 1861 as an officer of the Third Tennessee Infantry, with John Calvin Brown as his colonel (Horn, 1: 182). The Third Tennessee was captured at Fort Donelson and Cheairs spent several months in Fort Warren in Boston Harbor. Following his exchange, Cheairs appears not to have won reelection as major and returned to his home, Rippa Villa, near Spring Hill, Tennessee. In early 1863, Forrest asked the major to join his staff as a volunteer aide, a role Cheairs would fill until July 1863. At that time, Gen. Joseph E. Johnston asked Cheairs to become a commissary officer, buying cattle in west Tennessee and getting them out as best he could to the main Confederate army. In performing these duties, Cheairs was captured a second time and spent several months in Camp Chase, Ohio. He returned to duty just in time to fight with Forrest at Selma (Hughes, *I'll Sting*, 6-7).

Thomas Gorum Cheairs had served in the Escort during much of the war, although he was only eighteen when the war began. He never married but worked as a helper on various farms run by his father, Major Cheairs, and died in 1909. His obituary said, "He was General Forrest's ideal of a good soldier. Ever near his chief, he was ready to go and do whatever ordered, however dangerous it might be" (CV 17: 609).

The note about the old men sitting around the campfire all night preceding the meeting of the Veterans Association stirs the imagination as one wonders what stories were told there under the stars. With each year, fewer were seated in the ruddy glow to tell their tale.

The Veterans Association did not meet in Spring Hill in 1892 but decided instead to meet in Franklin in conjunction with the convention of the United Confederate Veterans. The local units of the UCV were called "bivouacs," as noted in the following minutes.

> Pursuent to the call of the President the Eleventh anuel reunion of the Association convened in Lt Geo. L. Cowan's Grove in conjunction with the anuel reunion of the State Association and as time was limited we met under a large oak tree. President Geo L. Cowan presiding, the minutes of the last meeting being read and approved the Roll was called showing the following members present:

| | | |
|---|---|---|
| Adkinson | Hugh Boone | Geo L. Cowan |
| J.B. Cowan | Crump | Cheairs |
| Duzenberry | Duff | Ingle |
| Cummings | Hooper | Capt. Jackson |
| Morton | McKissack | Padget |
| Priest | W. L. Shofner | Wharton |
| Parks | John Eaton | G. C. Gillespie |

> On Motion a committee was appointed to Draft suitable resolution to the memory of our departed comrads S. W. Carmack, Jas. W. Newson, W. H. Matthews, and Henry Pointer. The following was the committee: Dr. J. B. Cowan, Chm J. O. Crump, G. C. Gillespie.

> On Motion, the following officers were elected for twelve months:

| | |
|---|---|
| President | W. L. Shofner |
| 1st Vic Pres | Orville McKissack |
| Rec Sect | George L. Cowan |

Cor Sect     J. N. Taylor
Treas          Thos Cheairs

The committee on arrangements: Capt. N. Boone, W. L. Shofner, H. L. H. Boone, Jno Eaton.

On Motion Booneville, Tenn was selected as the next place of meeting on Thursday Sept 7th 1893.

On Motion of Geo L. Cowan he was allowed to turn over the following amount of dues collected from the following parties towit:

| | | | |
|---|---|---|---|
| Geo. L. Cowan | 50 | J. B. Cowan | 50 |
| J. O. Crump | 50 | T. G. Cheairs | 50 |
| H. S. Dusenbury | 50 | J. C. Duff | 50 |
| B. B. Ingle | 50 | G. C. Gillespie | 50 |
| G. W. Hooper | 50 | D. C. Padgett | 50 |
| W. L. Shofner | 50 | Jno Eaton | 50 |
| O. W. McKissack | 50 | | |

Total amount Six 50/100 Dollars to T. G. Cheairs the Treasurer.

On Motion of G. C. Gillespie this Association do not meet again in connection with any other Bivouac. Adopted.

Moved that we do now stand adjourned to meet at Booneville Tenn Sept 7, 1893. Adopted

Geo L. Cowan Recording Sect     W. L. Shofner Pres

Escort

| | |
|---|---|
| 1. Capt J. C. Jackson | 10. B. B. Ingle |
| 2. Lieut Geo L. Cowan | 11. J. J. Cummins |
| 3. Lieut Jno Eaton | 12. G. C. Gillespie |
| 4. F. M. Adkinson | 13. G. W. Hooper |
| 5. H.L.W.Boone | 14. O. W. McKissack |
| 6. J. O. Crump | 15. D. C. Padgett |
| 7. T. G. Cheairs | 16. Tom Priest |
| 8. H. F. Dusenberry | 17. W. L. Shofner |
| 9. J. C. Duff | 18. W. T. H. Wharton |
| 19. M. L. Parks | |

Staff Officers Present

| | |
|---|---|
| Dr. J. B. Cowan C.S. | Capt. J. Morton C. A. |
| (Chief Surgeon) | (CommanderArtillery) |

The amount collected in dues gives a glimpse into the economy of the South in 1892. The total of $6.50 was sufficient to keep the Escort and Staff Veterans Association in postage and supplies for a year but was still a pitifully small amount. The *Confederate Veteran* is filled with calls for monuments to be erected, and on page after page the pledges to these funds were $1 or less per person. The passage of almost thirty years had done little to heal the economic devastation wrought by the Union army.

Clearly, the veterans of the Escort and Staff liked to meet with each other and visit, exchange reminiscences, and remember their dead. Meeting briefly while attending the state meeting of the United Confederate Veterans left them with too little time to reinforce the bond their unique past had created.

The Association was called to order by the President at 10:30 oclock in the beautiful grove adjoining the house of Comrad B. B. Ingle and after prayer by the Chaplin (Comrad T. C. Little and address of welcome in behalf of the citizens was offered by Dr. B. E. Noblett and responded too in behalf of the Company by Chaplain T. C. Little after which the Association adjourned until 2 oclock P. M.

At 2 P. M. the Association was called to order by President Shofner. The minutes were read and approved and an able and interesting address on the History of the Escort was delivered by the Rev. J. G. Woods which was listened too with rapt attention.

Letters of regret were read from Comrads Adj Gen C. W. Anderson, A.D. Adair, W. J. Biggs, H. D. Lipscomb and D. R. Bidford and On Motion of Comrad G. C. Gillespiewere noted and filed.

On Motion the accounts of the Corresponding Sect for $3.75 and Recording Sect. for $2.50 were allowed.

On Motion of comrad Gillespie a recess of five minutes were taken in order to let all present pay their dues. Motion amended by Comrad Taylor to reduce the dues from 50 to 25 cents. Carried.

On Motion of Comrad G. L. Cowan a page of the minutes was dedicated to all of our dead Comrads.

Comrad Morton called attention to the Association badges and requested all who wanted one to come forward and procure one.

By permission the Rev J. G. Woods suggested that the Escort have the History of Forrest Cavalry republished with a certificate.

On Motion of Capt Morton the President appointed the following Historical committee: Capt J. W. Morton, Chm, G. L. Cowan, Chas W. Anderson, H.L.W.Boone, and Dr. J. B. Cowan.

On Motion of Comrad G. L. Cowan the following committee was appointed to draft suitible resolution to the memory of Col John McGavock an honarory member of this Association. Capt J. W. Morton, W. A. Bailey, and J. O. Crump.

On Motion Vine Hill the home of Capt Jno W. Morton was selected as our next meeting place and time the 6th of Sept 1894. Capt Morton was appointed chairman of the committee of arrangements with power to select a committee to assist him.

On Motion the following officers were elected for the ensuing twelve months:

| President | Jno W. Morton | Nashville Tenn |
| 1st V. Pres | Geo C. Gillespie | Petersburg Tenn |
| 2nd V.P. | M. L. Parks | Lynchburg Tenn |
| 3 V. P. | Ed Sims | Shelbyville Tenn |
| Record. Sect | Geo L. Cowan | Franklin Tenn |
| Cor Sect | J. N. Taylor | Lynchburg Tenn |
| Chaplin | T. C. Little | Fayetteville Tenn |

On Motion Geo C. Carmack and W. T. Ferguson were elected honarary members.

On Motion the committee on the death of our comrad Judge S. W. Carmack be granted further time.

On Motion of comrad Little the thanks of this Association be here by tendered the good people of Booneville and vecinity for their uniform Kindness and hospitality and that we assure them we shall ever remember them with unfaigned pleasure. Carried.

On Motion of Capt Morton the thanks of the Association was tendered Rev. J. G. Woods for his entertaining, interesting, and trustfull address on the deeds of Forrest and his men.

On Motion an adjournment was taken until 7:30 oclock PM.

The President called the Association together at 7:30 oclock P.M.

On Motion Dr. J. N. Taylor, M. L. Parks and E. Clark was appointed a committee on the death of Comrad T. J. Eaton and on the death of Comrad Hyraim Neece, Ed Sims, L. H. Russ, and Emmit Fay, was appointed.

On Motion Maj C. W. Anderson and Capt J. W. Morton was appointed a committee on transportation for the next reunion.

On Motion of Comrad Cowan that M. C. Galloway, J. B. Cowan, C. W. Anderson, and D. C. Kelley be appointed a committee on the death of Mrs. N. B. Forrest.

Capt Morton urged everybody to give all the help possible to the Historical Committee in the noble work they were doing.

Moved by Capt Morton that an N. B. Forest monumental association be formed for the erection of a monument to our beloved General, N. B. Forrest. Unanimously elected. President W. L. Shofner Secretary and Treasurer with Capt Jno W. Morton general agent with power to issue an address and appropriate Sub-Committees.

The following comrads answered the roll call:

Lt. Geo. L. Cowan, Thomas Priest, J. O. Crump, D. C. Padget— all of Williamson County; T. G. Cheairs, Spring Hill; B. B. Ingle, Capt. N. Boone, H.L.W.Boone, B. F. Martin, J. C. Shofner, E. M. McClure, Geo Enochs, Geo Heath, Wm A. Wood of Booneville Tenn; Capt J. W. Morton of Nashville Tenn; Dr. M. A. L. Enochs of Flat Creek Tenn; Geo C. Gillespie, Geo Davidson, Jack Cummings of Petersburg; T. C. Little, W. L. Shofner of Fayetteville; Sgt. M. L. Parks, W. T. Taylor, J. N. Taylor Lynchburg Tenn; E. Clark, Lynchburg; Will A. Bailey, Eagleville, Jno Bryant, Flat Creek; Jas Duff, C.F. Blackwell, Mulberry; Geo W. Felps, Dean, Tenn; Joel Ruse, Belfast, Tenn; W. Ed. Sims, Shelbyville; H.C. Childs, Booneshill, Tenn.

There being no further business before the Association it adjourned to meet at Vine Hill, Tenn, on Aug 6th 1894 at 10 A.M.

Geo L. Cowan, Recording Sect.

Booneville is a rural crossroads community located between Fayetteville and Lynchburg. It should not be confused with Boonshill, which is west of Fayetteville. "The beautiful grove adjoining the house of Comrad B.B. Ingle" was to be known for many years simply as "The Ingle Place." The house stood atop the hill behind the present-day Booneville Community Center. Benjamin B. Ingle was a prominent citizen of the community and he represents the fact that, while the Escort was not literally a "band of brothers," it was a unit of cousins and in-laws. The Ingle family was related to the Dusenberrys and the Boones and had marriage ties to many of the other families of Escort members in the Lynchburg area.

It was fortunate that the meeting was held in the open on a day when the sun was shining, because no building in the area could have contained the crowd. The *Fayetteville Observer* noted on September 14, 1893, that 2,500 people were present. The veterans and guests gathered on Wednesday, the day before the meeting, and "tented that night as they had on the camp-ground." The article continued, "The scenes of camp life, the abandon of conventionalities and pranks for which soldiers are noted were enacted; memory was furbished and there was a recounting of the incidents of Donelson and Johnsonville and Stone's River and the Streight Raid and other brilliant engagements in which they participated." After a welcome from a member of the community and a response from a member of the Escort, "a charge was made on the dinner table," the newspaper reported. "Those people know how to feed a crowd and there was never a more sumptuous and inviting dinner spread in Lincoln County."

When the formal speaking began, J. G. Woods spoke of the causes of the war "and showed that the appeal to arms upon the part of the south was a dernier resort, that there was no other alternative save the surrender of self-respect and honor," the article stated. "He paid a tribute to the memory of the genius of their commander and eulogized the Escort for the valor and heroism displayed from the organization to the surrender at Gainesville, Ala."

Speaking was not the only form of entertainment for the occasion. The article continued, "The Elk Coronet Band made music for the occasion and were highly complimented. This is one of the best bands of the state and the masterly manner in which they rendered 'Dixie' and other martial airs filled the old soldiers with enthusiasm and would inspire anyone to deeds of daring." Charity was not neglected, as "the association raised a fund to name a room at the Confederate Soldiers' Home in honor of Capt. N. Boone."

George C. Carmack was a former first sergeant of the Eighth Tennessee Infantry. This unit had been raised in Lincoln County, especially that part that later became Moore County. Carmack was from Lynchburg and was the brother of S. W. Carmack, a deceased member of the Escort.

On September 15, 1868, John Morton had married Miss Annie Payne Humphreys, the daughter of a Federal and Confederate judge. They built a house near Nashville and named it "Vine Hill." It was described as crowning a hilltop, surrounded by cedars and oaks, with the door always open to ex-Confederates (Morton, *Artillery*, 346-47). Morton was active in numerous veterans associations and several had held meetings at his home. Serving as host for the relatively small Escort and Staff Veterans Association would have been a pleasant but not novel experience for Morton and his household.

## Minutes of the 1894 Reunion

The Reunion of Genl N. B. Forrest's Escort and Staff was held this year at the beautiful home of Capt John W. Morton who was chief of Artillery on Genl Forrests Staff and as President of the Association for 1894 called the association to order at Eleven and a half oclock under the beautiful and commodious Grand Stand of the Cumberland Driving Park. A beautiful prayer was made by Dr. D. C. Kelley after which the roll was called and the following answered.

STAFF

| Capt. John W. Morton | Chief of Artillery | Vine Hill |
| Dr. J. B. Cowan | Chief Surgeon | Tullahoma |
| Maj G. V. Rambant | Chief Commissary | Memphis |
| Maj Chas W. Anderson | AAA Genl | Florence |
| Capt. George Dashields | Chief Quartermaster | Memphis |
| Col. D. C. Kelley | Col. of Forrests | |
| | Old Regiment | Nashville |

ESCORT

| Capt. John C. Jackson | Rover, Tenn |
| W.A. Bailey | Eagleville,Tn. |
| Capt N. Boone | Bonneville |
| H. P. Dusenberry | Birmingham |
| Lieut Geo L. Cowan | Franklin |
| J.N. Taylor | Lynchburg |
| 1st Sgt M. L. Parks | Lynchburg |
| James Duff | Bonneville |
| 1st Corp L. H. Russ | Shelbyville |
| T. G. Cheairs | Spring Hill |
| H.L.W.Boone | Booneville |
| W. C. Cooper | Bellbuckle |
| Thomas Priest | Franklin |
| Mack Watson | Nashville |
| J. O. Crump | Franklin |
| F. R. (Bud) Evans | Winchester |
| S. H. Scales | Murfreesboro |
| F. N. Adkinson | Nashville |

The farewell address of Genl Forrest was read by Dr. J. B. Cowan in a very feeling manner.

Genl Andrew J. Coldwell of Nashville was introduced by the President and delivered a masterly and eloquent address on the life and career of Genl Forrest which was closely listened to and often applauded.

A beautiful Poem, on the lost cause, was composed and read by Mr. John Moore of Columbia, Tenn. Who when Genl Forrest was dashing over Middle Tenn at the head of his dauntless troopers was only a "knee britches little boy."

Col. D. C. Kelley in an eloquint and touching manner gave the Federal Side of the Fall of Fort Pillow and why they did not haul down their colors and surrender thc Fort. Showing that as they did not do so, the loss of life was much greater than it would have been.

The following comrads were reported dead since last meeting: Henry C. Troxler, Philip Dodd, James Garrett, Ed. Batts, D. C. Padgett.

On Motion the Sect was ordered to correct the number and dates of the Reunions held.

On Motion the committees on the death of comrads W. H. Matthews and Henry Pointer were granted further time as were the committees on the Death of Mrs Genl N. B. Forrest and Col John McGavock.

The committee on the Death of comrad T. J. Eaton made a report and on motion it was ordered spread on the Memorial Page which is no. 49.

On Motion of Dr. J. B. Cowan Genl Wm. H. Jackson who commanded a Division of Cavalry under Genl Forrest was placed on the Roll of Active Members which motion prevailed and Genl Jackson accepted with very appropriate remarks.

On Motion a vote of thanks was tendered Genl A. J. Coldwell for his address and Mr. John Moore for his Poem and by a unanimous vote they were made honorary Members of this Association. Also a vote of thanks to the Cumberland Park Assoc for the use of this beautiful park.

The Treasurer made a report of six and 25/100 Dollars in Treasury.

On Motion a vote of thanks was given the Ladies for the bountiful dinner served and the many kindnesses shown.

On Motion the next place of holding the Reunion was voted for, and Genl W. H. Jackson put Belle Meade his beautiful house in nomination which was unanimously carried by every body rising.

On Motion of Dr. Cowan a committee of conference was appointed composed of Genl Jackson, Col. Kelley, and Capt. Morton.

On Motion of Col Kelley ammended by Genl Jackson that every member of the Staff and Escort be requested to write all they could recollect about acts and deeds of Genl Forrest and his men and forward same to the Recording Secretary.

Letters of regret were received and read from Geo W. Adair of Atlanta, W. J. Biggs of Jackson, and D.R. Bedford of Fort Worth.

The following Resolution was offered and adopted that in the death of Capt. Montgomery Little, Lieut Joshua Holt, and the many others who were killed and who died in the service we all loved so well, are still held in dear remembrance and our sympathies are here tendered to their families.

Resolved that a page be left to their memories also to that of Maj J. P. Strange of Forrests Staff with following resolutions.

MEMORIAL ROLL

The following is a list of the deceased members of Genl Forrest's Staff and Escort

STAFF

Lieut Gen N. B. Forrest

Maj J. P. Strange

Maj C. S. Severson

Capt Henry Pointer


ESCORT

Capt Montgomery Little

Lieut Matt Cortner

Lieut Josh Holt

| | | |
|---|---|---|
| R. C. Keeble | C. C. McLemore | William Little |
| W. H. Livingston | H. C. Troxler | T. J. Eaton |
| S. W. Edens | J. M. McNabb | J. O. Martin |
| R. H. Maxwell | W. H. Mathews | Hines Miller |
| J. W. Newson | T. N. McCord | S. W. Carmack |
| Phil Dodd | F. G. Motlow | J. K. P. Neece |
| Sgt. Jake Crews | A. M. Spencer | S. J. (Pone) Green |
| W. T. K. Green | Thos. J. Brown | Sam Carrier |
| Robt Terry | Wm E. Lipscomb | D. C. Padget |
| John Wright | Alf Christopher | Pless Arnold |
| W. M. Strickland | James Warren | Capt. J. D. Scott |
| Geo. Strickland | W. H. Redman | R. H. Orman |
| Benj Duggin | Marcus Black | E. A. Roses |
| Ed Ruffin | Dick Shirlock | Wm. Thompson |
| Wm. Wood | T. H. Wood | Wm. Warner |
| Wm Dyer | P.S. Dean Orderly Sgt | Cicero Buchanan |
| E. W. Rainey | A. H. (Doc) Boone | F.M. Dance |
| John Jordan | J.R. Bivins | A. H. Hicks, Jr. |
| John Nield | Thos Butler | J. C. Cochran |
| H. C. Berry | Burl Buchanan, Colored | |

The following officers were elected for the ensuing year.

| | | |
|---|---|---|
| Gen. Wm H. Jackson | President | Nashville |
| Maj. G. V. Rambeaut | 1st Vice President | Memphis |
| Capt. J. C. Jackson | 2nd Vice President | Rover |
| W. C. Cooper | 3rd Vice President | Bellbuckle |
| Lieut G. L. Cowan | Rec. Sect. | Franklin |
| J. N. Taylor | Cor. Sect. | Lynchburg |
| Col D. C. Kelley | Chaplain | Nashville |

By invitation of Gen. W. H. Jackson, the next meeting will be held at Belle Meade, near Nashville, on the 1st Thursday in September 1895.

On Motion a committee of those composed of Jno W. Morton, Geo L. Cowan and D. C. Kelley was appointed to write up and have the minutes printed and distributed.

On Motion the President was authorized to select his own committee on arrangements.

There being no further Business the Association adjourned to meet at Belle Meade on Sept    1895.

Geo L. Cowan, Rec. Sect.

## SACRED TO THE MEMORY OF
## THOMAS J. EATON

WHEREAS IT
HAS PLEASED THE
SUPREME RULER OF THE UNIVERSE
TO REMOVE FROM OUR MIDST
OUR LATE COMRAD IN ARMS, THOMAS J.
EATON, WHO WAS BORN JUNE 1ST 1841 AND
DIED AT HIS HOME IN TULLAHOMA TENNESSEE
DECEMBER 19TH 1892. THEREFORE BE IT RESOLVED
THAT THE COMMUNITY HAS LOST A
VALUABLE CITIZEN, HIS WIFE AND CHILDREN
AN AFFECTIONATE HUSBAND AND FATHER, AND
THE ESCORT AND STAFF ASSOCIATION A GENIAL
COMPANION. RESOLVED THAT WE EXTEND TO HIS
FAMILY OUR HEART FELT SYMPATHY IN THEIR
SAD BEREAVEMENT, AND THAT A COPY OF
THESE RESOLUTIONS BE SENT TO THEM, AND BE
IT FURTHER RESOLVED THAT HIS NAME BE ENROLLED
ON THE MEMORIAL PAGE OF OUR RECORDS

J. N. TAYLOR, M. L. PARKS, E. CLARK—COMMITTEE

## Details on the 1894 Reunion

"Cumberland Driving Park" was a racetrack that occupied the location of the present-day state fairgrounds. Races were held there from 1891 until 1906 when the State Fair Association purchased the property. "Vine Hill," Morton's home, was on Franklin Pike about three miles from the 1894 city limits of Nashville. The Vine Hill Housing Development now occupies part of the Morton property, according to Dr. James Jones, public historian with the Tennessee Historical Commission. Apparently the veterans and their wives were welcomed at Vine Hill, while the public meetings were held at the racecourse. Since the reunions drew thousands of spectators wishing to hear the speeches, the grandstand would have been an appropriate place for the formal part of the meeting.

William Hicks Jackson, often called "Red" Jackson, was born in Paris, Tennessee, in 1835 and graduated from West Point in the class of 1856. He served briefly in the Confederate artillery until wounded at Belmont, Kentucky. On recovering from his wound, he became colonel of the Seventh Tennessee Cavalry and was promoted to brigadier for his role in the capture of Holly Springs, Mississippi, in December 1862. He served in the Atlanta Campaign under Wheeler and commanded the cavalry of the Army of Tennessee during Hood's invasion of Tennessee in 1864. In February 1865 he was placed in command of all Tennessee troops in Forrest's Corps. In 1868 Jackson married the daughter of William G. Harding, the owner of one of the largest plantations in middle Tennessee, Belle Meade. He became known nationally as a breeder of thoroughbred horses before his death in 1903 (Warner, 152-53).

John Trotwood Moore was born in 1858 and was indeed a child in short pants during the war years. A native of Marion, Alabama, Moore moved to Columbia, Tennessee, in 1885 and became known as a writer. His favorite subject was historical figures, but he also wrote outdoors stories and some poetry. In 1919 he became state librarian and archivist, in which post he developed a Civil War questionnaire. This was sent to 5,000 surviving Tennessee veterans and was returned by 1,650 of them. For several years Moore was coeditor with Robert L. Taylor of the *Taylor-Trotwood Magazine*

(West, 644). The poem Moorc read on this occasion was "Wearing the Gray." The second stanza says:

> Wearing the gray, wearing the gray—
> The old line marches in memory today,
> The old drums beat and the old flags wave—
> How the dead gray jackets spring up from the grave!
> They rush on with Forrest where young gods would yield!
> They sweep with Cleburne the shell-harrowed field!
> They laugh at the bolt from the batteries hurled,
> Yet weep around Lee when the last flag is furled.
> Wearing the gray o'er the foreheads of white,
> Time's banner of truce for the end of the fight;
> Wearing a gray that was worn long ago,
> With their face to the front and their front to the foe.

The *Nashville Banner* reported on September 6, 1894, that about sixty members of the Escort and Staff were still alive at that date and that about thirty-five had attended the reunion. Over one thousand other veterans and numerous visitors were also present.

## Declining Years

No information has survived regarding any meeting of the Veterans Association in 1895.

October 16th 1896
The Escort & Staff met in the commodious Carriage House at Belle Meade where Chairs for over one Hundred had been arranged, and at 10.30 oclock was called to order by the President, Genl William H. Jackson and opened with a beautiful and Pathetic Prayer by the Chaplin, Rcv D. C. Kelley.

On Motion of Lieut Geo L. Cowan the calling of the roll was dispensed with.

The minutes of the last meeting was read and approved on motion of Capt Morton. The farewell address of General Forrest was read by Dr. J. B. Cowan.

Genl Jackson read his address, which on motion of Capt Morton was ordered spread on the minutes and will be found on page ___.

On Motion, John B. McEwen a citizen of Franklin Tenn, who was a guest of the association was called on for some remarks. He spoke touchingly of Genl William G. Harding the founder of Belle

Meade, of his loyalty to the Confederate cause, and how he mustered many soldiers into the service in 1861. Mr. McEwing spoke of the bloody Battle of Franklin, and many incidents about Genl Forrest, after which an adjournment was taken for dinner. The Dinner was set on tables on one side of the Carriage House with plates for 200. It is unnessary for me to try to describe the feast there spread enough to say it was in keeping with the well known hospitality of Genl Jackson & Belle Meade.

On reassembling after Dinner Dr. D. C. Kelley was called on and spoke touchingly of the killing of the gallant C. E. Merriweather at Sacramento Ky in 1862 and of just being introduced to his sister who was present with us today. Dr. Kelley spoke of how he was the only officer now living who sat at Genl Forrests mess table the first three months of the War, and Dr. J. B. Cowan joined the Mess soon after that. He spoke feelingly of Genl Forrest at Fort Donelson and how he tried to persuaid the Council of War held there that they could carry every man out without the loss of one, and how after the council decided to surrender Fort Donelson, he took all of his Regiment out without even firing a gun. He spoke of the insight he had into manhood and what confidence the men had in him. That it did not matter what the surroundings, even they would say it was all right, "Forrest is here." He also spoke of the dread the Federals had of Forrest, and how his name was a power at any time. How after the victories of Athens Ala and Sulphur Trussell he crossed the county to Fayetteville in the face of a corps of cavalry. And of his knowledge of the general character of the country, how he divided his command and sent Genl Buford with his Wagon Trains, Artillery, and Prisoners by way of Huntsville Ala. And he would go towards Nashville with the remainder of his command. And the result was as he had anticipated. The Yankies followed him and let Genl Buford pass out beyond the river unmolested. How he anticipated the moves of the enemy, how he thought they would try to intercept him with Gunboats on the Tennessee River, and how he sent the speaker to guard against such a move, and how he found that his conjectures were true. And what insight he had to know, what the other fellow knew. He spoke of how Genl Hood had turned his army over to him and asked Genl Forrest to take it out of Tennessee for him. How Genl Forrest sent orders to Genl Hood what roads to take and what pontoons and other things to abandon. I said to him, Genl Forrest, Genl Hood will have you arrested. He is not used to being ordered by subordinates, but it made no difference with him. He ordered as he thought best and Genl Hood thanked him for it at Corinth, saying I would not have gotten out if you had not told me of the many little things to do. Old friends always spoke highly of him. I never knew him to take but two drinks of whiskey during the War, he did not use tobacco, his grait means of recuperation was sleep. When the Battle was over he was like a tiger at bay untill he got a good sleep and during that time we always kept out of his way. His horses could go farther than any others in a day. Although he swore it was his notion to turn to prayers and at his own request I always had prayers in his tent. He never cursed twice before me, and always carried his mother's Bible with him. When out of temper he would say "send for 'Old Miss'" (His Wife). Addresses were made by Dr. J. B. Cowan, E. H. Douglas, and Mr. Bell of Ky.

Dr. Cowan made a report of his visit to the reunion at Richmond, Va.

Committee to select time and place of next meeting: Kelley, Morton, & Boone.

Committee to report the death of all members of Escort & Staff either during or since the war: Cooper, Sims & Biggs.

The committee on time and place of next meeting reported that Nashville be the place and that we be the guests of Cheatham & Brown Bivouac and the time be during the Reunion of U.C.V. in June. Carried on motion of Dr. Kelley. Capt Morton and Capt Boone will be the committee of arrangements.

On Motion the following officers were elected for the ensuing year:

| | | | |
|---|---|---|---|
| W. C. Cooper | President | W.J. Biggs | 1st V.P. |
| J. O. Crump | 2nd V.P. | Geo L. Cowan | Rec Sect |
| J.W. Taylor | Corasponding Sect | Dr. D. C. Kelley | Chaplain |

On Motion the following committee was appointed to have the address of Genl W. H. Jackson published, Vis Capt Morton, Dr. Cowan & Geo L. Cowan.

On Motion of Dr. J. B. Cowan the following were elected honary members: Mrs Jno Overton, Mrs. V. L. Kirkman, Mrs M. G. Goodlet, Miss Nina Spofford, Miss White May and all the Wifes, Daughters, & Mothers of Escort & Staff.

Members of Staff Present

Maj C. W. Anderson, Dr. J. B. Cowan, Capt Jno W. Morton, Col D. C. Kelley, Maj. Genl W. H. Jackson.

Escort Present

Capt N. Boone, Lieut Geo L. Cowan, Serg W. E. Sims, Serg W. C. Cooper, Color Bearer J. O. Crump, W. J. Biggs, T. G. Cheairs, "Bud" Evans, & T. M. Adkinson.

Visitors Present

Col Briggs, Orphan Brigade Ky; Lieut E. H. Douglas, Freemans Battery; Privates Jno M. Gault & Frank Eilbeck

Citizens

Jno B. McEwan, Franklin; Jas Lipscomb, Nashville; Dr. J. B. Lindsley & Mr. Bell of Ky.

Address of Genl W. H. Jackson will be found in front of this book page YZ

Adjourned to meet at Nashville in June 1897.

Geo L. Cowan, Rec Sect    W. C. Cooper, Pres

One of the visitors at the meeting was a most distinguished Tennessean, Dr. John Berrien Lindsley. Dr. Lindsley was a Presbyterian minister, educator, and civic leader. As a minister he worked with slaves before the war and with the poor after it. He was one of the founders of the Medical Department of the University of Nashville and of Peabody Teachers College. He served as surgeon to Confederate hospitals in Nashville and, after Union occupation, as surgeon to Confederate prisoners. He edited and published the *Military Annals of Tennessee, Confederate,* was a founder of the Tennessee Historical Society, and served as the first superintendent of public schools for Nashville following the war. He also helped found Montgomery Bell Academy (West, 543). Dr. Lindsley died in 1897, the year after attending the meeting of the Veterans Association.

Caroline Meriweather Goodlett was the national president of the United Daughters of the Confederacy when the Belle Meade meeting was held. During the war she had spent large sums of money helping her Kentucky neighbor who wanted to move South to join the Confederacy and, later, helping Confederate prisoners of war. She and her husband moved to Nashville soon after the war, and Mrs. Goodlett became a charter member of the Monumental Association, which raised the money for the Confederate monument in Mount Olivet Cemetery in Nashville. She was also active in establishing the state Confederate Soldiers Home at the Hermitage (CV 2: 307).

Nina Spofford was a member of a prominent Giles County family associated with Martin College in Pulaski. Her family had been generous in its financial support of Confederate causes, including the erection of the Sam Davis Monument at the court-house in Pulaski (CV 16: 136).

Harriet Overton was the wife of Col. John Overton, Jr. The military rank was honorary, so John Overton had no military service during the Civil War. Mrs. Overton, however, was mistress of

Travelers Rest, the couple's plantation, during most of the war, since her husband had a price placed on his head by Union authorities and spent most of the war in exile. During the Battle of Nashville, Gen. John B. Hood made his headquarters at Travelers Rest for about two weeks. During that time, Forrest and members of his Staff came to the house for a conference and perhaps met Mrs. Overton, so there may have been a connection of friendship and admiration with the Staff dating to that time. Mrs. Overton was active in supporting the effort to gather Confederate dead from the battlefield around Nashville and having the bodies reinterred at Mount Olivet Cemetery in the area now known as Confederate Circle. She was also a leader in the U.D.C. and, at the time of the meeting at Belle Meade, was the first president of the Woman's Board for planning the Tennessee Centennial (Dehart).

Miss White May, a niece of Col. John Overton, had become well known during the war for her support of Confederate soldiers and her attempts to aid prisoners. She was at Travelers Rest during the Battle of Nashville, had served on the committee raising money for the Sam Davis Monument in Pulaski, and was the first vice-president of the U.D.C. for Tennessee. One Confederate officer recalled her as "a most accomplished and partiotic young lady who contributed very much to our pleasure and who won the admiration and esteem" of all she met (Dinkins, 239-40). She died in Atlanta in 1898 on the last day of the Confederate Reunion held there. The *Confederate Veteran* said of her: "She lived and died a true Confederate" (CV 1: 17, 2: 306, 6: 534).

Lt. E. H. Douglas had served in the battery that gained fame as Freeman's Battery. After Freeman's murder by the Fourth U.S. Cavalry, the battery was known as Huggin's Battery. This unit was associated with Forrest until Braxton Bragg broke up Forrest's command following the Battle of Chickamauga (Horn, 1: 131-32).

Pvt. John M. Gault had been a member of Company C, "The Rock City Guards," of the First (Field's) Tennessee Infantry (Horn, 1: 172-73). His company took its sobriquet from the fact that Nashville, in 1860, had many buildings standing on limestone foundations.

The 1896 reunion was held in conjunction with a meeting of the United Confederate Veterans, which had met on October 14 and 15. The latter organization had put on a parade down Broadway, with the Orphan Brigade as the leading unit

(*Nashville Banner*, October 15, 1896). This explains the presence of a representative of that unit at the Veterans Association meeting.

> Nashville Tennessee June 1897
> There was no meeting of the Escort and staff this year.
> Geo L. Cowan Sect

No information has survived as to why there was no meeting of the Veterans Association in 1897, but the next year the group had moved back into its home country, the area from which the men had been recruited in 1862.

> Reunion of Lieut. Genl N. B. Forrest's
> Escort and Staff
> at Bellbuckle Tenn
> Sept 1st 1898
> The Association of Genl Forests Escort & Staff met in anual session in the Hall of Webb School in Bellbuckle Tenn. this A. M. and was called order by the President W. C. Cooper. Prayer was offered by Rev. John W. Hanner. After which the welcome address was made in behalf of the Citizens by Rev Jno W. Hanner, and responded to by Dr. James B. Cowan, after which the Roll was called and the minutes of last meeting read and approved.
> W. C. Cooper and _____ was appointed a committee on the dead and made the following report towit:
> Whereas, since our last meeting death has entered our ranks and summoned to the "Last Roll Call" our beloved comrades Col. Mat C. Galloway and Maj Gilbert Vincent Rambaut of General Forrest's Staff and Capt John C. Jackson, B. F. Duggen, W. A. Woodard, and Joe Cunningham of his Escort.
> Resolved, That in the Death of Col. Galloway and Maj Rambaut this Association has lost two staunch comrads, and that we treasure their memories and extend to their surviving families the deepest sympathy of Comrads who knew and loved them well.
> Resolved, that we treasure many kind memories of Capt Jackson and B. F. Duggan, W. H. Woodard and Jo. Cunningham whose names are inseperately linked with the immortal Escort, and to their families we stretch out in deepest sympathy the hand of genuine comradship. Submitted and ordered spread on Minutes.          W. C. Cooper, Chm
> Dr. Cowan and others discussed in touching and feeling manner the beauty, grases, and bravery of all the dead and the Association ordered a memorial page set aside for them.
> *Treasurer's Report*          The Treasurer T. G. Cheairs made his

annuel report showing twenty one dollars in the treasury, with not a cent expended for the year just closed.

*Dues Remitted*     Moved and carried that the dues for the year ending Sept 1st 1898 be remitted. Dr. Cowan remarked that no institution _____

*Roll Ordered*     The Secretary was ordered to make a roll of all the officers and men to be called at our reunions and notice caller of sick.

*Honery Members*  The following old comrads were made honorary members to it. John Bennett and J. R. Jackson the latter being a son of our deceased Captain, it was also mooved and carried that the children of all members be made honary members.

*Election of Officers*  It was then mooved and carried that we now go into the election of Officers for the ensuing year, wit the following result:

| For president | L. H. Russ | Shelbyville Tenn |
|---|---|---|
| 1st V. Pres | George C. Gillespie | Petersburg Tenn |
| 2nd V. P. | Orville McKissick | Pulaski, Tenn |
| Recording | SectGeo. L. Cowan | Franklin, Tenn |
| Treasurer | T. G. Cheairs | Spring Hill, Tenn |
| Chaplain | Dr. D. C. Kelley | Columbia, Tenn |

*Next Place of Meeting*  On Motion, the following place was selected for next reunion Via Petersburg Tenn, and the time of meeting the 3rd Thursday in Sept.

*Sympathy to Capt Boone*     It was mooved and carried by a rising vote that the Corresponding Sect convey to our absent comrad Capt N Boone our sympathy and good wishes for his continued long life and happyness.

*Thanks to Citizens*     Mooved and carried by a rising vote that the thanks of this Association be extended to the good citizens of Bellbuckle for their heartfelt good wishes and cheerful hospitality and to Professor Webb for the use of school chapel.

*Allowance for Sect*     Mooved and carried that the corresponding sect be allowed two 25/100 dollars for stationary and stamps.

*Orator for Next Meeting*     On Motion, Maj Charles W. Anderson was unanimously elected to deliver our historical address at our next reunion.

*Committee*     On Motion, Geo C. Gillespie, E. E. McEwen, Geo Davieson and Jas Cummings was appointed an executive committee for the next reunion.

*Adjournment*     No further business the Association adjourned to meet at Petersburg Tenn the 3 Wednesday in September 1899.

This meeting of the Veterans Association took place at a school that even then was well known and that today is known internationally, The Webb School. "Professor" Sawney Webb was a veteran of the Ninth North Carolina Infantry and the Second North Carolina Cavalry. He had been a prisoner of war for several weeks after the end of the conflict, having been captured on the retreat to Appomattox. He had discovered his talent for teaching while recovering from a wound received during the Seven Days in 1862. Webb was famous for the discipline he demanded from his students and from himself. His biography is *The Schoolmaker,* by Laurence McMillin.

Arrangements for the Bell Buckle meeting of the Veterans Association had been made by W. C. Cooper, a resident of the village who had served as sergeant in the Escort. Cooper's tombstone in the Bell Buckle cemetery is marked with an engraved battle flag.

John Bennett was a member of Company C, Twenty-third Infantry Battalion, a unit that was raised in what is now Moore County and Bedford County. His unit had served with Forrest at Murfreesboro in the 1864 Campaign and had been a part of the fabled rear guard on the retreat to the Tennessee River (Horn, 1: 167).

Grave of Sgt. W. C. Cooper, who had arranged the meeting at Bell Buckle, Tennessee, 1898

## REUNION OF LIEUT. GENL N. B. FORREST'S
## ESCORT & STAFF AT
## PETERSBURG TENN
## THE 20TH DAY OF SEPTEMBER A. D. 1899

The Association of General Forrest's Escort and Staff met in annuel session in the Chapple of the _____ and was called to order by the President Lee H. Russ and after a prayer by Professor Minter the rutine business was taken up. The following deaths were reported via Captain Nathan Boone, Privates Hugh L.W.Boone and George Hooper. And the following committee was appointed to draft sutible resolutions to be inscribed on the memorial page. Via. Capt John W. Morton, J. N. Taylor, and T. C. Little. An adjournment was taken until 7:20 P. M. in order that all could attend a Barbeque given by the citizens. After adjournment a general hand shaking and love feast was indulged in.

The Association was called to order at 7:30 P. M. and short speeches were indulged in by many of the members.

The chairman of the Historical committee Lieut Geo L. Cowan made a strong appeal to all present to write up and forward to him all events worth recording in each ones experience, particularly the accounts of all battles and skirmishes, that they took part in.

It was mooved that we go into the selection of the next place of meeting and Pulaski Tenn was unanimously selected. And the following committee was selected for that event:

C. W. McKissack   F. C. Renfro     Geo Dismukes

Corp J. M. C. Wharton

The account of the corrasponding Secretary for Stationary and Stamps was allowed it being two 50/100 Dollars.

The Treasurer reported Fifteen dollars in the Treasury and on motion the dues for the year was remitted.

The following Officers were elected for the ensuing year:

| | |
|---|---|
| President | George C. Gillespie |
| 1st V. P. O. | W. McKissack |
| 2nd V. P. | W.A. Bailey |
| Recording Sect | Geo. L. Cowan |
| Cor Sect | J.N. Taylor |
| Treasurer | T. G. Cheairs |
| Chaplain | T. C. Little |
| Segt at Arms | F. C. Renfro |

The Ladies, the good citizens, and the School Board, by a rising vote were declared the Cream of the Earth.

On Motion, a vote of thanks was given the Executive committee especially the Chairman comrad Geo C. Gillespie for the very efficant maner in which the meeting was managed.

Nothing further coming before the Association it adjourned to meet in Pulaski in Sept. 1900.

NAMES OF THOSE PRESENT

STAFF

Capt John W. Morton     Chief of Artillery

ESCORT

1. Lieut Geo. L. Cowan
2. J. N. Taylor
3. W.A. Bailey
4. E. F. Tucker
5. J. C. Shofner
6. Geo. W. Heath
7. L. H. Russ
8. Geo. C. Gillespie
9. Geo Davidson
10. J. J. Cummings
11. A. A. McEwen
12. T. G. Cheairs
13. Felix Renfro
14. O. W. McKissack
15. Geo. W. Enocks
16. E. M. McClure
17. Geo. W. Foster
18. W. F. Buchanan

The years were taking their toll on the veterans of the Staff and Escort, as can be seen in the small number attending these latter reunions. As the group began meeting regularly in the small towns of southern-middle Tennessee where they had been recruited, the number of well-known visitors declined, as did the practice of naming honorary members. However, public support and approval of the Veterans Association remained high. The *Fayetteville Observer* estimated on September 28, 1899, that over three thousand people attended the meeting at Petersburg, far more than could fit into any building in the town. "There was not a thing transpired to mar the pleasure of the occasion," the paper said. But age would wear on the old men; the organization would not last many years into the twentieth century.

There are no minutes for the meeting scheduled for Pulaski in 1900 and no mention is made of any assembly in the *Confederate Veteran* or *Pulaski Citizen*. The next recorded meeting convened in Memphis on May 27, 1901.

The Escort and Staff met in the rooms of Capt. George Dashid on the corner of Madison and Main Street, Memphis, Tenn, and was called to order by the President George C. Gillespie.

The reading of the minutes of the last meeting was dispensed with.

The Roll being called the following members were found present:

STAFF
Maj Chas W Anderson    A.A.G.
Capt Jno W. Morton     Chf Art.
Capt Geo Dashid        I. G.
Capt Will Forrest      A. D. G.
and
Col D. C. Kelley a Brigade Commander

ESCORT
Lieut Geo L. Cowan     H. D. Lipscomb
Lieut Jno Eaton        J. C. Shofner
First Sgt M. L. Parks  R. F. McKnight
J. O. Davidson         Jack Cummins
Will McGhee            W. J. Biggs
C. H. Shurtock         Joel Reece
Geo. Foster            J. N. Taylor

The Escort being asked to join in the Procession on the next day, and the Association offering to furnish Homes, the Escort accepted the invitation and agreed to go mounted.

The account of the corrasponding Sectary for stationary and stamps, $2.25 was allowed.

On Motion, Jackson Tenn was selected as the last place of meeting.
The following officers were elected for the ensuing year:
Pres       B. A. Persons    V.P.       H. D. Lipscomb
Rec Sect   Geo. L. Cowan    Cor Sect   J. N. Taylor
Treas      T. G. Cheairs
A letter from Com L. H. Russ was read and filed.
The Association adjourned to meet at Jackson in 1902
Geo L. Cowan    Rec Sect        Geo C. Gillespie    Prs

The Veterans Association meeting for 1901 was held in connection with the reunion of the United Confederate Veterans. This was a very special occasion, one that overrode the earlier expressed decision of the Veterans Association not to meet in connection with other Confederate reunions. As a part of the 1901 UCV reunion, the Forrest Memorial Committee laid the cornerstone of the Forrest Monument, which today stands over the general's grave in Forrest Park in Memphis. It is understandable that the Escort and Staff would have made an exception to their rule in order to be present, and it is further understandable that, despite the advanced age of some of them, the old veterans wanted to visit the general's grave mounted on horseback.

The meeting of the Veterans Association took place in the law office of George Dashiel, former paymaster under Forrest.

## REUNION OF LIEUT GENL N. B. FORREST
## ESCORT AND STAFF ASSOCIATION
## OCTOBER 8TH 1902

The Escort and Staff of Genl Forrest met in Nashville Tenn on Oct 8 1902 and not at Jackson Tenn as per appointment at the meeting in Memphis in 1901 on account of meeting with the General reunion of U.C.V.

The Association was called to order by the President B. A. Persons and was opened with Prayer by Rev D. C. Kelley.

The Roll being called the following members answered:

STAFF
Maj C. W.Anderson
Capt John W. Morton
and Col D. C. Kelley

ESCORT

| | |
|---|---|
| Lieut Geo. L. Cowan | T. G. Cheairs |
| C. W. Cooper | J. O. Crump |
| Lee H. Russ | B. A. Persons |
| O. W. McKissack | F. N. Adkinson |
| Joel Reese | J. N. Taylor |
| Felix Renfro | J. J. Cummins |
| W.A. Bailey | |

The amount of $3.50 was collected for dues and turned over to the Treasurer.

The account of the Cor Sect for Stationary and Stamps $1.50 was allowed.

The following officers were elected for ensuing year:

| | | | |
|---|---|---|---|
| Pres | C. W. Anderson | V.P. | O. W. McKissack |
| Rec Sect | Geo. L. Cowan | Cor Sect | J. N. Taylor |
| Treas | T. G. Cheairs | | |

The following deaths were reported Sgt W. E. Sims, Corp. W. T. H. Wharton and J. H. C. Duff

This meeting was held in connection with a meeting of the United Confederate Veterans at the Tabernacle, now known as the Ryman Auditorium. Members of the Escort and Staff Veterans Association attended that meeting before holding their own. At the UCV meeting, the United Daughters of the Confederacy announced plans to build a dormitory at Peabody College so that descendants of Confederate soldiers would have a free place to

live while attending college to become teachers. D. C. Kelley proposed a rising vote of thanks to the ladies for this effort. That
evening the Veterans Association met at Tulane Assembly Hall,
where Kelley and John Morton were in charge of the program
(*Nashville Banner,* October 8, 1902).

The minutes of the Veterans Association end at this point.
There were several more reunions of the group, but the accounts
below of these meetings are gleaned from the pages of the
*Confederate Veteran* and local newspapers.

## A Final Victory

The year 1905 was a memorable one for the surviving members of
the Escort and Staff. After years of talk and planning, and four years
after a cornerstone had been laid, a monument to General Forrest
was erected over his grave in Memphis. According to the account in
the *Confederate Veteran,* "At 2:30 P. M. on May 16 Miss Kathleen
Bradley pulled the cord that released the veil from the magnificent
equestrian statue of her illustrious great-grandfather, Lieut. Gen.
Nathan Bedford Forrest. There was a momentary silence . . . then
wild cheer broke from hundreds of his old surviving followers
clustered around the base" (CV 13: 389). W. F. Taylor, a member of
the Escort, was the grand marshal of the parade that led the dignitaries from downtown Memphis to the park, and while numerous
speeches were made, it was fitting that a member of the Escort and
Staff Veterans Association had the last word. The benediction was
given by D. C. Kelley (*Memphis Commercial Appeal,* May 16, 1905).

The next year, the Veterans Association met in Fayetteville,
Tennessee, on September 6, 1906. The *Confederate Veteran* says of
that meeting:

Doubtless no company in the Army of Tennessee was more widely
and favorably known or did more perilous service than Forrest's
Escort. It was organized in October, 1862, ninety strong, by Capt.
Montgomery Little of Bedford County, Tenn., who was killed at
Thompson's Station, Tenn., in March, 1863, and who was a warm
personal friend of General Forrest before the war, and had been with
him after the fall of Fort Donelson. Though often depleted, this
company received many recruits, so that it numbered over one
hundred men at the surrender at Gainesville, Ala., May 10, 1865.
About thirty are still living. Those present at Fayetteville were Dr. J. B.

Cowan, Staff Chief Surgeon; Escort T. C. Little, President; W. L. Shofner, G. W. Foster, Joel Reese, O. W. McKissick, J. B. Pearson, Geo. Davidson, G. W. Enochs, H. T. Childs, E. M. McClure, E. G. Montgomery, and Col. D. C. Kelley, who commanded Forrest's Old Regiment.

The officers elected for next year are: O. W. McKissick, President; J. N. Taylor, Corresponding Secretary; G. L. Cowan, Recording Secretary; Tom Cheairs, Treasurer; T. C. Little, Chaplain. (CV 14: 441)

This was a far grander affair than the report sent to the *Confederate Veteran* would lead one to believe. For several years, the United Daughters of the Confederacy had been raising funds to place a memorial Confederate statue on Fayetteville's courthouse square. By 1906, their goal had been met, and the statue had been commissioned. The County Court deeded a plot on the court-house lawn for the statue, and a program of music, oratory, and poetry was planned to mark the unveiling. The Escort and Staff held their annual meeting in conjunction with the festivities ded-icating and unveiling the Confederate statue. The *Fayetteville Observer* reported, "There were fully three thousand people pres-ent at the unveiling of the Monument and the exercises were of a character that was gratifying in the extreme to those who were participants in the bloody drama of forty years ago. It was an object lesson of most potent influence to the young that patriot-ism is the most noble virtue which finds lodgement in the human breast and that the performance of deeds of valor on behalf of one's native land encircles the soldier with a halo of glory which will never fade, that the lapse of time will not dim." The reporter was lifted to flights of oratory that must have challenged the skill of those who spoke on the occasion.

The paper described the program as including a short speech by Mrs. J. P. Gillespie. Then:

As the clock in the tower struck eleven the cord was pulled and the drapery floated down, revealing the statue in all its beauty. The thirteen states which furnished troops for the Southern cause were represented by thirteen little girls dressed in white. In their beauty and purity they fittingly represented the justice of the Southern Cause and the purity of Southern motives. They came forward, removed their crowns of roses, and laid them at the base of the mon-ument. It was also the time and place of the meeting of the veterans of General Forrest's Escort and Staff and Colonel D.C. Kelley made a speech on their behalf. (*Fayetteville Observer,* September 13, 1906)

A dinner was served for the Veterans Association in the building on the west side of the square, which had been the Confederate headquarters. Following the meal a business meeting was held. The old veterans chose not to move far for their next reunion. George L. Cowan seems to have been the member who traveled the farthest, from Franklin to Fayetteville; most of the others were rather local. So it was decided to accept the invitation of Clara Mason, daughter of Nathan Boone, to meet in 1907 in Prospect, Tennessee, in adjacent Giles County (*Fayetteville Observer,* September 13, 1906). However, for reasons unknown, that meeting did not take place. There is no mention of a reunion in either the pages of the *Confederate Veteran* or *Pulaski Citizen.*

The next year, 1908, the Veterans Association met at Booneville, Tennessee, only a few miles east of Fayetteville. A correspondent informed the *Confederate Veteran:*

The annual reunion of Forrest's Escort [was] held at Booneville, Tennessee, which had a programme of music and recitation on Tuesday evening, with welcome address by N. R. Bonner and response by T. C. Little.

Fifteen years have elapsed since the Escort met here, and many faces were missing and several members who had entertained them then are not here no longer, among them being Capt. Nathan Boone, . H. L.W.Boone, J. H. C. Duff, B. B. Ingle, and Perry Logan. The feeble state of Dr. J. B. Cowan's health prevented his being present, and George L. Dismukes was reported sick.

The deaths reported since the last meeting were: Capt. William Forrest, Maj. Charles W. Anderson, Dr. J. N. Taylor, John W. Snell, John P. Hoffman, and Jordan Womack.

A large crowd welcomed the 'boys who wore the gray' to a lovely grove on Wednesday; and after a speech by Col. E. Shapard, of Shelbyville, a sumptuous dinner was spread.

Forrest's followers are ever welcome to Booneville.

The following officers were elected for the ensuing year: President, W. C. Buchanan; Vice President, R. C. Garrett; Recording Secretary, George L. Cowan; Secretary and Treasurer, N. F. Boone; Chaplain D. C. Kelley.

The next meeting will be at Shelbyville. (CV 16: 566)

The *Lynchburg Falcon* on September 17, 1908, reported that

members of the Veterans Association attending the reunion were:

| | |
|---|---|
| George L. Cowan | W. L. Shofner |
| Robert Reeves | A. A. McEwen |
| R. C. Garrett | B. F. Martin |
| M. L. Parks | Joel Reece |
| George W. Foster | J. C. Shofner |
| W. F. Buchanan | E. M. McClure |
| T. C. Little | E. Clark |
| W. F. Robinson | |

The *Fayetteville Observer* for the same date waxed eloquent in its description of the reunion.

Not many of the Escort and Staff are now living, the ranks are thinning out, and each reunion is sadder than the last. . . . The meeting on Tuesday evening was at the school house which could not seat all who were present to welcome the soldiers. . . . A program of music and recitations was rendered. . . . On Wednesday morning a great crowd of people from this and surrounding counties assembled with the soldiers in a beautiful grove, where a stand had been erected and seats prepared. . . . Then came the noon hour, the time for feasting, and we were glad to once more break bread with these old gray-haired boys of Gen. Forrest's Escort and Staff and we rejoice that we could give them more than bread, that beneath those trees was spared with the bread, meat, cakes, pies and more than enough. We Booneville folks are not pigs, we do not live for the mere joy of eating, but you just ask any one who was ever here at a reunion or other gathering if we don't know how to "spread on" the grounds the dinner. There was no programme in the afternoon, the time was allowed for chats and reminiscences, for many other soldiers were there, all honored, all welcome, and then when the sun light and shadow fell about us, and the first brown leaves of autumn fluttered to our fee, where sweet breezes blew and the golden-rod waved its golden head, we bade the comrades good-bye.

Col. Evander Shapard had been a second lieutenant in the Forty-first Tennessee Infantry. This unit had fought throughout the war and had been in the brigade of Otho Strahl, one of the Confederate generals killed at the Battle of Franklin (Horn, 2: 263-64). "Colonel" was Shapard's position in the United Confederate Veterans. This group did not necessarily call its officers by their actual military rank, a practice that has created vast problems for generations of genealogists.

The *Confederate Veteran* announced:

General N. B. Forrest's Escort Company will hold the annual meeting of its members in Shelbyville, Tenn., September 7, 1909. It is
understood that there are surviving about thirty members, half of
whom were at the Memphis Reunion. W. F. Buchanan of
Shelbyville, is President for this year. (CV 17: 359)

The *Shelbyville Times-Gazette* on September 16, 1909, gave a full
account of the meeting, which was held in the city auditorium
beginning at 8:00 P.M.

There was soul stirring song and speech galore for the next two
hours. Elder T. C. Little of Fayetteville . . . held his audience
spellbound as he told of running away from his home in
Shelbyville, a mere boy in his early teens, to join the Escort. . . .
Hon. Evander Shapard . . . spoke with the ease, power and eloquence of an old stager on the rostrum. We have never heard the
brilliant genius of the great Nathan Bedford Forrest more splen-
didly portrayed and ably illustrated than by this speaker.

The next morning, a business meeting was conducted and
resolutions were adopted in memory of the members of the
Veterans Association who had died during the last two years.
These included J. N. Taylor of Lynchburg and Maj. Charles W.
Anderson of Murfreesboro. A resolution of sympathy was also
adopted on behalf of Sumner A. Cunningham, whose mother
died a few weeks before the meeting. John Morton then read a
paper, and an oration by the Rev. John B. Erwin closed the formal
meeting. A dinner was then served at the courthouse, and the
reunion concluded with the singing of old war songs.

With these few words, the account of the meetings of the Veterans
Association of Forrest's Escort and Staff comes to an end. They were
indeed "a band of brothers," although not all of them were "native
to the soil." One of their most faithful members, George L. Cowan,
was an Irish immigrant. One can envision them, as they complete
their meeting at Shelbyville. In 1862, 105 enlisted men had formed
up on the south side of the public square and ridden away to war. In
1909, a handful of grizzled survivors looked one last time at the
Shelbyville square and rode away into eternity. They are all long
since gone. They will not soon be forgotten.

Pvt. Monroe Shofner

# Roster of Escort at Organization

## Shelbyville, Tennessee, October 1862

Alfred, Christopher
Allison, G. W.
Arnold, P. P.
Arnold, F. F.
Atkinson, F. M.
Auman, R. H.
Bedford, D. R.
Bivins, John R.
Bivins, J. R.
Black, B. F.
Black, Marcus
Boone, A. B.
Boone, H. L.
Brown, Thomas
Bryant, J. C.
Buchanan, R.
Buchanan, W. R.
Call, D. H.
Carpenter, M. D.
Christopher, Alf.
Clark, E.
Cochran, John C.
Cooper, W. C.
Cox, T.
Crenshaw, H. J.
Crump, J. O.
Cruse, Jacob
Dance, T. M.

Dean, T. M.
Dean, P. S.
Derryberry, H. F.
Dismukes, Geo.
Duggan, B. F.
Dyer, W. R.
Eaton, John
Eaton, J. T.
Ekin, Spencer
Enochs, M. A.
Erwin, J. B.
Floyd, F. K.
Garrett, J. S.
Garrett, R. C.
Gibson, J. W.
Girdner, J. S.
Gowan, H. C.
Green, S. J.
Green, W. T. K.
Hastings, G. D.
Hicks, Felix
Hudson, Crockett
Huffman, J.
Huffman, M. D.
Huffman, W. C.
Jackson, D. C.
Jordan, J.
Kinnard, A. C.

Lipscomb, H. D.
Little, T. C.
Long, A. J.
Long, William C.
Lucas, C. W.
McCord, W. H.
McFarland, J. S.
McKnight, R. F.
Martin, W. K.
Matthews, W. H.
Miller, W. K.
Moon, W. H.
Moore, Hise
Motlow, Felix G.
Nash, A. J.
Neal, J. J.
Newsom, J. W.
Nolan, F. C.
Padgett, D. C.
Parton, A.
Poplin, W. R.
Rainey, E. W.
Redman, W. H.
Reeves, F. M.
Russ, L. H.
Rutledge, W. A.
Ryall, J. S.
Scales, S. H.

Shelborn, J. M.
Shofner, James C.
Shofner, Monroe
Sims, William E.
Snell, J. W.
Spence, M. C.
Strickland, Wm.
Taylor, J. N.
Taylor, W. F.
Terry, Rbt. M.
Troxler, G. R.
Troxler, M. P.
Tucker, Granville
Ward, G. F.
Warren, John
Watson, W. F.
Webb, J. H.
Wharton, W. T. R.
Wood, T. H.
J.Wood, Wm.
Woodward, J. W.

# Officers

| | |
|---|---|
| Captain: | Montgomery Little |
| 1st Lieutenant: | Nathan Boone |
| 2nd Lieutenant: | Matthew Cortner |
| 3rd Lieutenant: | D. P. Dunnaway |
| 1st Sergeants: | Joseph Holt, Martin Livingston Parks |
| 2nd Sergeants: | C. A. Arnold, W. Edward Sims |
| 3rd Sergeants: | William Brown, W. A. E. Rutledge |
| 4th Sergeant: | W. W. Hasting |
| 5th Sergeants: | B. B. Ingle, William H. Matthews |
| 1st Corporals: | John Smith, H. J. Crenshaw |
| 2nd Corporals: | Alex Cortner, W. T. H. Wharton |
| 3rd Corporals: | J. P. Lorance, P. L. Richardson |
| 4th Corporals: | T. N. McCord, R. C. Keeble |

# Members of the Escort Present at the Surrender

The Escort had very high morale because they knew they were the premier soldiers in a premier combat unit, Forrest's Cavalry Corps. When men of the Escort were wounded, they usually returned to the command once their wounds healed. As the end of the war approached and Confederate units disintegrated, those determined to continue the fight were attracted to the Escort. As a result, the Escort is the only Confederate unit known to the author whose numbers were greater when they surrendered than they had been when the unit was organized. When the Escort rode out of Shelbyville, Tennessee, in October 1862, there were 105 enlisted men, as listed in Appendix A. There were 110 when the surrender took place in 1865 (Lindsley, 771). Following are the names of those who were present at the surrender.

Capt. John C. Jackson
1st Lt. Nathan Boone
2nd Lt. Matthew Cortner
2nd Lt. George L. Cowan

1st Sgt. Martin Livingston Parks
2nd Sgt. W. Edward Sims
3rd Sgt. W. A. E. Rutledge
4th Sgt. C. C. McLemore
5th Sgt. W. H. Matthews
1st Corp. H. J. Crenshaw
2nd Corp. W. T. H. Wharton
3rd Corp. P. L. Richardson
4th Corp. R. C. Keeble
Bugler W. F. Watson

| | | |
|---|---|---|
| Adair, Robert | Battes, E. | Boone, H. L. |
| Alford, Chris. | Bennett, P. P. | Bridges, J. W. |
| Anderson, N. J. | Bivins, J. H. | Buchanan, W. R. |
| Bailey, W. A. | Boone, Abner | Call, D. H. |

| | | |
|---|---|---|
| Carmack, S. W. | Gillespie, G. C. | Poplin, W. R. |
| Cheairs, T. G. | Green, W. T. K. | Priest, T. R. |
| Childs, Thomas | Holland, H. A. | Reece, Joel |
| Clark, E. C. | Hooper, G. W. | Reeves, J. K. P. |
| Clark, S. J. | Hudson, Crockett | Renfroe, F. C. G. |
| Cooper, W. C. | Jackson, D. C. | Roland, D. G. |
| Cortner, Alex | Key, A. W. | Ruffin, C. H. |
| Crenshaw, C. A. | Key, J. F. | Scales, Noah |
| Crump, J. O. | Latimer, C. T. | Scales, Sam'l Clark |
| Cunningham, Joseph | Lipscomb, H. D. | Scott, J. D. |
| Dance, T. M. | Little, T. C. | Shaffner, U. R. |
| Davidson, G. W. | Livingston, Geo. W. | Shofner, W. L. |
| Davidson, J. Q. | Livingston, W. H. | Snell, J. W. |
| Dismukes, G. R. | Lynch, E. E. | Spencer, A. M. |
| Dodd, Philip | McCord, T. N. | Spurlock, Richard |
| Dusenberry, H. P. | McEwing, A. A. | Stephens, J. K. |
| Dwiggins, G. A. | McGehee, W. T. | Stephenson, G. W. |
| Dyer, W. R. | McKissick, O. W. | Stephenson, J. W. |
| Eaton, John | McKnight, R. F. | Strickland, G. W. |
| Eaton, T. J. | McNabb, J. M. | Taylor, J. N. |
| Edens, S. W. | Martin, B. F. | Taylor, W. F. |
| Elder, Wm. D. | Martin, J. O. | Thompson, N. F. |
| Emmons, N. M. | Maxwell, R. H. | Thompson, W. A. |
| Enocks, M. A. L. | Moore, F. H. | Troop, J. R. |
| Fay, R. E. | Neece, J. R. P. | Troxler, Geo. R. |
| Felps, G. W. | Newsom, J. W. | Troxler, M. P. |
| Fletcher, J. D. | Nolan, F. C. | Tucker, E. F. |
| Floyd, R. E. B. | Oakley, E. P. | Watson, Mark G. |
| Forrest, A. | Padgett, D. C. | Whatron, W. T. R. |
| Foster, George | Pearson, A. A. | White, A. L. |
| Garnett, J. L. | Pearson, J. B. | Wood, T. H. |
| Garnett, R. C. | Person, B. A. | Woodard, W. A. |

Leander H. Ross and W. H. Moon were in Camp Chase as POWs at the surrender (CV 31: 47-48, 17: 426).

# Complete Roster of Forrest's Escort and Staff

Much of the information in this list comes from two roll books from the Carnton Plantation Archives. These roll books were found with papers belonging to George L. Cowan.

## Escort

Adair, Robert
Alfred, Christopher
Allison, G. W.
Anderson, Newton
Arnold, C. C.—discharged
Arnold, F. F.—missing, returned
Arnold, Pleasant Polk—killed at Hattiesburg, Mississippi, 7/14/64
Atkinson, F. M.—discharged
Auman, R. H.—killed at Chickamauga, 9/19/63

Bailey, W. A.
Baldridge, Robert—missing
Batts, Edward—missing
Bedford, D. R.
Bell, Richard—transferred
Bennett, Powhatan
Berry, Henry C.
Biggs, W. J.—captured
Bivins, James R.
Bivins, John R.—wounded, later killed at Shelbyville, May 1865, after the surrender
Black, B. F.
Black, Marcus—killed near Pulaski, 12/24/64
Blackmore, Tom—missing
Blackwell, C. F.—transferred
Boone, A. B.
Boone, Alfred H. -killed at Somerville, Tennessee, 12/3/63

Boone, W. H. L.
Broom, N.
Brown, Thomas J.-killed near Lynchburg, Tennessee, 12/30/64
Bridges, J. T.
Bryant, J. C.—wounded
Buchanan, Burrell
Buchanan, Cicero
Buchanan, George
Buchanan, R.
Buchanan, W. R.
Butler, Thomas—discharged, died of brain fever at Gainsboro, Alabama

Call, D. H.
Carmack, S. W.
Carmack, Samuel C.
Carpenter, M. D.—missing
Carrier, Sam
Cheairs, Thomas Gorum
Childs, H. C.—wounded
Childs, Thomas—wounded
Christopher, Alfred—discharged with dysentery, died
Clark, Elijah C.
Clark, S. J.
Cochran, John—died of dysentery at Jackson, Tennessee
Cooper, W. C.
Cortner, Alexander
Cox, Tom—missing
Crenshaw, C. A.
Crenshaw, H. J.
Crump, J. O.
Cruse, Jacob—killed at Chickamauga, 9/19/63
Cummings, James—transferred
Cunningham, Joseph

Dance, T. M.
Darnell, W. A.—deserted
Davidson, George—missing
Davidson, John Quincy
Dean, P. S.—killed at Hillsboro, Tennessee, July 1863
Dean, T. M.

Derryberry, H. F.
Dismukes, George
Dodd, Philip
Duff, H. C.—sick
Duggan, B. F.—missing
Dunnaway, D.—missing
Dusenberry, H. P.—sick
Dwiggins, George
Dyer, William R.

Eaton, John
Eaton, Thomas J.
Edens, S. W.
Ekin, Spencer
Elder, W. D.
Emmons, N. M.
Enochs, M. A.
Erwin, J. B.—missing
Evans, F. R.—missing

Faye, R. E.
Felps, G. W.
Finley, Clabe
Fletcher, Jack
Floyd, F. K.
Floyd, R. E. B.
Floyd, William—went home, returned
Forrest, A.
Foster, G. W.
Frater, G. W.

Garnett, J. L.
Garrett, James S.
Garrett, Robert Cannon
Gibson, J. W.
Gill, R. S.—flesh wound to right leg, Murfreesboro, Tennessee, 12/8/64
Gillespie, George C.—captured
Girdner, J. S.
Gowan, H. C.—missing
Green, S. J.—killed near Tuscaloosa, Alabama, April 1865

Green, W. T. K.—killed near Lynchburg, Tennessee, 12/30/64, after surrendering

Harrison, R. F.—severe wounds to right wrist and hip, Murfreesboro, Tennessee, 12/8/64
Hastings, G. D.—severe wound to ankle, missing
Heath, George
Hicks, A. H., Jr.
Hicks, Felix—killed at Hattiesburg, Mississippi, 7/14/64
Holland, H. A.
Holt, Josh—killed
Hooper, G. W.
Hopkins, J. S.—missing
Horton, W. T. H.
Hudson, Crockett
Huffman, George—transferred
Huffman, Joshua
Huffman, M. D.—captured, exchanged, and transferred
Huffman, W. C.

Ingle, Benjamin B.—discharged
Irvine, Joseph

Jackson, Davy Crockett
Jackson, F. M.
James, R. M.—transferred
Johnson, John
Jones, A.—transferred
Jordan, John—captured

Key, A. W.
Key, John
Kinnard, A. C.

Latimer, Charles
Lawrence, J. P.—wounded
Lipscomb, H. D.
Lipscomb, William E.—killed at Fouche Springs, Tennessee, 11/23/64
Little, M.—killed
Little, T. C.

Little, William—missing
Livingston, W. H.—wounded at Okolona, Mississippi, 2/21/64
Long, Albert J.—captured
Long, William C.
Lucas, C. W.
Lynch, E. E.

McBride, James—captured
McClure, E. M.—transferred
McCord, T. N.—wounded
McCord, Dr. William—transferred to infantry
McEwen, Alexander A.
McFarland, J. S.—wounded at Franklin, 3/10/63
McGhee, William
McKissick, Orville W.—wounded during Nashville Campaign, December 1864
McKnight, R. F.—captured
McLemore, C. C.—died
McNabb, J. M.
Martin, B. F.—missing, returned
Martin, J. O.
Martin, W. K.
Mash, A. J.—missing
Massey, C. S.—missing
Matthews, W. H.
Maxwell, R. H.—wounded at Okolona, Mississippi, 2/21/64
Miller, Hiran—missing
Miller, W. K.
Moon, W. H.—wounded, captured
Moore, F. Hise
Motlow, Felix Grundy—killed at Trenton, Tennessee, 12/20/62

Nash, A. J.
Neal, John J.—killed while carrying a dispatch from Forrest to Hood, November 1864
Neece, J. K. P.—missing
Newsome, James W.
Nolan, F. C.

Oakley, Bud
Orman, R. H.

Owsley, Polk—missing

Padgett, D. C. "Lim"
Parks, Will—missing
Parsons, Alexander
Partin, Al—missing
Parton, A. J.
Pearson, A. A.
Pearson, James B.
Perry, Jessy—discharged
Persons, B. A.
Poplin, William Richard
Porter, A. J.—missing
Priest, Thomas R.—wounded
Pybas, K. M.—missing

Rainey, Eley W.—wounded, missing
Redman, W. H.—wounded at Franklin, 4/10/63
Reese, Joel—transferred
Reeves, Francis Marion—missing
Reeves, J. K. P.
Reeves, Robert M.—killed
Renfroe, F. C.
Rice, Joel
Richardson, T. M.
Robinson, W. F.—killed
Roland, D. G.
Rose, E. A.—discharged
Ross, Leander H.
Ruffin, C. H.
Ruffin, Edward—deserted
Runnell, James—missing
Russ, Lee H.—captured
Rutledge, W. A.—missing
Rydall, J. S.—captured

Scales, Noah
Scales, S. H.—killed
Schurtock, C. H.
Scott, J. D.—wounded

Shaffner, U. R.
Shelborn, J. M.
Sherlock, Dick
Shofner, James. C.—killed
Shofner, R. W.
Shofner, Monroe
Shofner, W. L.
Simmons, George—missing
Sims, W. E.
Snell, J. W.
Spence, John—discharged
Spence, M. C.
Spencer, A. M.
Spurlock, Richard
Stephens, J. K.—captured
Stephenson, James White
Stevens, J. King—captured
Stevenson, "Doc"
Stevenson, George—transferred
Stevenson, Wing—transferred
Strickland, G. W.
Strickland, William—killed near Pulaski, Tennessee, 12/25/64
Summerford, William—missing

Taylor, Jasper Newton
Taylor, W. F.—wounded
Terry, George
Terry, Robert M.—discharged, died of disease in west Tennessee
Thompson, Joseph
Thompson, N. F.
Thompson, William—wounded
Troop, Jim
Troxler, George—transferred
Troxler, Henry C.
Troxler, M. P.
Tucker, E. F.—missing
Tucker, Granville—missing

Ward, G. F.
Ward, William D.

Warner, William
Warren, John—killed at Okolona, Mississippi, 2/21/64
Watson, Mack—captured
Watson, W. F.
Watson, W. F.
Webb, J. H.
Wharton, T. H.
White, Sandy—discharged
Wise, Dave—missing
Wood, T. H.—wounded
Wood, William—killed at Fouche Springs, Tennessee, 11/23/64
Woodard, H. W.
Woodard, T.
Woodard, W. A.
Woodward, J. W.
Womack, Jordan H.
Wright, John—discharged

Yowell, Will

# Officers

*Captains*
Dysart, A. A.—killed at Thompsons Station, Tennessee, 3/5/63
Jackson, John C.—wounded at Shelbyville, November 1864
Little, Montgomery—killed at Thompsons Station, Tennessee, 3/5/63

*1st Lieutenants*
Boone, Nathan
Eaton, John

*2nd Lieutenants*
Cortner, Matthew—captured
Cowan, George L.

*3rd Lieutenants*
Dunnaway, D. P.
Holt, Joshua—severely wounded at Okolona, Mississippi, 2/21/64, killed near Demopolis, Alabama, April 1865, after surrendering

*1st Sergeants*
Holt, Joseph—killed at Okolona, Mississippi, 2/21/64
Parks, Martin Livingston

*2nd Sergeants*
Arnold, C. A.
Crews, Jake
Sims, W. Edward

*3rd Sergeants*
Brown, William
Rutledge, W. A. E.
Shofner, W. L.—wounded at Okolona, MS 2/21/64

*4th Sergeants*
Arnold, C. C.
Hasting, W. W.
McLemore, C. C.

*5th Sergeants*
Ingle, Benjamin B.
Matthews, William H.—captured
Stegall, D. M.

*1st Corporals*
Crenshaw, H. J.
Russ, Lee H.
Smith, John

*2nd Corporals*
Cortner, Alex—captured
Wharton, W. T. H.

*3rd Corporals*
Lorance, J. P.
Richardson, P. L.

*4th Corporals*
Keeble, R. C.
McCord, T. N.

# Staff

Anderson, Maj. Charles W
Cheairs, Maj. Nathaniel
Cowan, Dr. J. B.
Dashiels, Capt. George
Donelson, Capt. Samuel
Galloway, Capt. M. C.
Kelley, Col. David C.
Morton, Capt. John
Pointer, Capt. Henry
Rambaut, Maj. Gilbert V.
Scott, Capt. J. D.
Strange, Maj. John P.

# Forrest in Literature

Nathan Bedford Forrest was one of the first Civil War generals to have a book published about his campaigns. Thomas Jordan and J. P. Pryor published *The Campaigns of General Nathan Bedford Forrest* in 1876. This is an essential text for anyone wanting to learn about the military career of Forrest. The book is very accurate in its description of military actions, but it does deal with events and controversies that the passage of time has made insignificant to modern readers. The major value of the book is that Forrest probably read and corrected the manuscript himself.

A Confederate veteran who served under Gen. Joseph Wheeler, John Allan Wyeth, wrote *A Life of General Nathan Bedford Forrest* in 1899. Republished in 1959, the book carried a new header above the original title, *That Devil Forrest,* and is now usually called by that name. The new title comes from a dispatch sent by Gen. William Sherman ordering his western area commander to "track down that devil." As a veteran of cavalry combat, Wyeth had an unusual appreciation of what Forrest and his men accomplished during the war. The evaluation and analysis in this book of military events show the insights of a man who has known war. In addition to the usual photographs and maps, this book contains an excellent collection of drawings made by nineteenth-century artists showing Forrest's men in action.

In 1931, Andrew Nelson Lytle published *Bedford Forrest and His Critter Company.* Lytle was a member of the famous Vanderbilt Agrarians, a group noted for its defense of traditional Southern values. The Agrarians later produced several leading fiction writers, poets, and literary critics, but Lytle was not a historian and his book reflects this. The research for the book depends heavily on secondary sources, some of them not directly related to the subject at hand. From the use of "Critter Company" in the title to the interpretation of historical facts, Lytle took a romantic view of Forrest that softened all the rough edges of the man and his career and blurred the contradictions in the general's character.

However, Lytle was a good writer and he tells the story of Forrest's life with literary grace, even while omitting the sorts of details that make Forrest come alive in other biographies.

Robert Selph Henry did a yeomanly piece of work with his 1944 *First with the Most Forrest*. Henry was a historian who wrote extensively on the War Between the States and who continued his work on Forrest with a second book, *As They Saw Forrest*. This is a collection of firsthand accounts written by people who met Forrest. As a historian who was familiar with the broader features of the war, Henry set Forrest and his achievements in their proper context.

Lonnie Maness broke an almost fifty-year silence on Forrest with the publication of his *Untutored Genius: The Military Career of Nathan Bedford Forrest* in 1990. The book maintained an older interpretation of Forrest and his career in the face of historiographical trends that had turned decidedly anti-Forrest and anti-Confederate at the time it was published. In his biography, Maness argues that, had the Confederate government heeded Forrest's advice on the proper strategy for fighting the war, the South might have won its independence.

During the 1990s, two more books about Forrest appeared. Brian Steel Wills wrote *A Battle from the Start*. Although informed by the current historiogaphical theories and biases, this 1992 publication has little new to say about Forrest. More interesting is Jack Hurst's *Nathan Bedford Forrest: A Biography* (1993). Hurst, a newspaperman, brought to his book considerable research skills, especially in news archives, and avoided falling prey to the anti-Forrest biases prevalent among academic professional historians. Hurst had a personal interest in Forrest since his ancestors include a Union soldier from Tennessee who fought against him. The most interesting part of Hurst's book is his account of Forrest's postwar life and the evolving racial attitudes of a complex man.

Richard L. Fuchs' *An Unerring Fire* is published as history but is an excellent example of politically correct bias masquerading as fact. Fuchs takes as true the atrocity stories told to the congressional investigation committee that looked into the Fort Pillow affair. This investigation was carried out during the closing days of the war, when bitterness and anti-Confederate hysteria were at their height. The congressional committee printed the atrocity stories but rejected them in reaching its conclusions. As an attorney, Fuchs should know better than to base judgments on discredited testimony.

Other historians and writers have given some brief accounts of Forrest. The general appears in all the histories of the western theater of the war. Bennett H. Young produced *Confederate Wizards of the Saddle,* which includes a chapter on Forrest, but the brevity of his treatment prevents Young, or those who followed in his footsteps, from doing more than repeating what others have said.

These books ably tell of the life and military career of Forrest, and those who wish to focus on the general, or who want additional details about his battles, are referred to these sources.

Paul Ashdown and Edward Caudill published *The Myth of Bedford Forrest* in 2005. These two men are professors of journalism and electronic media at the University of Tennessee. They provide a thumbnail sketch of the military career of Forrest but focus their attention on the process by which the man became a myth, beginning with the war years and continuing to the present. The authors are unable to refrain from expressing their anti-Forrest bias. Every event from Forrest's life that is unusual is labeled "mythic" and described in sarcastic language. Critics of Forrest are freely quoted, while his defenders are said to be representatives of outdated historiography or presenters of a biased point of view. The strength of this book is that it gives a relatively full list of the works of fiction in which Forrest and Forrest-like figures appear. The authors further allow their bias to intrude when they describe the contemporary controversies over the naming of streets and schools for Forrest. In these descriptions, those who oppose the memorializing of Forrest are quoted, but those who uphold it receive short shrift. The authors fail to recount that the controversies frequently have been resolved in favor of retaining the memorials.

As a legendary figure, Forrest has also attracted the attention of fiction writers. Some have used Forrest as a model; others seem to have drawn on him for inspiration for characters that never existed outside the imagination of the author.

In 1905, Thomas Dixon wrote *The Clansman,* a romanticized novel about the Ku Klux Klan and its role in overthrowing the Reconstruction government in North Carolina, a process that was repeated in all the Southern states by 1876. Dixon wrote at a time when a belief in Anglo-Saxon superiority was rampant throughout the western world, a time when European colonialism had dominated Africa and Asia and the United States was consolidating something of an empire in the Philippines and Puerto Rico following the 1898 war with Spain. The Supreme Court of the United States had only recently ruled that the races could be kept separate if the facilities provided were equal (Plessy vs. Ferguson). Dixon reflected the racial views of his time and made the Klan the great heroes of the book by saving the South from ruin at the hands of Negro leaders and their Northern white supporters. This novel was the basis for the 1915 motion picture *Birth of a Nation*. Because the Klan is so prominent in the novel, some literary critics have argued that the book is based on Nathan Bedford Forrest. I do not agree. Forrest does not appear in the book, and the life of the protagonist is not at all similar to that of Forrest. *The Clansman* is a work of fiction with a "hero" who existed solely in the mind of the author.

Jesse Hill Ford based his novel, *The Raider*, on Forrest although the name "Forrest" is never used. The entire book is a thinly disguised biography of Forrest with some invented conversations inserted among the facts to move the narrative along. Often Ford repeated conversations recorded in historical sources, simply placing them in the mouths of his characters.

Recently, Bob Armistead wrote *Never to Quit: The Story of Two Confederates*. In this book, the military skill of Forrest is recognized by the Confederate high command and the general is placed in command of a major Southern army, with the result that the South wins the war. A similar theme informs Harry Turtledove's *Guns of the South*, in which South Africa introduces AK-47 automatic rifles into the 1864 campaign, via a time machine. This technology makes the South victorious and Forrest becomes president of the independent Confederacy.

Robert S. Chambers' recent *The God of War* also features General Forrest. Chambers creates a fictitious officer, Lt. Henry Wylie, who rides with Forrest through the entire war. This book is well researched and uses a fictitious narrator to carry the story.

Another good novel is *Fightin' with Forrest*, by Charles Gordon Yeager, a "blood and thunder" tale with a fictitious hero who relates his battle experiences to his family back home.

Aileen W. Parks has a children's book about Forrest, *Bedford Forrest: Boy on Horseback*. The venerable Alfred Leland Crabb has numerous books about the Civil War in Tennessee, including *A Mockingbird Sang at Chickamauga*, *Supper at the Maxwell House*, *Dinner at Belmont*, and *Home to Tennessee*. Forrest appears as a character in these books but is not the major feature.

Forrest also figures in Howard Bahr's *Black Flower*, a novel set at the Battle of Franklin. In this account, Forrest appears at Carnton, the home of the McGavock family, and uses the upstairs porch as an observation post. Indeed, Forrest's command was in the vicinity of Carnton, and from the porch of the house the general could have observed his men crossing the Harpeth River to turn the flank of the Union position. Though Forrest is not the focus of the book, this is one of the best of the "cameo appearances" he makes in a number of stories, by writers from William Faulkner to O. Henry.

In 2004, Barry Barnes published *Whipping Post.* In this novel, the North and South have decided to play a football game to settle their differences. Forrest is one of the three Confederate captains for the contest.

The earliest novel that features Forrest, by name, as a major character is a little work titled *The Shadow Between His Shoulderblades,* written by Joel Chandler Harris. If anyone remembers Harris today, they remember him as the creator of the Uncle Remus stories about Brer Rabbit, Brer Fox, and Brer Bear. But Harris was a journalist who also wrote prolifically about the South and the Civil War. At one time, Harris was as well known as Mark Twain, and the two traveled and lectured together.

In *The Shadow Between His Shoulderblades,* two pro-Confederates go to Mississippi to join Forrest. One of them is over military age and the other has been discharged because of wounds, but both are looking for ways to fight the Yankees. These two men scout out a route for Forrest's raid into Memphis and comfort a young woman who has been wronged by a Tory (a Southern man who supports the Yankees). They are caught and jailed for their efforts but are rescued by Forrest when he comes charging into Murfreesboro. Forrest catches the Tory and provides summary justice at the end of a rope.

Harris is very careful about historical details in this little book. He has Forrest riding in a buggy just before the Memphis raid because of a wound to the foot, an injury Forrest actually received just weeks before the Memphis incursion. But Harris has no qualms about rearranging the dates of events to suit the flow of the story. The Memphis raid took place in the summer of 1864. The Murfreesboro raid, in which civilians were rescued from a burning jail precisely as depicted, took place in 1862.

*The Shadow Between His Shoulderblades* has long since passed out of print, but copies can be found on used-book Web sites.

# APPENDIX E

# Forrest and Race

One of the more interesting features of the career of Nathan Bedford Forrest was his relationship with Negroes. Forrest was a slave trader before the war, an occupation that even slave owners did not hold in high esteem. Although such an attitude by slave owners was illogical, Forrest saw slave trading as legal and profitable and was not much concerned with the views of the "planter aristocracy." This attention to the law and the profits, as opposed to social opinions and moral niceties, makes Forrest quite modern in his approach to business. As the owner of a large plantation, he owned a number of slaves because, like many people of his time, Forrest saw nothing wrong with slavery. The institution was of ancient usage; sanctioned, as many nineteenth-century theologians told Christians, by the Bible; and clearly was protected by the Constitution of the United States. The Dred Scott Decision of 1857 had placed slavery beyond the reach of the president or Congress by declaring that only individual states had the legal authority to end slavery.

Forrest also shared the nigh-universal belief in Anglo-Saxon superiority. This attitude, shared by Abraham Lincoln, saw Negroes as inherently inferior to white men and incapable of achieving equality. In the United States, this attitude justified the destruction of the Indian cultures, while in Europe, it became the pretext for colonizing Africa and much of Asia.

Because we today see moral problems with Forrest's actions as a slave trader and owner, we can be thankful for the changes our society has made, but we cannot reasonably apply the moral codes and values of today to the past. To attempt to do so involves one in the unhistorical practice of "presentism"—the assumption that current standards are absolutely right and all others are wrong. This sitting in judgment prevents the student of history from understanding the people of the past, since the past is condemned out of hand for not being the present. All earlier people are deemed to be wrong because they are not us.

The people of the past understood issues by the light of information and attitudes current to their day, just as we are guided by the knowledge available to us. "Presentism" would have us use our knowledge and values to judge the actions of the past, even though our knowledge and values were not accessible to the people of the past. Not only is this an illogical approach to the past, it should make us realize that we and our actions will be condemned by future historians. Assuredly our values will not be those of the future; our code of ethics will one day be "old-fashioned" and outmoded. One day a "presentist" will be asking how we could have been so stupid as to believe what we now hold as true. Our only defense will be that we walked by the light we had. And that is the defense of the people of the past.

This honest admission does not condone or advocate the continued practice of past standards of behavior, but it does lead to understanding the past rather than merely reacting to it. Unfortunately, many academicians and students do not understand this simple point. They wish to condemn people of the nineteenth century for not practicing the moral and social values of the twenty-first century. How can we say that no people before our time ever made a correct choice unless that choice reflects our current ideas? What moral arrogance! What historical ignorance!

Some may find it ironic that a belief in slavery and white superiority did not prevent Forrest, and thousands of others of that era, from forming personal relationships with people of color. Forrest certainly had a personal relationship with the most famous group of African-Americans who rendered service to the Confederacy, the teamsters who drove his wagons. In testimony before a congressional committee, Forrest said that he called these men together when the war began and offered them a proposition. "I said to forty-five colored fellows on my plantation that it was a war upon slavery, and that I was going into the army; that if they would go with me, if we got whipped they would be free anyhow, and that if we succeeded and slavery was perpetuated, if they would act faithfully with me to the end of the war, I would set them free. Eighteen months before the war closed I was satisfied that we were going to be defeated, and I gave these forty-five men, or forty-four of them, their free papers, for fear I might be killed" (Wills, 316-17).

It may be that Forrest freed some of his slaves at that point, but he was still freeing some others only days before the surrender. George Washington Cable, later to become one of the prominent writers telling stories of Creole life in Louisiana and antebellum life along the Mississippi River, was a soldier in the Thirteenth Mississippi Cavalry. While recovering from wounds, he was assigned to duty as an assistant clerk and, on April 14, 1865, found himself in Gainesville. He recalled that Forrest came to the headquarters building and asked in a loud voice for "that clerk Major Strange had told him about." Cable was soon presented with a sheet of paper and was told, "Here's the legal form for you to follow, and the niggers'll come to you one by one as you want 'em. Here, Tom! You be first." And so, the slaves came forward, one after the other, until Cable had written out manumission papers for each one, a task that consumed the working hours of three days. This event is fully described by Prof. Arlin Turner in "George W. Cable's Recollections of General Forrest," which appeared in *The Journal of Southern History* in May 1955. Cable described his experiences in letters to his mother, which are now in the library of Tulane University. The names of these freedmen seem to be lost to history.

Other African-Americans served in positions of responsibility under Forrest and exercised a degree of independence in carrying out their duties. The preparation of food for Forrest's men while they were in camp, and the disbursement of the funds necessary for this duty, rested in black hands. At least one of the enlisted men in the Escort was a Negro, so there were nights when Forrest slept guarded by a black man. The relationship that grew up between soldiers and servants, or between soldiers of different races, withstood the test of war.

Following the war, events in the North made it clear that opposition to slavery did not mean belief in racial equality. While the Thirteenth Amendment to the Constitution legally ending slavery was easily ratified by Northern states, the Fourteenth and Fifteenth amendments creating legal equality failed. So many Northern states rejected the equality amendments that it became necessary to coerce Southern states to approve them as a condition of ending military occupation and reentering the Union. It was against this background of Northern opposition to equality that Forrest publicly advocated allowing the freedmen to rise to the level of their ability. On July 5, 1875, Forrest was invited to address the Independent Order of Pole-Bearers Association in Memphis. This organization had been formed to promote the economic and civil rights of Negroes. To this audience Forrest said:

> Ladies and Gentlemen, I accept these flowers [a bouquet had just been presented him by Miss Lou Lewis, the daughter of one of the officers of the Association] as a memento of reconciliation between the white and colored races of the southern states. I accept them more particularly as it comes from a colored lady, for if there is any one on God's earth who loves the ladies I believe it is myself. I came here with the jeers of some white people, who think that I am doing wrong. I believe I can exert some influence, and do much to assist the people in strengthening fraternal relations, and shall do all in my power to elevate every man and to depress none. I want to elevate you to take positions in law office, in stores, on farms, and wherever you are capable of going. I have not said anything about politics today. I don't propose to say anything about politics. You have a right to elect whom you please; vote for the man you think best, and I think, when that is done, you and I are freemen. Do as you consider right and honest in electing men for office. I did not come here to make you a long speech, although invited to do so by you. I am not much of a speaker, and my business prevented me from preparing myself. I came to meet you as friends, and welcome you to the white people. I want you to come nearer to us. When I can serve you I will do so. We have but one flag, one country; let us stand together. We may differ in color, but not in sentiment. Many things have been said about me which are wrong, and which white and black persons here, who stood by me through the war, can contradict. Go to work, be industrious, live honestly and act truly, and when you are oppressed I'll come to your relief. I thank you, ladies and gentlemen, for this opportunity you have afforded me to be with you, and to assure you that I am with you in heart and in hand. (Forrest Historical Society Web Site)

In the mind of Forrest, according to his wartime experience and the evidence of peacetime accomplishments, a black person was not his brother but he was a man. This thinking was in advance of many opinions, North and South. This attitude was present in the ranks of the Escort and Staff as well. Daily life in the antebellum South was spent in the presence of those of another race. The absence of privacy in camp and on campaign increased the degree of intimacy in which the two races existed. While there was never any question that the white men were dominant, there grew up a bond among these men who shared the same hardships; who ate, literally, out of the same pot. This bond accounts for the welcome that black veterans of all ranks and categories found at the reunions, even to the extent of placing these black men on the official program and of electing them to office. Some people will see in this degree of acceptance nothing more than paternalism. This is, however, superior to antagonism, and these were men of the nineteenth century. We have no reason to expect them to share the views of post-civil rights movement America.

African-Americans served under the command of Forrest in a variety of capacities. The names of five of them are found in Confederate pension application records. Polk Pleasant Arnold was born in Shelbyville, Tennessee, in 1844. He joined the Confederate army in 1863 and served as a private in the Escort under the command of Capt. J. C. Jackson in the platoon of Lt. Nathan Boone. Arnold was killed at the Battle of Harrisburg, Mississippi, on July 17, 1864. His widow, Caldonia Arnold, received a Confederate pension for the service of her husband.

Ben Davis was born March 4, 1836, in Fayette, Tennessee. Davis applied for a Confederate pension on July 12, 1921. He claimed to have been a teamster with Forrest and was present at Gainesville.

Jones Greer was born in Lincoln County, Tennessee, in 1844. He served as a servant for Lt. George Cowan of the Escort. Greer lived in Marshall County, Tennessee, after the war and owned ten acres of land.

Preston Roberts enlisted in 1861 and served as head of the mess for the cavalry when it was in camp. Roberts was in charge of all funds to purchase the food that was not provided by the commissary, and he commanded seventy-five cooks. He was awarded the Southern Cross of Honor by the United Daughters of the Confederacy after the war.

Nim Wilkes was born in Maury County, Tennessee. Wilkes was a teamster but did not join Forrest until the spring of 1863. In August 1915 he applied for a Confederate pension from his home in Crestview, Tennessee.

# APPENDIX F

# George L. Cowan's History of the Escort

This short history was found at Carnton Plantation with papers belonging to George L. Cowan. It was written in a small notebook in Cowan's hand.

## History of Lt. Genl. N. B. Forrest's Escort

After the battle of Shiloh, Miss. Col. N. B. Forrest being promoted to Brigadier General and placed in command of all the cavalry around Chattanooga, Tenn., found it necessary to have a body of well mounted & disciplined men to act as escort so as to enable him to execute with dispatch and rapidity the plans for his future movements. To raise and equip such a company would take a man of no ordinary ability and capacity as a disciplinarian, and for this reason he selected Capt. Montgomery Little, one of the bravest of his staff officers and a life long friend. Capt. Little, after accepting the Commission entered Medina, Tenn. And came to his home at Shelbyville, Bedford Co. and also the home County of Genl Forrest. Shelbyville was at that time occupied (September, 1862) by a small detachment of Federals, and Captain Little had to act in secret and very quietly, but soon succeeded in organizing a company of about 85 men. A little incident occurred just at this time that will show to some extent what kind of material the company was to be composed of. Nathan Boon, a farmer of Lincoln Co., who in after years became one of the bravest and most dashing officers in Forrest's command, hearing of the smallness of the garrison at Shelbyville, collected five of the young men of his neighborhood and with that recklessness and dash for which he was afterwards noted, dashed in on the garrison and dispersed it before they knew how small a force he had.

Shelbyville was one of the largest distributing points for the garrisons around, and was well stocked with Commissary & Q.M. stores. So Mr. Boone, finding it impossible to carry the stores off with him, loaded two six-mule wagons with tents and camp equipment, and after destroying all the stores—all he could without firing the town—succeeded in making his way back to Lincoln Co. with his trophies.

It is needless to say that Capt. Little soon got Mr. Boone to enlist with him, and at the organization of the company, Mr. Boone was elected First Lieut., and afterwards, when Capt. Little was killed, succeeded him to the Captaincy.

The company was organized in the last days of September, 1862, and as they were mostly sons of the best citizens of Bedford and adjoining counties, and were able to mount and equip themselves, they went into the service the best armed and equipped body of men that ever entered the Confederate service. Each man had a fine horse rigged with a double-barrel shot-gun, and clothes enough for a regiment.

The company was organized by the election of Montgomery Little, Capt.; N. Boone, 1st Lieut; Mat Cortner 2nd Lieut; and Dan'l Dunnaway as 3rd Lieut. Joshua Hold was the first orderly sergeant.

The first days march was from Shelbyville towards Murfreesboro, and our first nights' camp was at Ransom's Spring, about 12 miles from Shelbyville. Early the next morning, the camp was aroused before day by the noise of firing in the direction of Murfreesboro, and soon the company was on the march towards Murfreesboro. We soon met stragglers who informed us of the fight at Laverne. We pressed on to Murfreesboro where we met Genl. Forrest for the first time. Capt. Little soon reported to the Genl. and was ordered to bring his company up for him to look at. At casting his eagle eye down the line, he exclaimed, "What a fine body of men, Capt. Have you any more where they come from?" Capt. Little, proud of his men, said, "No, Genl., they can't be found that will equal my boys," and in after years the proud name they made justified the assertion of their noble Capt., for the fame they won was only equaled by the fame won by their noble Genl. The service rendered Genl. Forrest by his escort in gathering up the scattered forces around Laverne and Murfreesboro proved that they could be trusted in any emergency.

## Attack on Nashville, Tennessee

In this attack, so well planned but so unfortunately nipped in the bud by orders from Genl. Bragg, Forrest's Escort saw their first service. When Genl. Forest formed his lines of battle near the

Hermitage, he sent Capt. Little with his escort down the Murfreesboro and Nashville Pike in the direction of Nashville to drive in the pickets, and reconnoiter the position of the enemy. They met with no opposition until within three miles of the city, when, at the first toll gate, they found the enemy's pickets, which they charged and dispersed with only the loss of two men wounded. Capt. Little, finding the enemy in force not far from the tollgate, reported the fact to Genl. Forrest, when he was relieved by some of the cavalry.

In the several little engagements of that day, the escort behaved so well that Genl. Forest was satisfied that he had a company he could rely on on all occasions.

The escort went into camps at Maury's Springs in the suburbs of Murfreesboro and remained there doing courier duty for Genl Forrest until he moved his command to Columbia to make preparation for his famous raid through West Tenn. They were with him on that entire raid and did good service at Lexington, when Genl. Forrest first met the enemy, and they led the advance on that successful flank movement on the enemy's position which secured such a rapid and successful victory. They also united with Capt. Gurley in the successful charge on Col. Ingersoll and his batteries and were the first to reach the guns of the enemy, and as this might be said to be the first real fight they were in, they behaved like old veterans, and you might say now, for themselves, in the first battle, honors that they never let fade until the last gun had roared and the last battle cry had died in the death of an infant Confederacy.

From Lexington the escort moved with Genl. Forrest to Jackson and on to Trenton, where Forrest had occasion to again try the mettle of a company he in after years was proud of. On the 20th of December, 1862, on reaching the vicinity of Trenton, Genl. Forrest ordered them to charge the town, which they did with that dash peculiar only to themselves, and they soon drove the enemy—some 400 men—through the streets into their breastworks of cotton bales and hogsheads of tobacco around the Depot House, on which they advanced to within 50 yards., when the fire from the enemy became so warm that they fell back behind a large frame house and dismounted, not more when the enemy's reinforcements came up, and Forrest's command was compelled to retire they covered the retreat with their usual dash and hardihood.

# APPENDIX G
# Abbreviations Used in Citations

Full citations may be found in the bibliography.

BCHQ: *Bedford County Historical Quarterly*
CV: *Confederate Veteran* magazine
MCHQ: *Marshall County Historical Quarterly*
OR: *Official Records of the War of the Rebellion*

# Bibliography

Bearss, Edwin C. *Forrest at Brice's Cross Roads*. Dayton, Ohio: Morningside, 1994.

*Bedford County (Tennessee) Historical Quarterly*, 1981-88.

Bradley, Michael R. *Tullahoma: The 1863 Campaign for the Control of Middle Tennessee*. Shippensburg, Pa.: Burd Street, 2000.

———. *With Blood and Fire: Life Behind Union Lines in Middle Tennessee, 1863-65*. Shippensburg, Pa.: Burd Street, 2003.

Burton, Annie Cooper. Annie Cooper Burton Collection of Papers. Author's Collection.

*Confederate Pension Records*. 3 vols. Nashville: Tennessee State Historical Society, 1886.

Cowan, George Limrick. "History of Lt. Genl. N. B. Forrest's Escort." Author's Collection.

Cunningham, Sumner A., ed. *Confederate Veteran*. 40 vols. 1893-1932.

Dehart, Rob. Conversation with author, Travelers Rest, Tenn., April 2, 2004.

Dinkins, James. *1861-1865, Personal Recollections and Experiences in the Confederate Army*. Dayton, Ohio: Press of Morningside Bookshop, 1975.

Dyer, Gustavus W., and John Trotwood Moore. *The Tennessee Civil War Veterans Questionnaires*. 5 vols. Easley, S.C.: Southern Historical, 1985.

Dyer, William R. Diary. Civil War Collection. Tennessee State Library and Archives.

*Fayetteville Observer*, September 14, 1886; October 3, 1906.

Forrest Historical Society Web site, www.Tennessee_SCV.org/ ForrestHistSociety.

Henry, Robert Selph. *First with the Most Forrest*. Jackson, Tenn.: McCowan-Mercer, 1969.

Hill-Freeman Camp, SCV. "The Battle of Trenton." Author's Collection.

Horn, Stanley. *Tennesseans in the Civil War*. 2 vols. Nashville: Civil War Centennial Commission, 1964.

Hughes, Nathaniel Cheairs, Jr. *Brigidier General Tyree H. Bell, C.S.A.: Forrest's Fighting Lieutenant.* Knoxville: The University of Tennessee Press, 2004.

———. *I'll Sting If I Can: The Life and Prison Papers of Major N. F. Cheairs, C.S.A.* Signal Mountain, Tenn.: Mountain, 1998.

Hurst, Jack. *Nathan Bedford Forrest: A Biography.* New York: Alfred A. Knopf, 1993.

Jackson Family Papers. Dick Poplin Collection. Shelbyville, Tenn.

Johnson, Robert Underwood, and Clarence C. Buel, eds. *Battles and Leaders of the Civil War.* 4 vols. New York: Castle, 1956.

Jordan, Thomas, and J. P. Pryor. *The Campaigns of General Nathan Bedford Forrest and of Forrest's Cavalry.* 1868. Reprint, New York: Da Capo, 1996.

Kelley, David C. "Nathan Bedford Forrest." *The Methodist Review* (Nashville) 26 (March-April 1900).

Kennerley, Dan. *Forrest at Parker's Crossroads: The Dawn of Lightning War.* 7th ed. Richmond, Tex.: Parker's Crossroads, 2001.

Lindsley, John Berrien. *The Military Annals of Tennessee.* 2 vols. 1886. Reprint, Wilmington, N.C.: Broadfoot, 1995.

Lytle, Andrew Nelson. *Bedford Forrest and His Critter Company.* 1931. Reprint, Nashville: J. S. Sanders, 1992.

McBride, Robert M., and Dan M. Robinson. *Biographical Directory of the General Assembly.* 3 vols. Nashville: Tennessee State Library and Archives & the Tennessee Historical Commission, 1979.

McCullough, Rob. Letter to author, May 16, 2001.

Maness, Lonnie E. *An Untutored Genius: The Military Career of General Nathan Bedford Forrest.* Oxford, Miss.: Guild Bindery, 1990.

*Marshall County (Tennessee) Historical Quarterly,* 2001-4.

*Memphis Commercial Appeal,* 1863-65.

Morton, John Watson. *The Artillery of Nathan Bedford Forrest's Cavalry.* Marietta, Ga.: R. Bemis, 1995.

———. "Fighting at Brices Crossroads." In *The New Annals of the Civil War,* edited by Peter Cozzens and Robert Il Girardi. Mechanicsburg, Pa.: Stackpole, 2004.

*Nashville Banner,* 1863-65.

*Official Records of the War of the Rebellion.* 119 vols. Washington, D.C.: United States War Department, 1899.

Ryall, Johnston S. "Letters of Johnston S. Ryall." Author's Collection.

Speer, William S. *Sketches of Prominent Tennesseeans.* Nashville: Southern Historical, 1978.

Tippah County (Mississippi) Historical County Papers. Tippah County Public Library, Ripley, Miss.

Warner, Ezra. *Generals in Gray: Lives of Confederate Commanders.* Baton Rouge: Louisiana State University Press, 1959.

Watt, Martha. Letter to author, June 4, 2002.

West, Carroll Van, ed. *The Tennessee Encyclopedia of History and Culture.* Nashville: Rutledge Hill, 1998.

Willett, Robert L. *The Lightning Mule Brigade: Abel Streight's 1863 Raid into Alabama.* Carmel, Ind.: Guild, 1999.

Wills, Brian Steele. *A Battle from the Start: The Life of Nathan Bedford Forrest.* New York: HarperCollins, 1992.

Wyeth, John Allan. *That Devil Forrest: A Life of General Nathan Bedford Forrest.* 1899. Reprint, Baton Rouge: Louisiana State University Press, 1959.

# Index

Adair, A. D., 140, 168
Adair, Geo W., 173
Adimson, F. M., 162
Adkinson, F. M., 144, 148-49, 166-67
Adkinson, F. N., 172, 188
Adkinson, M. M., 148
Adkinson, T. M., 179
Anderson, C. W., 34, 65, 70-71, 76, 84, 94, 96, 109, 112, 114-19, 122, 133, 138-40, 149, 151-52, 154-55, 157-61, 164, 168-69, 172, 179, 183, 187-88, 191, 193
Arnold, C. C., 140
Arnold, Caldonia, 48
Arnold, Frank F., 140, 144, 149
Arnold, Pleasant, 117, 174
Aydelott, J. G., 161

Bailey, W. A., 142, 144, 149, 155, 164, 168, 170, 172, 185-86, 188
Barteau, C. R., 92
Bate, William B., 130
Batts, Ed., 173
Baxter, Nat, Jr., 57
Bedford, D. R., 48, 140, 173
Bell, Mr., 179
Bell, Tyree H., 113, 115
Bell's Brigade, 92, 100, 112
Bennett, Evand, 143
Bennett, John, 183-84

Berry, Henry C., 151, 174
Bidford, D. R., 168
Biffle, J. B., 51
Biffle's Ninth Tennessee, 71
Biggs, W. J., 143, 168, 173, 179, 187
Bird, Henry, 75
Bivins, J. R., 174
Black, Marcus, 48, 174
Blackwell, C. F., 170
Blackwell, O. F., 140
Blakemore, R. M. ("Dick"), 143-44
Blanton, W. L., 157
Bloodgood, E., 70
Bobo, Mary, 153
Bonner, N. R., 191
Boone, A. H. ("Doc"), 174
Boone, Daniel, 44
Boone, Hugh L. W., 49, 140, 142, 144, 149, 152, 154-55, 157, 159, 164, 166-69, 172, 185, 191
Boone, Nathan, 34, 43-44, 46, 69, 122, 132-33, 139-40, 142-44, 148-50, 152, 155, 157-59, 162, 167, 169, 171, 179, 183, 185, 191
Boone, Sam, 87
Booth, Lionel, 98, 107
Bradford, William F., 98, 107
Bradley, Kathleen, 189
Bragg, Braxton, 26, 29-30, 35,

37, 39, 63-64, 66, 73, 81-82, 84-86, 181

Brand, W. H., 42, 116

Breckenridge, John, 79

Brewer, Theodore F., 97

Briggs, Colonel, 179

Bright, John M., 156

Brown, John Calvin, 165

Brown, Thomas J., 49, 174

Bryant, John, 60, 170

Buchanan, Burrell, 158-59, 161-62, 174

Buchanan, Cicero, 174

Buchanan, W. C., 191

Buchanan, W. F., 49, 186, 192-93

Buckner, J. D., 144, 161

Buell, Don Carlos, 25, 44, 47

Buford, General, 113, 117, 130

Bull Pups, 39-40, 120

Burch, Jno C., 140

Butler, Thos, 174

Cahill, Frank P., 140

Campbell, Alexander William, 148

Campbell, W., 119

Carmack, Edward W., 42

Carmack, George C., 169, 171

Carmack, S. W., 151, 153-54, 158-60, 162, 164, 166, 169, 171, 174

Carnes, W. W., 86

Carr, Shannon, 75

Carrier, Sam, 174

Carroll, Charles, 58

Chalmers, General, 99-100, 104, 109, 123

Chalmers' Brigade, 92

Cheairs, Nathaniel, 164-66

Cheairs, Thomas Gorum, 50,

142-44, 149, 159, 164, 166-167, 169, 172, 179, 182-83, 185-88, 190

Cheatham, Benjamin Franklin, 40

Chick, Mr., 154

Childs, H. C., 170

Childs, H. T., 190

Christopher, Alf, 174

Clark, E., 144, 149, 159, 169-70, 192

Coburn, John, 67

Cochran, J. C., 174

Coldwell, A. J., 173

Cook, V. Y., 52

Cooper, C. W., 188

Cooper, W. C., 140, 145, 148, 151, 172, 175, 179, 182, 184

Cortner, Matthew, 43-44, 140, 142, 144, 149, 154, 161, 174

Cowan, George Limrick, 44-45, 81, 88, 90, 111-12, 124, 133, 139-40, 143, 145, 149-52, 154, 160-70, 172, 175, 177, 179, 182-83, 185-93

Cowan, Hannah, 46

Cowan, James B., 37, 54-55, 83-84, 93, 115-17, 139-40, 142-44, 146-49, 152, 154-55, 157-59, 161-62, 164, 166-69, 172, 177, 179, 182, 189, 191

Cowan, Mrs. James B., 148, 164

Cox, Nicholas Nichols, 51, 55, 60

Crenshaw, J. H., 46

Crews, Jake, 174

Crittenden, Thomas T., 27

Crump, J. O., 46, 154, 161, 166-69, 172, 179, 188

Cummings, James J. ("Jack"), 142, 166-67, 169, 187-88

Cunningham, Joseph K., 144, 149, 182
Cunningham, Sumner A., 193

Dance, F. M., 174
Dashiel, George, 37, 172, 186-88
Davidson, Geo, 169, 186, 190
Davidson, J. O., 187
Davieson, Geo, 183
Davis, Bill, 49
Davis, Jefferson, 149
Dibrell, George Gibbs, 51, 148-49
Dinkins, James, 118, 123
Dismukes, George L., 185, 191
Dodd, Philip, 173-74
Dodge, Grenville, 73
Donalson, Samuel, 38, 115-16, 139-40, 151, 154, 164
Donelson, Daniel, 38
Doughty, Capt, 152
Douglas, E. H., 164-65, 179, 181
Duff, J. H. C., 142, 149, 166-67, 170, 172, 188, 191
Duggin, Benj, 174, 182
Dunaway, Daniel P., 44, 46
Dunham, C. T., 57
Dunnington, Frank C., 42
Dusenberry, H. F., 140, 166-67
Dusenberry, H. P., 172
Dwiggins, H. C., 90
Dwiggins, R. S., 90
Dyer, William R., 87, 174
Dysart, A. A., 68

Earle, S. G., 69
Eaton, Jack, 46, 105
Eaton, John, 34, 44, 46, 140, 142-44, 148-49, 151, 160, 162, 164, 166, 187
Eaton, Thomas Jackson, 46, 140, 144, 149, 169, 173-75
Edens, S. W., 140, 174
Eilbeck, Frank, 179
Enochs, G. W., 169, 186, 190
Enochs, M. A. L., 47, 140, 169
Erwin, John B., 48, 193
Evans, F. R. ("Bud"), 140, 149, 172, 179
Evans, T.R., 144

Fay, R. E., 144, 169
Felps, Geo W., 140, 144, 170
Ferguson, W. T., 105, 169
Floyd, John, 25
Forrest, Jeffrey, 56, 93
Forrest, Jesse, 141, 143-44
Forrest, Mrs. Nathan Bedford, 38, 84, 139, 142, 169, 173
Forrest, Nathan Bedford, 139, 174
Forrest, William M., 38, 68, 75, 99, 134, 187, 191
Foster, George W., 155-56, 186-87, 190, 192
Freeman, Samuel, 36, 38-39, 52, 57, 67, 86, 133
Fry, Jacob, 55
Fry, R. E., 149

Galloway, Lt. Aide-de-Camp, 115-116
Galloway, Matthew C., 99, 122, 169, 182
Galloway, Robert, 109
Galloway, William, 109
Garrett, James, 173
Garrett, Robert Cannon, 47, 191-92
Gartrell, Henry, 111

Gault, John M., 179, 181
Gentry, Wat, 164-65
Gillespie, George C., 149,155, 158-59, 161, 166-69, 183, 185-86
Gillespie, Mrs. J. P., 190
Gillespie, T. C., 152
Goodlett, Caroline Meriweather, 179-80
Goss, George, 93
Gould, A. W., 74, 79
Grady, Henry W., 111
Green, S. J. ("Pone"), 174
Green, W. T., 49
Green, W. T. K., 174
Greer, Jones, 46
Gurley, Frank B., 52-53

Hanner, John W., 182
Hamner, Mary A., 133
Harding, William G., 176-77
Harris, G. W. D., 97
Harris, Isham, 36-37, 133
Harris, J. R., 67
Harris, Joel Chandler, 111
Harris, Robert, 144
Harrison, James C., 53
Harton, John W., 143-44, 148
Hastings, Geo., 140
Hawkins, Isaac R., 53
Hayes, Rutherford B., 138
Heath, George W., 169, 186
Helm, Mrs. Ben Hardin, 34
Hicks, Felix, 117
Hicks, Felix, Jr., 174
Hill, Charles S., 40
Hill, D. H., 84
Hoffman, John P., 191
Holt, John, 143
Holt, Joshua, 143, 174
Hood, John Bell, 124

Hooper, George W., 166-67, 185
Horton, J. W., 149
Horton, W. T. H., 162
Hudson, Crockett, 50
Huffman, Joshua, 140
Hughes, Nathaniel C., Jr., 98
Humphreys, Annic Payne, 171
Hurst, Fielding, 25, 94, 96, 109
Hunter, J. N., 62

Ingersol, Robert, 52-54
Ingle, B. B., 140, 142, 144, 148-50, 155, 159, 166-69, 191
Irvine, Joseph B., 160-61

Jackson, Davy Crocket, 149
Jackson, J. R., 183
Jackson, John C., 44, 47, 61, 69, 110-11, 113, 115, 140, 142-44, 149, 152, 154, 166-67, 172, 175, 182
Jackson, William Hicks, 173, 175-77, 179
Johnson, Andrew, 35
Johnson, T. W. H., 143
Johnston, Albert Sidney, 25, 34
Johnston, John, 152
Johnston, Joseph E., 165
Jordan, John, 174

Keeble, Richard C., 150, 174
Kelley, David C., 24, 40, 42, 109, 143, 147-50, 158, 160, 169, 171-72, 175, 177, 179, 183, 186-91
Key, A. W., 154
King, Henry R., 76
Kirkman, Mrs. V. L., 179
Kyle, R. B., 79

Lamar, L. Q. C., 38

Lee, S. D., 86, 109, 116-17
Lindsley, John Berrien, 180
Lipscomb, H. C., 164
Lipscomb, H. D., 154, 168, 187
Lipscomb, Henry, 46
Lipscomb, Jas, 180
Lipscomb, Thomas, 152, 154
Lipscomb, William E., 126, 154, 174
Little, Montgomery, 42-44, 48, 51, 61, 68-69, 174, 189
Little, Thomas Cheatham, 148-49, 154-55, 168-70, 185, 190-92
Little, William, 174
Livingston, W. H., 174
Logan, Perry, 191
Long, J. B., 93
Lyon, Hylan, 111, 123

McClain, W. E., 127
McClure, E. M., 169, 186, 190, 192
McCord, Thomas N., 144, 148-49, 154, 174
McCulloch, Robert A., 92
McEwan, Jno B., 180
McEwen, A. A., 156, 159, 186, 192
McEwen, E. E., 183
McEwen, John B., 177
McFarland, J. S., 140
McFarland, J. T., 143
McGavock, Hattie, 46
McGavock, John, 46, 164-65, 168, 173
McGhee, Will, 187
McGregor, Andrew, 121
McKissack, Orville W., 155, 164, 166-67, 183, 185-86, 188, 190

McKnight, R. F., 187
McLemore, C. C., 174
McLemore, W. S., 144
McNabb, J. M., 174
McNairy, Frank, 65
Mann, John G., 40
Marks, Albert S., 140-41, 156
Marshall, James, 107
Martin, B. F., 169, 192
Martin, J. O., 174
Massey, C. S., 140
Mastin, Charles J., 79
Matthews, William H., 140, 143 166, 173-74
Maxwell, R. H., 174
Merriweather, C. E., 178
Metcalf, J. M., 59
Miller, Hines, 174
Milroy, Robert, 130
Mitchell, Ormsby, 81
Montgomery, E. G., 190
Moore, John Trotwood, 172, 176
Morton, John W., 21, 39-40, 52, 57, 67, 82, 115-16, 119, 124, 130, 138, 145, 152, 154, 157-60, 164, 166-69, 171, 172, 177, 179, 185-89, 193
Morton's Battery, 54-55, 57, 74, 92, 112, 123
Motlow, Felix Grundy, 55, 174

Neece, Hyraim, 169
Neece, J. K. P., 174
Newly, R. P., 60
Newsom, James W., 142, 149, 152, 166, 174
Nield, John, 174
Noblett, B. E., 168
Northrupp, Lucius, 64

Orman, R. H., 174

Orphan Brigade, 181
Otey, James, 38
Otey, Mercer, 38, 109, 116
Overton, Harriet, 179-80
Overton, John, 179

Padget, D. C., 166-67, 169, 173-74
Padget, Lim, 164
Palmer, Joseph B., 163
Parks, M. S., 140
Parks, Martin Livingston., 47, 142, 144, 149, 157, 159, 166-67, 169-70, 172, 187, 192
Pearson, J. B., 190
Pearson, James, 156, 159
Peck, W. H., 76
Persons, B. A., 187-88
Piper, Sam, 55
Pitman, R. W., 122
Pointer, Henry, 77, 166, 173-74
Polk, Leonidas, 38, 80
Price, Sterling, 42
Priest, Thomas R.,46, 166-67, 169, 172
Prince, Edward, 87
Pybas, K. M., 140

Rainey, E. W., 140, 174
Rambaut, Gilbert Vincent, 36, 56, 122, 140, 145, 172, 174-75, 182
Redman, W. H., 174
Reece, Joel, 158, 187-88, 190, 192
Reed, Wiley, 108
Reeves, F. M., 140
Reeves, Robert, 192
Renfro, Felix C., 185-86, 188
Rice, T. W., 112

Richardson, R. V., 87
Robinson, W. F., 192
Roddey, Philip D., 73, 120, 131
Roosevelt, Theodore, 49
Rosecrans, William S., 63, 80-81
Roses, E. A., 174
Rounds, Oliver Cromwell, 28
Rousseau, Lovell, 130
Rucker, E. W., 123, 127
Ruffin, Ed, 174
Ruse, Joel, 170
Russ, C. H., 150
Russ, Lee H., 50, 109, 140, 142, 145-46, 148-49, 151, 169, 172, 183, 185-88
Russell, A. A., 51, 53
Ryall, Johnston S., 43, 60, 91
Ryan, Abram, 153

Salmon, Ezekiel Young, 151, 153
Salmon, Nannie, 152
Sansom, Emma, 77
Scales, S. H., 172
Scott, J. D., 174
Second Georgia Cavalry, 27
Second Kentucky Cavalry, 86
Second Tennessee, 112
Seventh Tennessee, 115
Severson, C. S., 36, 114, 174
Shapard, Evander, 191-92
Sherman, William, 91
Shirlock, Dick, 174
Shofner, H. L. W., 151
Shofner, J. C., 169, 186-87, 192
Shofner, R. W., 140
Shofner, W. L., 140, 142, 144, 148-49, 151, 155-57, 159, 166-67, 169-70, 190, 192

Shofner, W. R., 144, 149
Shurtock, C. H., 187
Simmons, Geo., 143
Sims, M. B., 144
Sims, W. Edward, 140, 142-44, 149, 151, 169-70, 179, 188
Smart, H. T., 144
Smith, A. J., 116
Smith, Baxter, 161-62
Smith, Green Clay, 71
Smith, Sooy, 91, 94
Snell, John W., 191
Sparks, Jesse, 161-62
Spencer, A. M., 174
Spofford, Nina, 179-80
Starnes, James W., 51, 56, 70, 144
Starr, Matthew, 118
Stegall, D. M., 68
Story, Tom, 60
Strange, John P., 36, 42, 55-56, 60, 88, 99, 119, 122, 125-26, 130, 152, 174
Street, Solomon, 109
Streight, Abel, 73-74, 78, 111, 119
Strickland, Geo., 174
Strickland, W. M., 174
Strickland, W. W., 47
Sturgis, Samuel D., 110

Tate, Thomas T., 94
Taylor, J. A., 144
Taylor, J. W., 179
Taylor, James D., 132
Taylor, Jasper Newton, 140, 142, 144, 148-50, 153, 155-56, 158, 160-62, 164, 169-70, 172, 175, 185-88, 190-91
Taylor, Robert L., 176

Taylor, W. F., 189
Taylor, W. T., 170
Taylor, William Ford, 153
Tenth Tennessee, 70-71
Terry, Robert, 46, 174
Terry's Texas Rangers, 26, 162
Third Arkansas, 69
Third Tennessee Cavalry, 23
Thompson, Alice, 69
Thompson, Wm., 174
Tillman, James D., 158, 160
Tolley, W. P., 140, 142
Travis, James M., 143-44, 148-49
Troxler, Henry C., 140, 173-74
Tucker, E. F., 186
Turney's First Tennessee Infantry, 47, 55, 153
Twelfth Kentucky, 94

Utley, William, 68

Van Dorn, Earl, 39, 66

Waring, George E., 94
Warner, Wm., 174
Warren, James, 174
Watson, Mack, 113, 172
Webb, Sawney, 184
West, Lydia, 128
Wharton, J. M. C., 185
Wharton, John A., 66
Wharton, W. T. H., 143, 152, 166-67, 188
Wheeler, Joseph, 30, 63-66
Whitsett, W. H., 39
Wilder, John, 80
Will A., 170
Williams, Charles, 143
Wilson, D. M., 95, 115
Wilson, James, 131

Wisdom, John, 77
Witherspoon, J. G., 71
Womack, Jordan H., 140, 191
Wood, T. H., 174
Wood, Wm A., 169, 174
Woodard, W. A., 182
Woods, J. G., 168-70

Woodward's Kentucky
  Battalion, 58
Wright, John, 174
Wright, Luke E., 49
Wyeth, John Allan, 61

Young, J. P., 103, 121